Careers In and Out of Organizations

FOUNDATIONS FOR ORGANIZATIONAL SCIENCE
A Sage Publications Series

Series Editor
David Whetten, *Brigham Young University*

Editors
Peter J. Frost, *University of British Columbia*
Anne S. Huff, *University of Colorado* and *Cranfield University* (UK)
Benjamin Schneider, *University of Maryland*
M. Susan Taylor, *University of Maryland*
Andrew Van de Ven, *University of Minnesota*

The FOUNDATIONS FOR ORGANIZATIONAL SCIENCE series supports the development of students, faculty, and prospective organizational science professionals through the publication of texts authored by leading organizational scientists. Each volume provides a highly personal, hands-on introduction to a core topic or theory and challenges the reader to explore promising avenues for future theory development and empirical application.

Books in This Series

Douglas T. Hall
Boston University

Careers In and Out of Organizations

Foundations for
Organizational
Science
A Sage Publications Series

Sage Publications
International Educational and Professional Publisher
Thousand Oaks ▪ London ▪ New Delhi

For information:

Sage Publications, Inc.
2455 Teller Road
Thousand Oaks, California 91320
E-mail: order@sagepub.com

Sage Publications Ltd.
6 Bonhill Street
London EC2A 4PU
United Kingdom

Sage Publications India Pvt. Ltd.
M-32 Market
Greater Kailash I
New Delhi 110 048 India

Printed in the United States of America

Library of Congress Cataloging-in-Publication Data

Hall, Douglas T., 1940-
  Careers in and out of organizations / by Douglas T. Hall.
    p. cm. — (Foundations for organizational science)
  Includes bibliographical references and index.
  ISBN 0-7619-1546-X (c) — ISBN 0-7619-1547-8 (p)
  1. Career development. I. Title. II. Series.
  HF5381 .C13162 2001
  650.14—dc21   2001006095

01 02 03 04 05 10 9 8 7 6 5 4 3 2 1

Acquisitions Editor:	Marquita Flemming
Editorial Assistant:	MaryAnn Vail
Production Editor:	Diane S. Foster
Copy Editor:	Dan Hays
Typesetter/Designer:	Denyse Dunn
Proofreader:	Taryn Bigelow
Indexer:	Molly Hall
Cover Designer:	Jane Quaney

Contents

To Marcy (and I'll be right home ...)

Introduction to the Series

The title of this series, **Foundations for Organizational Science** (FOS), denotes a distinctive focus. FOS books are educational aids for mastering the core theories, essential tools, and emerging perspectives that constitute the field of organizational science (broadly conceived to include organizational behavior, organizational theory, human resource management, and business strategy). Our ambitious goal is to assemble the "essential library" for members of our professional community.

The vision for the series emerged from conversations with several colleagues, including Peter Frost, Anne Huff, Rick Mowday, Benjamin Schneider, Susan Taylor, and Andy Van de Ven. A number of common interests emerged from these sympathetic encounters, including enhancing the quality of doctoral education by providing broader access to the master teachers in our field, "bottling" the experience and insights of some of the founding scholars in our field before they retire, and providing professional development opportunities for colleagues seeking to broaden their understanding of the rapidly expanding subfields within organizational science.

Our unique learning objectives are reflected in an unusual set of instructions to FOS authors. They are encouraged to (a) "write the way they teach"—framing their book as an extension of their teaching notes rather than as the expansion of a handbook chapter; (b) pass on their "craft knowledge" to the next generation of scholars—making them wiser, not just smarter; (c) share with their "virtual students and colleagues" the insider tips and best bets for research that are normally reserved for one-on-one mentoring sessions; and (d) make the complexity of their subject matter comprehensible to nonexperts so that readers can share their puzzlement, fascination, and intrigue.

We are proud of the group of highly qualified authors who have embraced the unique educational perspective of our "Foundations" series. We encourage your suggestions for how these books can better satisfy your learning needs—as a newcomer to the field preparing for prelims or developing a dissertation proposal, or as an established scholar seeking to broaden your knowledge and proficiency.

—DAVID A. WHETTEN
Series Editor

Preface

This book is in part a revision of my 1976 volume, *Careers in Organizations* (and thus the similarity in the titles) and in part a new piece of work. I started this project with the intention of revising the original book, but then it became clear that there are now career issues that simply did not exist in 1976, such as the changing career contract, work/family balance, career metacompetencies such as identity growth and adaptability, and tools for working on these metacompetencies such as personal reflection and relational processes. Thus, the book took on a life of its own and has emerged as a combination of a new book and a revision.

Plan for the Book

Now that we have some common understanding of the term *career*, we can examine how people's careers are influenced by (and sometimes influence) organizations.

The book is organized into three parts. Part I provides an overview of contemporary careers. In Chapter 1, we review the overall terrain of the career landscape and provide a definition of the term career. In Chapter

2, we consider the ways careers have changed during the past 25 or more years. In particular, we focus on the changing career contract and what I have called the protean career.

Part II examines the specific components or elements of the career. In Chapter 3, we examine the process of career choice and discuss different approaches that have been taken to study career decision making. For many people, this occurs mainly at the beginning of their work lives. Today, however, it often occurs at various points in one's career, particularly in midcareer and even in late career. In Chapter 4, we examine the general developmental stages people pass through during the course of their working lives in organizations. Although a person's specific experiences will depend greatly on the particular occupation and type of organization he or she enters, current studies suggest that there are certain general phases that seem to occur in fairly regular order. Chapter 4, then, will give us a broad overview of the person's total life/career experience. Chapter 5 examines what happens after a career choice has been made, in particular, how the individual level of performance can be predicted. Performance will be viewed as one of four important dimensions of career effectiveness.

Chapter 6 discusses factors related to two other dimensions of career effectiveness: identity and attitudes. Again, we examine the possible predictability of these dimensions, although there has been far more research on performance. Chapter 7 examines the final element of career effectiveness, career adaptability. Together, adaptability and identity represent what I call *career metacompetencies*. By this I mean that if a person has the capacity for adaptability and for gaining self-knowledge, that person has the capacity to learn how to learn.

Chapter 8 examines the career in the broader context of the full set of the person's life roles. Because in countries such as the United States more than half of workers are part of a two-income family, these issues of integrating career and personal life are critical to a person's well-being and success.

In Part III, we turn from research to the practical issues involved in applying theory to actuality in career and organizational effectiveness. Chapter 9 examines how a person can tap more of the potential learning that can result from challenging work experiences. We have often heard that "experience is the best teacher." What we are learning from recent research, however, is that experience may be the best teacher—if you can learn from it.

In Chapters 10 and 11, we examine how organizations and individuals can "put it all together." Here, we discuss some of the current and not so obvious problems of organizational careers and how our understanding of career dynamics can be employed to make careers work better for individuals and for the work communities in which they are employed.

Following Chapter 1, which is primarily definitional, the end of each chapter contains some questions or implications for further research. Because many of the readers of this book may be graduate students, this section of each chapter attempts to provide some guidance for people who are beginning to do research on issues related to careers. These ideas are not meant to be exhaustive or the "final word" about future research; rather, they are just my "top-of-the-head" musings about issues that I would like to explore if I had the opportunity, and they are presented in that spirit.

Acknowledgments

This book has had a long journey since appearing in its original form as *Careers in Organizations* in 1976, and there have been many people to thank along the way.

The editor of the original Goodyear Series in Management and Organizations was Lyman Porter. He envisioned the books in this series as stressing key issues related to a given topic, and he asked the authors to "distinguish figure from ground." I believe that this activity is even more critical in the this book because the field of careers has become so much more mature during the past 25 years. Thus, although Porter is not formally involved in the current project, I still hear and benefit from his wisdom from years ago. He has also been a strong supporter throughout the years for the use of the concept of career in management research as well as a strong supporter of me personally—and a good friend.

Three other long-term supporters and guides for me are Chris Argyris, Ed Schein, and Warren Bennis. Chris was my first teacher in organizational behavior, back when there was no field by that name. The term existed only in the title of Chris's senior-level undergraduate course. It was a large fall lecture course, out of which he selected a small group to take a course with him the second semester. More than half of the small group of 12 undergraduate seniors went on to get doctorates in organizational behavior or other fields of management (including Clay Alderfer and Lee Bolman, who are still active publishers today). Chris remained in contact with me when I was in graduate school at the Massachusetts Institute of Technology Sloan School, where I came in contact with Ed Schein and Warren Bennis, who were my dissertation committee and helped shape my interest in and ways of approaching careers. Throughout the years, they have been role models for their ability to make fresh contributions to many fields and their long-term passion for melding theory, research, and practice.

After graduate school, when I went back to Yale to teach, Chris was department chair, and those 5 years working under his leadership I now view as the world's best postdoctoral education. By teaching with him, working collaboratively on research (such as the priest study, in which he consulted me and Ben Schneider), helping him build a strong organizational behavior group, and even being in a couples group together, I had incredibly rich opportunities to grow personally and professionally. Also, I have always thought that Chris's ideas on the relationship between the organization and the individual are, in fact, career theory because they explain the changing work experiences and attitudes of the individual over time. Through all this relational development, Chris has been a true mentor to me.

Specifically related to this book, the person I thank most of all is my old friend and sometime collaborator, Ben Schneider. As an editor of the Sage series Foundations for Organizational Science, in which this book appears, Ben has nudged, cajoled, sweet-talked, threatened, begged, and flattered me into producing this book. (He referred to me as "The Whip" years ago for pushing him to complete a research paper, and he has more than returned the favor and claimed title to the nickname for himself.) This has been one of my more difficult books to write, perhaps because the original volume was so important to me and because it is very challenging to cover 25 years of the birth of a field without writing a completely new and different book. Ben was there when I started the first one (in fact, we were working on another one at the same time), and he has been there with me in various ways, personally and professionally, throughout the years, so he understands this project in a very deep way. In our book authored together (*Organizational Climates and Careers: The Work Lives of Priests*, 1973), we discovered the notion of supportive autonomy to describe a balance of help (but not oversupervision) and freedom (but not abandonment) that supports a person's growth. Ben applied that concept well to this project. He is a dear friend.

It has also been a delight to discover a new publisher in this process. The various editors I have had the pleasure to work with at Sage have been extremely good and efficient at their respective tasks. Marquita Flemming, acquisition editor for Sage, who has overall responsibility for this series, has been incredibly enthusiastic and supportive at every step of the way. There is nothing like the feeling of finishing something after a long, hard slug of work, feeling exhausted, e-mailing it to her, and then receiving a very prompt and excited reply from Marquita. It does serve to keep one going! On the production side, Diane Foster, Senior Production Editor and Dan Hays, the book's copy editor, have made my least favorite part of the process, dealing with the production process, almost bearable work—and a very pleasant interpersonal experience. Not only do they know copyediting but also the psychology of authors, and their patience and understanding make everything work smoothly. Even the permissions process, which to me makes root canal work seem almost attractive by comparison (my parents did not raise me to be an accountant or any other kind of detail person), has been surprisingly painless. Although I have definitely been a challenge to work with for Anna Howland, the permissions editor, she has been incredibly helpful and patient, simplifying and clarifying just what I needed to do and providing good encouragement along the way.

I also thank the various reviewers who have greatly strengthened the final version of the manuscript. In particular, Ben Schneider and Susan Taylor gave early coaching and feedback when there were basic decisions to be made about tone and direction. Later reviewers who read and commented on the completed manuscript include: Michael Arthur, Ayse Karaevli, and Samuel Rabinowitz.

Like many other books in our field, this one has a special group of "godfathers" (I mean this in the spiritual/familial sense, not the underworld meaning of the term). Specifically, I have been blessed to be a member of a men's support group, variously called the Brookline Circle (although no one lives there anymore), the Boys' Group, the Mystic Knights of Marginality (although most are now pretty central to their respective systems), and simply The Group. We meet every month or two to solve the problems of the world, deal with personal and professional crises, explore intergenerational interfaces, develop grand theory, support one another's dreams, and figure out the meaning and purpose of life. It is very comforting to know that when a major problem occurs, one answer for me is always, "I'll bring this to the Boys' Group." Deep thanks to Lee Bolman, Dave Brown, Todd Jick, Bill Kahn, Phil Mirvis, and Barry Oshry.

Another strong source of support has been colleagues, students, and institutions in the School of Management at Boston University. Under the leadership of Dean Lou Lataif, two research centers have supported my research and writing in various ways—The Human Resources Policy Institute (under the leadership of Fred Foulkes) and the Executive Development Roundtable (EDRT), which I direct. Faculty colleagues, such as Kathy Kram, Lloyd Baird, Aimin Yan, and Gerry Leader, have played strong roles in these research centers, and our collaborations in various spheres have been tremendously helpful and satisfying to me. The members of EDRT have been valuable sources of wisdom about career development processes as they affect managers and directors. In particular, EDRT members who have been especially insightful coaches about this process in relation to this book are Lisa Cheraskin at Eli Lilly, Laurie Hutton-Corr at Marsh and McLennan, Ellen Johnston at Sun Microsystems, and Paul Yost and Mary Mannion-Plunkett at Boeing. Administrators for EDRT, such as Patti Collins, Leslie Steinberg, and Susan Casey Bourland, have been very helpful to the completion of this project. One "ace" student assistant in particular, Sarah Leivick (mock trial star, U.S. Senate intern, and future lawyer who has also had experience in the publishing industry), has made several key editorial contributions at critical points.

Most important, of course, has been my family's support and encouragement—along with the occasional urgings to "balance your life!" (Marcy Crary, personal communication, August 17, 2001). (In other words, leave that book alone for a while and remember what it is all about, anyway!) A major part of what it is all about are my children and grandchildren: Elizabeth (Liz) and my son-in-law Scott, Chip and my daughter-in-law Christina, Mary Lauran, and grandchildren Matthew, Sabrina, one little person who is on the way, and perhaps others to come. I have already learned much about the new careers from Elizabeth and Chip and Christina and Scott, now in their 30s and pursuing very protean careers. They have a way of occasionally asking me for career coaching (since their dad is the "expert," right?). The result of the conversation is usually that I am the one who ends up enlightened about how careers really work in this new environment. I hope that by the time Matthew and Sabrina and any future cousins of theirs start their careers, many of the career problems described in this text will be long resolved. May they have the identity strength and adaptability to cope masterfully with those new challenges that will have emerged in their future careers, in and out of organizations.

My wife and soul mate, Marcy, is always ready to discuss some idea or issue that I am working on (or that she is working on), to listen patiently to my rants about various facets of the project, and to help me disengage from it at times. She helps ground me and try to keep in touch with what this is all about, anyway. She is a graceful, generous, and loving lady. And did I mention strong? This book is dedicated to her, with my love and gratitude.

I

Contemporary Careers

1   The Study of Careers

The Changing Context of Careers

This book is based on one of my first books, *Careers in Organizations*, published in 1976. How is the world different today from the world of this original book? Consider the history of the book's publisher (and my career as its author) as a case in point. Shortly after its first printing, Goodyear was acquired by Scott, Foresman. Most of the copies of this book bear the Scott, Foresman imprint. Then, Scott, Foresman merged with Little, Brown & Company. When I first considered revising this book, my discussions were with the editors at Little, Brown. Then, in quick succession, during the 1980s, came four rounds of acquisition, culminating with my being "owned" by Rupert Murdoch and his publishing empire. At that point, someone made the decision to let the book go out of print and not revise it. *Careers in Organizations* was dead before it reached its 10th birthday. (I do not know if there is a ratio for converting book-years to human-years, as there is for dog-years, but this was probably a pretty respectable life span for a publication that was somewhat short of the *New York Times* best-seller list.)

My career as author of *Careers in Organizations* reflects several aspects of the current context of careers. First, we are seeing many forms of organizational transformation. Companies are merging, acquiring, growing exponentially, downsizing, delayering, reinventing their missions, and undergoing many other fundamental changes. In 1976, any one of these changes would have probably been the "story of the decade" for a company. Now, it might at most be the story of the quarter, and perhaps story of the year.

Two key qualities of these transformations are speed and complexity. The changes, like the rounds of the book's acquisitions, are occurring with increasing frequency. The much-vaunted Internet boom (in which the "New Economy" was supposed to defy all the traditional rules of business) came and went. The basic laws of economics still hold—businesses do, in fact, need to make a profit. Also, the nature of other changes is becoming ever more complicated: Firms are merging with partners in quite different industries, even different economies (e.g., AOL in the New Economy and Time Warner from the "Old Economy"); younger, smaller firms are acquiring older, larger companies (same example); and companies are abandoning their original businesses (e.g., Qualcomm got out of the equipment business and focused on the knowledge business).

As Peiperl, Arthur, Goffee, and Morris (2000) and their contributors show, in settings ranging from Canadian biotechnology firms to the executive suite of large corporations, the world of professional service firms, and the film industry (and other places in between), this turbulence in the larger economy projects clearly on the lives and careers of the people who work there. The traditional career contract, with its promises of a long-term employment relationship and security, has been replaced by a shorter term transactional understanding: The contract is "renewable" daily based on current needs and performance.

At the end of *Careers in Organizations*, there was a discussion of an emerging form, the *protean career*, which was characterized by frequent change and self-invention, autonomy, and self-direction—driven by the needs of the person rather than the organization. (The term is taken from the Greek sea god Proteus, who could change shape at will.) As we will see in Chapter 2, the protean career has now emerged full blown. A rich description of many cases of these enacted careers can be found in Arthur, Inkson, and Pringle's *The New Careers* (1999).

As the nature of these protean changes suggests, boundaries have become much more permeable. In fact, careers in their current state have been termed *boundaryless* (Arthur & Rousseau, 1996). This suggests that not only is the book dead but also perhaps the main idea of the book (careers inside organizations) is dead as well (Hall & Associates, 1996). Although you will note that the current version of the book that you are now reading has a somewhat expanded title, I will argue that careers, even today's careers, are not totally boundaryless. The boundaries of organizations (such as levels, projects, products, functions, and locations—all necessary for any system to operate), however, are far more permeable than they were in the past, and movement through them has become much more essential, more frequent, and more accepted.

This change in the boundaries of the career landscape shows up in a variety of ways. First, it has now become much more common—and more acceptable—for a person to be in transition, on one's own, exploring new career options, and deciding what to do next. In the past, we would probably describe this condition as being "out of work," and it would clearly be viewed in a negative light. In a world in which, as Daniel Levinson (1986, 1996) pointed out, half of our adult lives are spent in transitions, this state is a normal part of living.

The "silver lining" in this context of continuous change and transition is the reality that the person is forced to find his or her own "path with a heart," in the words of Herb Shepard. Because the paths to the top have been largely removed, the smart person will take this as an opportunity to pursue his or her own path. We are seeing that there is now more concern for seeking a sense of personal meaning and purpose in one's work. We are hearing more explicit discussion of spirituality in careers—the notion of the career as a calling or vocation (Weiss, Skelley, Hall, & Haughey, 2001). (Ironically, this notion of career as vocation is as old as it is new because the whole field of vocational psychology deals with how people make choices that help them integrate their personal choices with occupational opportunities.) These ideas are discussed in detail in Hansen's book, *Integrative Life Planning* (1997), which describes a process of identity development through spiritual and secular quests for personal and professional purpose. Thus, I argue that the career has become much more of an internal, subjective matter than it was in 1976.

As we go deeper inside people to understand career dynamics, we are also seeing that the internal boundaries in people's lives are becoming more important and more at issue. Some examples of problematic boundaries might be those between work and home, between being at home and working and being at home and being with family, and between being psychologically present in the current physical location and being psychologically involved somewhere else. As one CEO recently stated, "The worst thing for an executive's family is not when you are absent from home. The worst thing is when you are at home and psychologically absent." Indeed, the topic of work/life balance was largely absent from our discussions in 1976.

Also, the notion of boundaries leads naturally to the topic of gender issues in careers. In 1976, the topic of work/life or work/family balance was largely absent from our discussions of career, although there was an emerging literature on "women's roles." This literature, however, was pretty small and undifferentiated. Now, there is a separate literature at the intersection of virtually any issue and gender. In particular, there are many literatures on the varied facets of work/life issues and two-career couples. (Again, to continue the differentiation, the two-career literature now includes work that does not span gender boundaries.)

In a similar vein of boundary changing, as a result of downsizing and outplacement, we have seen a tremendous increase in self-employment, independent contracting, private consultants, entrepreneurship, and the like. The largest employer in the United States now is a temporary placement firm, Manpower, Inc. Also, the fastest growing segment of the U.S. economy is women-owned small business. *We Are All Self-Employed*, proclaims the title of a book by Cliff Hakim (1994)—well, maybe not quite, but the trend is in that direction. For this reason, the words "and out of" were added to the title of the book you are reading.

As part of the bittersweet experience of seeing my book go out of print, the rights to the book passed from the publisher to the author. Thus, although the book in its original form was now dead, it was now under my control. This realization, in fact, was the inspiration for the title I gave another book (*The Career Is Dead—Long Live the Career* [Hall & Associates, 1996]). For most people, although the old organizational career, with its career paths and ladders and all its formulas and rules of thumb (remember the notion of "earning your age"?), was gone, in its place was the realization that the person was in charge (Hall & Moss, 1998). The new career, which I have called the protean career (Hall, 1976; Hall & Associates, 1996), is being managed by the person, not an organization, and the driving force is the person's own needs, values, and desire for psychological success (as opposed to some external definition of success). Thus, although there is less security provided by the organization, there is instead more freedom and the opportunity to create security from one's skills and one's ability to learn (Hall & Mirvis, 1996).

Another important feature of the journey of my book-author career for this book is that it started in San Diego, California, moved throughout the United States for most of its life, and completed its final stage with ownership in Australia. Thus, not only are careers less bounded but also in particular they are increasingly global (Black, Gregersen, & Mendenhall, 1992). As businesses grow to tap global markets, they need employees in key roles to function with ease in diverse locations and to communicate and cooperate across cultural, national, and ethnic boundaries. Part of the staffing to accomplish this global expansion is accomplished through international expatriate assignments, although these moves are often fraught with many problems (Black & Gregersen, 1999). Many organizations now require that a person have significant international experience to be considered a strong candidate for higher-level executive positions (Seibert, Hall, & Kram, 1995).

As I started doing my literature reviews for this new version of the book, my searches were aided greatly by another major difference between now and 1976: the emergence of the information economy or, as some call it, the New Economy. For the original book, it was necessary to go in person to the library, pore through the card catalogue, and obtain physical copies of books and journals. Now, probably 20%, at most, of the references I use are in paper form, whereas the rest exist electronically. For example, just a few minutes ago, when I wanted to write the sentence about Cliff Hakim's (1994) book, I had to check out the exact title, date, and publisher. For my original book, the simple task of finding one reference, probably would have required a total of at least 1 hour and perhaps more, for me to either personally to go to the library or to arrange for a research assistant to get the reference. I checked the clock while I did it this time, and it took me 2½ minutes to find the information on the Web.

For careers, as well, after years and decades of calls for more use of computers in career planning and decision making, the career "industry" is one of those most heavily impacted by the Internet. Web sites abound for career and job information, for career testing and self-assessment, for advice and peer coaching, for communicating with mentors and proteges, for finding career-related readings, and the like.

Why Study Careers?

Why should we study career development, and how should we study it? We might as well start with the tough question first. Why should the reader, a student, and future practitioner of business, education, law, social work, medicine, or some other profession need to learn about career development in organizational settings? Certainly, there is little material about careers in most graduate and professional school curricula. Isn't the career a private matter, of concern only to the individual employee and not to his supervisor or organization? Isn't career development the domain of counseling psychologists and personnel or guidance specialists rather than the line manager?

Obviously, the position taken in this book is that career processes are of great interest both to the individual and to the management of an organization. To support such a stand, we should consider exactly what the term career means and why it is relevant to professionals and organizations.

What Is a Career?

The term *career* suffers from surplus meaning. If "career" were used in a free-association test, it would undoubtedly elicit an impressive range of meanings and feelings. Career conjures visions of political gamesmanship, the "organization man," the Wall Street jungle, and government civil servants, slowly but steadily working their way upward, grade by grade. In both the popular and the behavioral science literature, there are four distinct meanings in which career is used:

1. Career as advancement: Most of the free-association examples given previously entail the notion of vertical mobility—moving upward in an organization's hierarchy. By this definition, career represents the sequence of promotions and other upward moves (e.g., lateral transfers to more responsible positions or moves to "better" organizations or locations) in a work-related hierarchy during the course of a person's work life. It is not

necessary that the person remain in one single occupation to "advance." For example, the university president who becomes a cabinet member in the federal government is generally considered to have moved upward in the overall status hierarchy of the world of work. This concept of *directionality* ("up is good, low is bad"), then, is a pervasive theme in our thinking about careers.

2. Career as profession: A less common way of viewing careers is that certain occupations represent careers, whereas others do not. This is related to the career-as-advancement theme because career occupations are generally those in which some clear pattern of systematic advancement (a "career ladder") is evident. For example, in the legal profession, there is a clear advancement ladder from law student to clerk (preferably for a Supreme Court judge) to associate (preferably for a major New York firm) to partner (again, preferably for a major New York firm). Within the group of partners, there are varying degrees of status (and share of the firm's income) based on influence and performance. Politics and government service are available as additional career moves for the lawyer. Doctors, professors, businessmen, teachers, and clergymen as well as other professional people also have a generally understood path of career movement. They periodically pass through what sociologists call "regularized status passages," which are regular movements from one status to another. For example, in the management career, the following is one frequent path: undergraduate science or engineering major, student in MBA program, management trainee, staff specialist, supervisor, and then manager and executive at various levels. (The concept of career stages is discussed in more detail later.)

In contrast, jobs that do not generally lead to advancement or to a long-term series of related positions are often viewed as not constituting a career. According to this idea, keypunch operators, secretaries, and parking lot attendants are not considered to have careers. (As we will see later, people in these occupations do in fact have careers by the definition used in this book.)

These first two meanings of career are likely to be found in popular writings. The next two are more representative of behavioral science writings on the subject.

3. Career as a lifelong sequence of jobs: By this definition, the person's career is his or her series of positions held, regardless of occupation or level,

during the course of his or her work life. According to this definition, all
people who work— all people with work histories— have careers. No value
judgment is made about the type of occupation or the direction of movement. Career here is a more neutral, less value-laden term than it is under
our first two definitions. Everett Hughes, one of the foremost scholars in the
sociological research on occupations and careers, refers to the person's
sequence of jobs as the *objective career* and the particular experiences he has
in those jobs as his *subjective career* (Hughes and Coser, 1994).

4. Career as a lifelong sequence of role-related experiences: By this definition,
career represents the way the person experiences the sequence of jobs and
activities that constitute his work history. This is the subjective career, as defined by Hughes—the changing aspirations, satisfactions, self-conceptions,
and other attitudes of the person toward his work and life. To understand
fully the course of a person's work life, both the subjective and the objective
careers must be considered together as two facets of the same process.

Using this career-as-life-process view, it is even possible to consider
careers independent of work; the term could refer to the history of a
person in any particular role or status, not just in a work role. Thus, it is
possible to refer to the career of the housewife, a nonprofit board member, or a hospital patient. One of the earliest organizational sociologists,
Erving Goffman (1961), described the concept of career as follows:

> Traditionally the term *career* has been reserved for those who expect to enjoy
> the rises laid out within a respectable profession. The term is coming to be
> used, however, in a broadened sense to refer to any social strand of any per-
> son's course through life. The perspective of natural history is taken: Unique
> outcomes are neglected in favor of such changes over time as are basic and
> common to the members of a social category, although occurring independ-
> ently to each of them. Such a career is not a thing that can be brilliant or dis-
> appointing; it can be no more a success than a failure. (p. 127)

A Working Definition of Career

We now consider what the working definition of career will be within
this book. We will start with the following assumptions:

1. Career per se does not imply success or failure or "fast" advancement or "slow" advancement. Our focus will be on understanding what happens during the process of the career rather than on evaluating how successful the person is in managing in it. Therefore, the career-as-advancement approach will not be employed here.

2. Career success or failure is best assessed by the person whose career is being considered rather than by other interested parties, such as researchers, employers, spouses, or friends. This important assumption is made for two reasons, one pragmatic and one normative. First, because there are no absolute criteria for evaluating a career (the most likely criterion, advancement, has been eliminated in Assumption 1), the evaluation can best be performed by the person in relation to his own particular criteria. Second, consistent with an ethic of self-direction or internal control, it would be inappropriate for one person to evaluate another person's career. It seems that one element at the core of recent social movements—civil rights; women's liberation; national liberation; job redesign; reform of laws regarding sex, birth control, and drugs; and so on—is an increasing recognition of the person's right and responsibility to make his or her own life choices. One effect of these social changes has been to make people examine their own careers more closely and consider what their own career interests and goals are rather than those someone else (such as parents, employers, family, or friends) may have for them. Therefore, external criteria of career success seem inconsistent with the emerging ethic of personal choice as a key element in career development.

3. The career is composed of both behaviors and attitudes (i.e., things the person does and feels). Thus, one aspect of a career (the subjective career) consists of the changes in values, attitudes, and motivation that occur as the person grows older. Another aspect (the objective career) is composed of the observable choices one makes and the activities one engages in, such as the acceptance or rejection of a particular job offer. Thus, both the subjective and the objective facets must be considered in obtaining a full understanding of a person's career.

4. The career is a process—a sequence of work-related experiences. Any work, paid or unpaid, pursued over an extended period of time can constitute a career. Thus, the career-as-profession concept will not be accepted here. (Indeed, it is not accepted in most behavioral science writings on the subject.) This also means that the career-as-life concept is not endorsed

here; much as the career-as-profession and the career-as-advancement views are too restrictive, the career-as-life idea is too broad. Our focus is on work and organizational settings. The work need not necessarily be a formal, paid job: It could be volunteer work, homemaking, political work, school work, or job work. This puts our orientation, then, somewhere between the career-as-sequence-of-jobs approach (Definition 3) and the career-as-life-experiences view (Definition 4).

Putting all these assumptions together, the following working definition of career emerges:

The career is the individually perceived sequence of attitudes and behaviors associated with work-related experiences and activities over the span of the person's life.

By saying "individually perceived," we are focusing on the subjective career experience of the individual, the way the person constructs or enacts the career. When we say "sequence ... over the span of the person's life," we view career as a lifelong process but restricted to work-related activities. By saying "attitudes and behaviors," we include both the subjective and the objective aspects of the career. We assume nothing about what sequence represents "up" or "down" for a particular person and nothing about the type of work in which the person is engaged.

Why Are Careers Important?

Career as Life

Now that we have a working definition of career, we can return to the original question: Why are careers important? First, the career represents the person's entire life in the work setting. Also, for most people, work is a primary factor in determining the overall quality of life. Work provides a setting for satisfying practically the whole range of human needs—physiological, safety, social, ego, and self-actualization (using Maslow's typology); achievement, affiliation, and power (using McClelland's trilogy); and other needs, such as aggression and altruism, autonomy, and applause. Indeed, there is some evidence that mortality rates increase immediately following retirement. Therefore, it is important to study careers because work plays a key role in a person's life.

Equality and Diversity Through Careers

A second consideration is that work is a fundamental area in which to achieve social equality, workplace diversity, and personal liberation. Many underrepresented groups have been seeking equality in job hiring and promotion practices for years, and the measures of results usually include assessments of career outcomes. There is legal and social pressure on organizations to eliminate job conditions that threaten the physical or emotional well-being of the employee. Indeed, in recent years job quality (not just employment per se) has been used in political campaigns as a means of fighting social inequality, and it may become an even more important issue in the future. Therefore, because the career is so important to the person, and because the work career is being recognized as a primary target in the politics of social change, organizations will be forced to give more attention to the nature of the career experiences they provide for their employees. This challenge has become more critical as organizations have outsourced work and produced legions of independent contractors and temporary workers, who often represent the downside of the "new" careers, with even more opportunities for exploitation.

Career Mobility

Another reason for the current emphasis on the importance of careers is the increased mobility resulting from the thrust toward personal liberation in our society. It is no longer necessarily seen as undesirable to have changed jobs frequently; rather than suggesting personal instability, it represents varied experience and personal drive (Arthur et al., 1999).

Taking advantage of better job opportunities and searching for a better match between job characteristics and personal interests and needs can cause frequent job changes. This is also a hedge against obsolescence; the person who specializes by staying in one job or organization too long may have difficulty finding and adapting to other work if technological, economic, or company policy changes force him out of his current job. Thus, with our current social norms favoring freedom of choice and "doing your own thing," employees—from storeroom clerks to company presidents—are far more likely today to change jobs and careers if they are not currently fulfilled or otherwise satisfied.

Related to this tendency toward greater career mobility is the growing reluctance to sacrifice personal and family gratifications for the sake of one's career. This may be reflected in more frequent refusals of job transfers, even with promotions and pay raises; more weight given to location and physical environment in selecting a job; and the challenging of work norms regarding work hours, personal appearance, and job involvement. More dramatically, this increased sense of career-related freedom is seen in the decisions of bright, high-performing youth not to go to college or to pursue conventional careers; the decisions of employees to opt for balance between families and careers; the decisions of gays and lesbians to come out in the work environment; and the decisions of many established professionals and executives to leave their current occupations and take up quite different lines of work, often requiring years of additional education. All these moves toward greater personal choice represent a significant change in the norms and internal environment of the organization. Increasingly, organizations and administrators will not be permitted the "luxury" of overlooking the impact of their actions on the personal lives and careers of their employees (Fletcher, 1998).

These three considerations represent external pressures that may force managers to become more concerned about employee careers. The picture is not entirely one of threat, however. There are three other factors that represent inducements or rewards to the administrator who takes careers into account in his decision making and problem solving.

The Employee's Prime Concern

The administrator's prime responsibility is to manage his or her subordinates. One of the subordinate's prime concerns, however, is to manage his career. He tends to view job and organizational situations in relation to the way they will affect him personally, not just in relation to what is best for the company. Therefore, the manager who can understand career interests and career dynamics will be more effective in managing people.

Change

A related factor is that much of the administrator's work involves managing change, if only a change in the work procedures of employees. Any change in the job or in the organization, however, implies a perceived change in the career of the employee; it will be viewed as either an aid or a threat (generally the latter) to his or her best interests at work. Again, by being sensitive to the career interests and aspirations of his subordinates, the manager will be able to bring about change more effectively.

The Manager's Career

Finally, and certainly not of least importance, any administrator needs to understand careers to manage his own career more effectively. Most people do not consider such vital issues as how to make well-informed career choices, how to cope with conflicts between work and personal life, and how to arrive at career goals. Many people adopt a passive stance toward their careers, letting important career decisions be initiated by others rather than by themselves on the basis of their own interests and goals. Many people fail to use outside knowledge and resources to determine their career goals. In fact, professionals and administrators probably make higher-quality decisions about managing their subordinates and their capital assets than they do about managing their own careers. This lack of career awareness can be very damaging. For example, when a fledgling professional leaves graduate or professional school, he or she will probably suffer what is termed *reality shock* in the first permanent job assignment. The formal knowledge and skills acquired in business school are often viewed as irrelevant to the low challenge and high personal resistance encountered in the first job. Schools, however, do little to prepare students by telling them what lies ahead or by helping them acquire interpersonal skills in overcoming resistance to change. Professional education does a far better job of preparing students for the work they will do than for the lives they will lead. Understanding of career processes can be a great aid to the individual's self-awareness and self-control.

Conclusion

In this chapter, we discussed the different meanings that the term career has in both everyday usage and social science writings. We investigated career as advancement, as profession, as lifelong sequence of jobs, and as lifelong sequence of work-related experiences. After reviewing these different interpretations, we arrived at a working definition to be used in this book: Career is the individually perceived sequence of attitudes and behaviors associated with work-related experiences and activities over the span of the person's life.

Next, we considered the "so what" question: Why are careers important and worthy of another book? Issues such as careers and quality of life, spirituality and personal calling, careers as a vehicle for social change, career mobility, and people's general lack of career awareness were examined as responses to this question.

 **2** The Protean Career Contract

We're brutalizing the workforce right now during this transitional period. If we're going to get what we need, the brutalization has to stop.

—James Champy (as quoted in Champy & Hammer, 1995, p. B1)

Although the era of restructuring began in the 1980s, the headlines continue to scream from the covers of major publications "What ever happened to the great American job?" "The pain of downsizing," "Downsizing government," "The end of jobs," and "Transforming the Army." The message is relentless: The deal has changed. The career contract is dead. Organizations are in constant flux. The job is a thing of the past.

Not surprisingly, there has been a reaction to the inhumane and incompetent way that many of these organizational changes were made. Even the champion of reengineering, James Champy, saw the corrosive effect of restructuring on employee commitment, as indicated by the opening quotation. In my view, this marked the beginning of the reaction, and since then there has been a greater awareness of the need to

AUTHOR'S NOTE: Portions of this chapter are adapted with permission from Hall and Moss (1998).

17

consider how employee careers are being affected and to seek ways to promote career development even in this context of massive organizational change.

It is clear that organizational transformation is taking place on a global scale (Friedman, 2000). To be competitive, firms have to be smaller, smarter, and swifter in their response to changing market conditions. It is also clear that the workplace has been similarly transformed for everyone. Employees must be equally flexible and adaptive.

It is unclear just how an organization and its employees can adapt in a satisfying and productive way to the new career contract. This chapter focuses primarily on a study by Hall and Moss (1998), with observations "from the trenches" of 49 people who were interviewed about the changing contract in their organizations. The study examined organizations that represented a range of time periods since their first business crisis or major environmental shock. AT&T, for example, had gone through divestitures in 1984 and again in the mid-1990s, and we wanted to determine how that organization had adjusted to its new competitive situation. Other firms, such as IBM and Apple Computer, had crises much later, and we wanted to determine the differences in the state of the psychological contract there compared to that of firms that experienced earlier crisis, such as AT&T. Also, some of the firms, such as First National Bank of Chicago (now part of Bank One) and Digital Equipment (now part of Compaq Computers), no longer exist as independent entities.

The Nature of a Psychological Contract

What Exactly Is a Psychological Contract?

First, we review the basic theory of the psychological contract. The idea of the psychological contract was discussed in the early 1960s by Chris Argyris (1957a), Harry Levinson (1962), and Edgar Schein (1965). Schein viewed the psychological contract as the foundation for the employment arrangement in that the continuation of the relationship, as well as the employee's rewards and contributions, depended on the degree to which the mutual expectations were met. At approximately the same time, David Berlew and Douglas Hall (1964), in a longitudinal study conducted at AT&T, found that if, in a given year, the contract was not met for either party, the employee was likely to leave the organization in the following year.

Later, Ian MacNeil (1980, 1985) discussed two forms of what he called the social contract. The first was *relational*, which was based on assumptions of a long-term relationship and trust that the relationship would be a mutual one. In contrast, the other form was *transactional*, based on a shorter term exchange of benefits and contributions. MacNeil discussed the role of an individual in a larger society, but his concepts seem applicable to organizations as well.

These notions were later extended by Michael Arthur and Denise Rousseau's *The Boundaryless Career* (1996). This book explored the concept of boundarylessness in contemporary organizations and its implications for new career competencies. A discussion of contemporary and future career contract issues was reported in a special issue (in two parts—November 1996 and February 1997) of the *Academy of Management Executive*, "Careers in the 21st Century," edited by Douglas Hall. Peiperl and Baruch (1997) and Rousseau, Schalk, and Schalk (2000) provided more detail on career networks that transcend organizational and geographic boundaries, including the role of information technology.In our interviews, these network and relational aspects of the old contract were mentioned frequently. Often, the metaphor of the family was used, representing perhaps the ultimate unconditional relationship. At Hewlett-Packard, one manager reported that a variety of "parental" benefits (lifetime employment and generous pension plans) led to a high level of financial security: "A trust was built, leading to employees' not thinking much about change or the future."

Another aspect of the old contract was identification with the organization. There was a sense of pride in being associated with the company. This feeling was often confirmed by the reactions of other people. Kevin Parker (a pseudonym, like all others used here), formerly in charge of management development at Digital, used what he called the "cocktail party test" for the status of the contract:

The cocktail party test told all. If you said you work for Digital, and the response was, "Gee, isn't that great?" then the contract was doing well. Later, as the contract began to change under crisis, responses were more varied.

The Myth That Everyone Was
Covered by the Old Contract

At this point, we need to pause and look a bit deeper. Consider not only what the old contract was but also where it existed. We argue that to a great extent the old contract is a myth. The long-term relationship-based employment arrangement that we just described was not the norm in U.S. business organizations (nor was it in other countries, we suspect, as well). In much the same way as employment security in Japan has existed only in certain large corporations during the post-World War II period, this old contract was found in only those U.S. organizations with strong internal labor markets and human resource policies favoring long-term employment security.

However, it was precisely these large firms with strong internal labor markets that, through their prominence and visibility, seemed to symbolize U.S. business, so it appeared that their mode of managing people was the norm. The firms with these long-term career cultures were those such as AT&T, IBM, Sears, Exxon, Digital Equipment Corporation, and Proctor & Gamble. These were hugely successful firms, which also tended to be relatively independent of fluctuations in the economic cycle. Many other equally successful companies, such as General Motors and General Electric, were more strongly affected by swings in the economy so that periodic layoffs were understood to be part of doing business. Of course, smaller firms had even less of a financial resource base to permit them to carry employees through an economic downturn.

Although no precise data exist on the number of firms or employees that operated under the so-called "old contract," we estimate that in 1975—to pick a year well in advance of the turbulent 1980s—fewer than 5% of American workers worked under what now has been labeled the old contract. Let us explain. Only approximately 50 firms, generally larger ones such as AT&T, IBM, and Proctor & Gamble, had full employment practices that guaranteed workers a certain number of paid weeks each year. (Our colleague, Fred Foulkes, identified 30 such firms in an earlier study, and we are assuming there were others that were simply less visible.) Also, the total employment of *Fortune* 500 companies in 1975 represented only approximately 17% of the total U.S. workforce. Therefore, even if these 50 full-employment firms represented as much as 20% of the total workforce of the *Fortune* 500 companies, this would yield only 3.4% of the U.S. workforce that had lifetime employment practices. (In fact, these were never stated as "guarantees" or "policies." They were referred to by ambiguous, nonbinding terms such as "traditions," "practices," "philosophies," or "intentions.") Thus, despite analyses that tout the old contract as part of the work arrangements for the U.S. workforce overall, this employment security was experienced only by those privileged workers in the "Fortunate 50." Also, even in these firms, it was rarely stated as a guarantee.

Decreased Job Stability and Increased Mobility

Of course, there was more of a sense of economic stability 30 or more years ago. Mobility was seen in more negative terms; a resume with job changes every 2 or 3 years was something that required explanation rather than a sign of one's energy and desire for continuous challenge and learning. Also, jobs seemed more secure and stable for professionals and managers then than now. When there were layoffs, it was lower-level employees who were affected, not the upper-level managers and professionals. As the old saying goes, "When your neighbor is laid off, it's a recession. When you get laid off, it's a depression!" In this New Economy, now that elite members have experienced turbulence in their work environments, it feels like a less secure world.

To be more specific, a study by the Employee Benefit Research Institute showed just how significant the decrease in job stability was in the 1990s (Koretz, 1997). Between 1991 and 1996, the median levels of job tenure for employed men between the ages of 25 and 64 decreased by an average of approximately 19%. For middle-aged to older employed men (35-64 years old), the decrease continued a trend that started in the early 1980s, following a post-World War II peak. For older men, the decrease in job stability was especially high, showing how difficult this group was hit by the layoffs of this era of downsizing. Since 1983, the median level for job tenure has decreased by 6 years, or 29%, for men between 55 and 64 years old and 25% for men 45 to 54 years old.

For women, the experience has been different. Their job tenure increased in the early 1980s and has remained relatively constant since 1983. We speculate that this may be due to the high influx of women into the labor market starting in the mid-1970s and to the heavier decreases experienced by men. Women were probably, on average, in lower-level positions and at lower pay levels and were thus less likely candidates for job elimination.

To give more of a feel for the magnitude of job mobility in the New Economy, Topel and Ward (1992) found in their study of white male U.S. high school graduates that the average worker held approximately seven jobs in his first 10 years in the workforce. They report that this U.S. job mobility rate is nearly twice as high as it is in Japan. For example, one fourth of all U.S. workers separated from a primary job in 1990 versus 14% or 15% in Japan. Also, in the United States, this turnover is less likely to be voluntary: There was a 60% voluntary job separation in the United States versus 80% in Japan. (In Japan, the reasons for separation were most likely to be child bearing and retirement.)

Topel and Ward (1992) also found that a major driver for voluntary job change in the United States was earnings improvement. For workers who stayed in a job, the average quarterly wage growth was 1.8%. In contrast, when workers switched jobs, their wages increased 18%. They report that job changes accounted for approximately one third of all earnings growth for people in their first 10 years in the U.S. workforce. (In Japan, wage gains are much smaller when workers switch jobs.) A related finding was reported in the "Shell Poll," a quarterly U.S. opinion survey conducted by the Shell Oil Company: 37% of the respondents viewed job mobility as a means of advancing their careers and career advancement opportunities. To that end, 57% of respondents expected to work for at least five employers in their careers, and half of that number expected to work for eight or more (Bellesi, 1999).

The Nature of the New Contract

From Relational to Transactional Contracts

Denise Rousseau (1995), in her book, *Psychological Contracts in Organizations: Understanding Written and Unwritten Agreements*, explored MacNeil's theory to examine contemporary changes in the psychological employment contract in organizations. She argued that employment contracts have moved in recent years from a longer-term relational basis to a shorter-term transactional one. As we heard in our interviews, some employees react by wanting the transaction to be a more explicit contract now, in contrast to the more implicit old contract. Sarah Lorey, vice president of Boston University Medical Center (now part of the merged entity Boston Medical Center) stated, "People are literally looking for a contract. They want to know what they will be doing for the next 12 months. They would like to know a little bit about what to expect."

From Organizational to Protean Contracts

Another way to frame this career contract change, from the perspective of the individual, is that we are seeing a shift from the organizational career to what we have described as the protean career, a career based on self-direction in the pursuit of psychological success in one's work. The new contract based on the protean career is summarized in Table 2.1. This table summarizes the issues we discuss throughout this chapter.

If the old contract was with the organization, in the protean career the contract is with the self and one's work. In a study comparing data collected in 1978 and 1989, Stroh, Brett, and Reilly (1994) found evidence of this shift from an organizational focus to an investment in one's own work; satisfaction with the company decreased from 1978 to 1989, but job involvement and job satisfaction increased. (They also reported that managers in 1989 were changing jobs and relocating more often than were those in 1978.)

The popular media have provided accounts of the new contract that support this move from an organization focus to a self focus. A *Fortune* cover story by Kenneth Labich (1995) was titled, "Kissing Off Corporate America: Why Big Companies Can't Hire the Best and the Brightest." Labich cited an Opinion Research Corporation study in which only 1% of the 1,000 adult respondents said they would choose to be corporate managers. Far more popular were careers that provided the autonomy of a protean career, such as law and medicine. In 1990, one fourth of Columbia's graduating MBAs went to work for large manufacturers; in 1994, only 13% chose this route. Similarly, at Stanford in 1989, approximately 70% of the MBA class went to work for large companies (e.g., those employing more than 1,000 employees); only approximately half did so in 1994. As John Martin, president of the Kellogg Graduate School of Management's 1995 MBA class, stated, "I don't know anyone who wants to be like Jack Welch or Jack Smith." In fact, one of the most

Table 2.1   The New "Protean" Career Contract

1.	The career is managed by the person, not the organization.
2.	The career is a lifelong series of experiences, skills, learnings, transitions, and identity changes ("career age" counts, not chronological age).
3.	Development is 　Continuous learning; 　Self-directed; 　Relational; 　Found in work challenges.
4.	Development is not (necessarily) 　Formal training; 　Retraining; 　Upward mobility.
5.	Ingredients for success have changed 　From know-how to learn-how; 　From job security to employability; 　From organizational careers to protean careers; 　From work self to whole self.
6.	The organization provides 　Challenging assignments; 　Developmental relationships; 　Information and other developmental resources.
7.	The goal is psychological success.

SOURCE: Hall and Mirvis (1996). *The career is dead—long live the career: A relational approach to careers.* San Francisco: Jossey-Bass.

important influences on work satisfaction is how much flexibility the work provides (Clark, 2001).

The Contingent Workforce

One of the ways that career mobility and protean careers are currently manifest is in the increase of contingent employment. In the United States, the largest employer at the time of this writing is a temporary agency, Manpower, Incorporated. More than 90% of U.S. employers use temporary workers as part of their staffing mix (von Hipple, Mangum, Greenberger, Heneman, & Skoglind, 1997), and approximately 3 million people worked as temporary workers in a single year (Hipple, 1998). It is clear that one of the major ways that careers have become boundary-less (Arthur & Rousseau, 1996) has been through the practice of temporary employment.

Contingent work entails frequent movement and transitions across organizational boundaries, which can have significant effects on the worker's attitudes and feelings of success (Peiperl & Lidewey, 1999). There is a real need to understand better how this rapid mobility can be facilitated as well as how the individual can quickly acquire, deploy, and share new knowledge and skills (von Hipple et al., 1997). Issues such as voluntarism (Ellington, Gruys, & Sackett, 1999) and commitment (McClurg, 1999) of contingent workers have received some attention, but there has still been insufficient attention paid to what behaviors make for the success of individuals, teams, and organizations when a large proportion of the work is done in a series of short episodes (O'Connell, 2001).

Research by O'Connell (2001) has addressed this need. He examined the behaviors of contingent workers who were working in the context of work teams. Through a modified case study approach (Eisenhardt, 1989; Miles & Huberman, 1994; Yin, 1994), he conducted in-depth interviews with contingent workers, their client company supervisors, and their client company coworkers. Using a modified case study approach, he identified a series of stages in the "career" of a contingent employee's engagement. The first stage was Finding, or making contact with the client company. This entailed assessing the match between the needs of the hiring manager in the client company and the qualifications of the employee; sometimes, a temporary staffing agency was involved. Stage Two was Adapting, which was a process of getting a "quick fit" between employee and the job. The next stage was Staying, which was the ongoing performance of the work, with the necessary flexibility and proactive information acquisition and communication as the demands of the work evolve. The final stage was Transforming, which was the completion of the work and moving on to the next assignment, which could entail either exiting the organization or remaining in the organization in a different role, perhaps as a regular employee. Appropriately, O'Connell calls this model of temporary work stages "FAST."

The FAST model is shown in Table 2.2. It shows the factors in the individual employee and in the supervisor and coworkers that were related to success in the temporary assignment. It seems clear that the process of forming a quick connection in a temporary assignment is complex and requires a wide range of skills on the part of the employee, the supervisor, and the coworkers. Thus, continuous learning is at a real premium in contingent work. In particular, as the acronym implies, speed—the creation of a "quick fit"—assumes a heightened role in the success of a contingent engagement. The FAST model seems to provide a specific description of how the career as a series of short learning stages might be played out. O'Connell (2001) describes this process as follows:

> The stage model developed in this research provides a microview of what happens within the Hall and Mirvis (1996) mini career stages. We know from industry research that contingent employment is, for many, a means of career *exploration* as people get a look at a variety of work before choosing a direction. We also know that temporary employment is a way for organizations and individuals to conduct a *trial* of the worker and the work. (p. 17)

This work on temporary employment also shows the importance of relational elements in successful career management. O'Connell (2001) notes the critical importance of "knowing whom," as suggested by Arthur and Rousseau (1996), and interpersonal knowledge, supported by Anakwe, Hall, and Schor (1999). As part of this relational component, there is also a large element of ongoing bargaining and exchange, as fits and mutual exchanges are negotiated. O'Connell points out how the employee's task success and skills create bargaining power, both for continuing the employment relationship and, later, for redefining the relationship, perhaps as a permanent employee.

Loyalty Versus Protean Careers?

In recent years, some researchers have argued for the opposite of contingent work. In his book *The Human Equation: Building Profits by Putting People First*, Pfeffer (1998) presents data from various studies that show that organizations with longer term relationships with employees tend to be more profitable than those with shorter employment relationships. Other support for this idea comes from Frederick Reichheld in his book, *The Loyalty Effect* (1996). Reichheld goes beyond Pfeffer's argument to include owners and customers in the loyalty equation. Using data from Bain Consulting's client database, Reichheld shows that the longer the firm's retention of customers, owners, and employees is, the more profitable it is. (Owner "retention" was defined in terms of how long a shareholder owned his or her stock.)

Table 2.2   Stages in Successful Contingent Employment Engagements

Stage	Individual Factors	Supervisor and Coworker Factors
Finding: Making contact	C1: Assess potential match in knowledge, skills, and abilities C2: Truth in advertising	C3: Clearly specify tasks and requisite skills C4: Make appropriate screening investment
Adapting: A process of quick fit to work setting and task demands	C5: Search for information C6: Demonstrate effort C7: Demonstrate skills	C8: Provide initial direction C9: Evaluate initial performance
Staying: Moving beyond the initial quick fit	C10: Be conscientious C11: Be flexible C12: Be proactive	C13: Provide clear expectations C14: Provide adequate support
Transforming: Changes in engagement status	C15: Communicate intent C16: Scan for opportunity C17: Continue high-quality output	C18: Clearly communicate status and direction of job C19: Do sufficient budgetary structural legwork

SOURCE: O'Connell, D. J. (2001). *FAST stages in contingent employment: Finding, adapting, staying, and transforming.* Davenport, IA: St. Ambrose University, College of Business. Reprinted with permission.

My view on this issue is that both perspectives have validity. The shorter term protean or contingent relationship has indeed become more common in today's organizations. The question of whether this form of employment is the most profitable for the organization or for the employee has not really been raised in most writings about protean and contingent work arrangements. Also, it does seem logical that longer term, high-loyalty employment relationships would be more efficient for the organization because human capital investments can be used, employees move up the learning curve, attitudes grow more positive, resulting in greater service to the customer (Schneider & Bowen, 1995), and the costs of retaining an employee become lower with each additional year of service.

Thus, I argue for an acceptance of the reality of the protean work environment—that both employees and employers have to operate on the assumption that the other party will remain only as long as its immediate needs are being met. The acceptance of this reality, however, would ideally be accompanied by the understanding that it is in the interests of both parties to work together toward a long-term relationship. This means constantly trying to satisfy the other with one's own performance and positive attitudes. Employers and employees win the loyalty of the other through delivering excellent performance and satisfaction of the other's needs. Also, this satisfaction of the other will feed back and lead to greater rewards for the originator. Thus, there is a positive spiral, as escalation of mutual commitment in the employment relationship. In other words, my hypothesis is that the most effective (for both parties) form of employment relationship is the high-loyalty protean career.

Is There a Role for the Organization in the New Contract?

If the new contract is with the self and not with the organization, what is the role of the organization in the new contract? Unfortunately, many employers are interpreting the new contract to mean that the employee should be completely responsible for his or her career, and that the employer bears no responsibility at all. This line of thinking views employees, even core employees, in sort of a "free agent" role, similar to contract workers.

Other employers, however, still see a responsibility for providing the resources and opportunities for core employees to grow and develop in their careers. In this group of forward-thinking companies, the employer's responsibility is seen to be providing opportunities for continuous learning, which will result in the creation of employability security for the employee. At the same time, the organization values the ongoing relationship it has with the employee and takes the long view in its employment practices.

To explore the role of the organization in the new contract in depth, we next discuss our company interviews and examine how different employers and their employees are dealing with the shift to the new contract.

Stages of Adaptation: Three Types of Companies

As we listened to our interviewees, we could hear three quite distinct types of company experiences based on what stage of adaptation they and their employees were in. To help explain their experiences, many people used the metaphor of getting lost in the woods and struggling to get oriented and find one's way out.

One type of firm was experiencing current trauma (still "lost in the trees"). A second group was either out of the woods (for the time being) or was at least able to "see the forest for the trees." Companies and employees in this group "can see the forest" and were accepting the new contract.

A third and very intriguing group never had a single traumatic event that marked an end of the old contract or the start of a new one. This type of company was characterized by a continuous learning process. To continue the wilderness metaphor, this type of firm has learned to adapt to continuously changing terrain and is now "comfortable in the forest." These groups of companies, with examples, are shown in Table 2.3.

Current Trauma: "Lost in the Trees"

One group of companies is currently undergoing radical instability from environmental economic trauma: Their employees cannot yet see the forest (the new contract required by the new competitive environment) for the trees (the latest business downturn or layoff announcement). They are still traumatized and grieving the loss of the old contract. Major turmoil for many occurred in the early 1990s (e.g., Digital, Philip Morris, Kodak, Nynex, Apple, and Texaco). These firms have been working for several years to evolve a different company/employee relationship. Most have not yet totally resolved how the company will survive but have made distinct strides in the direction of adapting to the new situation.

This experience of the "lost in the trees" firm is expressed by Janet Lancaster of Apple Computer as follows:

> There was a significant layoff. There had been other layoffs but this one hit the hardest. People who were doing a good job were laid off, too. It was a stiff psychological blow. There was a significant impact on people ... on loyalty.

Living the New Contract: "Sees the Forest"

For some companies, the drastic change was described as occurring "a long time ago": They can see the forest from the trees and have become clear on the nature of the new contract. In fact, many employees

Table 2.3   Status of the Psychological Contract in Three Types of Organizations in 1998

Current Trauma	Trauma Survivors	Continuous Learning
(Lost in the Trees) ——>	*(Sees the Forest)* ——>	*(Comfortable in Woods)*
Apple Computer	DuPont	Beth Israel Hospital
Digital Equipment Corporation/Compaq	First Chicago/Bank One	Hannaford Brothers
Kodak	Ingersoll-Rand	Hewlett-Packard
Philip Morris	Reader's Digest	Polaroid
Texaco	AT&T	Xerox
Nynex/Verizon	IBM	

now embrace the new contract, with its opportunities for greater freedom, responsibility, and psychological success.

One factor separating the "lost in the trees" companies from the "sees the forest" group is timing. The peak of the latter group's turmoil often occurred in the early 1980s. Since that time, people in these companies have had approximately 12 years to learn about and react to the changes in the environment, and they have implemented a new psychological contract that allows them to stay competitive and adaptable in the new business era.

A typical example of the experience of the new-contract firm was given by a manager at Ingersoll-Rand, which "hit the wall" in the early 1980s, in the wake of the energy crisis and a worldwide recession:

> We are trying to accommodate the change in the economy. We like loyalty though and don't want to jeopardize the loyal relationships. . . . We went through downsizing in '82-'83 and have returned. We are years ahead of many. Our people are more dedicated and educated than ever before. . . . People wonder about how it felt to go through a period where 20,000 people lost their jobs here, but I look at it differently, we saved the jobs of 35,000 people.

AT&T is another example of a company that experienced the contract change a long time ago (divestiture of the old "Bell System" by Judge Greene on January 1, 1984) and then implemented a second divestiture (actually a trivestiture) in the 1990s. Although the stress level is high, employees there seem to have an understanding of the new contract. Some other companies that seem to have experienced these changes long ago and are now functioning under the new contract, based on our interviews, are First National Bank of Chicago, DuPont, and Reader's Digest.

Continuous Learning: "Comfortable in Woods"

Some companies seem to have a contract that changed gradually but never was believed to be "broken" over the years. Organizations from our interviews that appeared to be in this group included Hewlett-Packard, Beth Israel Hospital, Hannaford Brothers, Polaroid, and Xerox. Although these firms have had some financial difficulties, they have generally been successful in staying competitive through exceptional leadership and high employee involvement. In the process of competitive adaptation, they have managed to maintain their core values about people through difficult economic and environmental changes.

We argue that as organizations learn how to learn, this continuous learning mode will become more common in the future through a natural selection process. That is, continuous learners will thrive and survive, whereas nonlearners and slower learners will not.

Companies in the continuous learning group have a fundamental respect for the individual—both the employee and the customer—and this value provides continuity between the old and new contracts in these firms. To illustrate, Helen Johnson of Beth Israel Hospital offers an idea of how the changes at her workplace have evolved:

> Dr. Rabkin came in as president in 1966. He was keen on the subject of personalized care and established it as a clear philosophy. He felt that the patient and employees are on an equal footing. Both people ought to be treated with respect and dignity by Beth Israel. ... The underlying commitment to the employee was evident several years ago as the private doctors cafeteria was discarded back in the 1960s. ... Even during rapid growth, the diverse workforce was taken into account. The culture and the philosophy of the hospital have a very narrow gap between them.

This new kind of loyalty is described by Fred Reichheld in his book, *The Loyalty Effect* (1996). Reichheld, head of what is called the "loyalty practice" at Bain Consulting, finds empirical evidence for loyalty based on performance, mutual value added, and satisfaction. Data from Bain show that the longer a company's relationships are with its employees and its customers, the more profitable is the firm. For example, it is much more expensive to attract a new customer, through special discounts, premiums, and extra advertising, than it is to maintain an old customer. (This is why, if you are a magazine subscriber, you get a better deal if you let your subscription expire and then be won back through lower rates, free issues, special videotapes, and other free gifts.) Similarly, it is more costly to recruit and train new employees than it is to train and develop experienced personnel. Also, in producing customer satisfaction, much greater value is created by experienced employees than by new employees. The key to the new loyalty, however, is that it has to be based on high performance and the ability to learn continuously.

In a fascinating discussion, Reichheld (1996) also finds that the same financial benefit of stakeholder retention holds for investors. Companies whose stock is held primarily by "high-churn" investors tend to be poorer performers than those who are owned by investors who are known for forming partnering relationships with companies in which they invest. These results show that a firm can have an effect on its economic environment by actively cultivating relationships with long-term investors and by not encouraging the high-churn pension fund or mutual fund.

A Clear Sense of Identity as a Compass

One important implication for the individual in a continuously changing organization is that he or she must have a clear sense of personal identity, to provide an internal "compass," keeping him or her headed on the "path with a heart" in the midst of all the turbulence. In fact, one of the ironies here is that one has more opportunities, not fewer, to pursue one's own path with a heart when the ground is constantly shifting because important new opportunities are always opening up. If the person lacks that internal compass, however, he or she will be constantly tempted and diverted from the path with a heart.

As discussed later, I think of identity development as a "metacompetency" that is needed to help the person experience psychological success during the course of the career. A metacompetency is a higher-order capability that enables the person to acquire other skills. An example is reading: If you know how to read, you can read how to learn other things, such as how to program your VCR or how to operate your new computer. In addition to the other key metacompetency, adaptability, identity growth has two elements. One is the ability to seek and take in feedback information about one's self, to learn about one's strengths and deficiencies. The other element of identity is self-awareness, the extent to which one has a clear understanding of one's own values, needs, interests, goals, abilities, and purpose. Thus, identity growth is not just about knowing yourself but also about knowing how to learn more about yourself. Of course, we need feedback and help from others to do this. Thus, much of identity development is a relational process (Hall & Associates, 1996).

One of the challenges of the boundaryless career is that people are open to many more stimuli and experiences that make up their sense of self, and the integration of this complexity is difficult (Kegan, 1994). In fact, as Kegan shows, it is precisely the integration of this complexity into an integrated self-concept that constitutes the growth of the identity. Therefore, although the turbulent world makes identity development more challenging, this challenge is in fact pushing us in the direction of growth.

If the person is not able to attain this identity growth, this strong internal compass, the result is likely to be a chameleon-like succession of quick changes that respond only to the shifting prevailing winds. This is the risk of having adaptability without identity. For sure, a successful protean career requires being highly flexible and adaptive, but the adaptability must be guided by a strong and clear sense of self.

Recycling

The three contract states are not as clear or as simple as the previous description may make them appear. When we asked some of our original interviewees how these categories fit with their experiences of the contract change process in their firms, our respondents pointed out some additional considerations. One idea they stressed was the fluidity of these categories. Although a firm may have survived an earlier trauma, and people believed they were out of the woods for awhile, a new force (e.g., a new CEO) could raise the uncertainty level again. Thus, a firm might recycle back through a previous state.

One example of recycling was the experience of AT&T in 1995, when employees were thrown back into a state of trauma regarding the uncertainties of the second divestiture, and again in 1997, with talk of a merger with SBC, one of the former "baby bell" telephone companies.

Our sense, however, is that when this recycling happens, it tends to happen at a higher level of awareness, with a higher degree of knowing how to learn and a somewhat higher level of comfort with the change process. Thus, it appears that AT&T is now back in the middle stage, "sees the forest." In other words, organizations may learn from prior experience, which may make future forays into rough terrain more hopeful.

Continuous Learning via Psychological Success

Psychological Success

Although the continuous learning culture has obvious benefits for the companies in our third group ("comfortable in woods"), what is in it for the employee? Perhaps the most important driver of learning for employees is the fact that the new career contract is not with the organization: It is with the self and one's work. The path to the top has been replaced by what Herb Shepard (1984) called the path with a heart. Shepard used this term to describe success in terms of one's unique vision and central values in life—in short, what we call psychological success. Shepard also noted that the path with a heart encompasses one's most-loved talents so that being paid in pursuit of one's work feels not like compensation but like a gift.

Unfortunately, it is too easy for a person to become successful in an organizational sense and even in a psychological sense (i.e., in terms of job satisfaction) and still lose sight of living out one's most deeply held values. For example, Karen Camp was an account manager with responsibilities in eight states. She was on a business trip just after her son Webb's first birthday. She called home and learned from the sitter that Webb had just taken his first steps. Her reaction was as follows: "I realized that his first year had gone by so quickly, I had been like a visitor in his life."

One of the reasons why a person loses sight of the path with a heart is that he or she may start off in that direction and then keep going in the same direction, through thick and thin, even though his or her "internal compass" has changed. Early career and life choices may not necessarily be the best fit for a person in midcareer. As one shocked 42-year-old manager exclaimed in the middle of a self-reflective career planning exercise, "Oh, no! I just realized I let a 20-year-old choose my wife and my career!"

Career Metacompetencies: Self-Knowledge and Adaptability

As mentioned earlier, pursuing the protean career entails a high level of self-awareness (personal identity) and personal adaptability. There is both good news and bad news. Many people cherish the autonomy of the protean career, but many others find this freedom terrifying, experiencing it as a lack of external support. There is a developmental or learning process here because people need time to adapt to this new freedom. Developmental psychologist Robert Kegan (1994) reports in his book, *In Over Our Heads: The Mental Demands of Modern Life*, that fewer than half of the adults in his samples had reached the level of psychological development at which they were comfortable operating independently in today's complex organizational environment.

To realize the potential of the new career, the individual must develop new competencies related to the management of self and career. The new career has become a continuous learning process. In particular, the person must learn how to develop self-knowledge (identity awareness) and adaptability. We call these metacompetencies because they are the skills required for learning how to learn. The need for adaptability is perhaps self-evident—to enable the person to be self-correcting in response to new demands from the environment without waiting for formal training and development from the organization. Without self-awareness, however, this adaptability could be a blind, reactive process, and the person could risk changing in ways that are not consistent with his or her own values and goals.

Adaptability alone might produce what Chris Argyris calls Model 1 reactive change, whereas adaptability plus self-knowledge promotes Model 2 generative change.

Implications for Organizational Career Management

A Relational Approach to Careers

In the future, the most effective organizations will take what I call a relational approach to the development of employees' careers and thus promote continuous learning. This means that firms will not "manage" employees' careers, as they did in the past. Rather, the employer will provide opportunities and flexibility and resources, particularly people resources, to enable the employee to develop identity and adaptability and thus be in charge of his or her own career. An example of an organization that provides many of these relational ingredients for psychological success is the entrepreneurial coffee company Starbucks, which is described in Box 2.1.

BOX 2.1

Starbucks: The New Loyalty[1]

Employees can develop a high degree of loyalty to an organization that is committed to them and with whose purpose they can identify. In turn, these loyal employees will produce loyal customers. Consider the fast-growing Starbucks Coffee organization run by entrepreneur Howard Schultz, who purchased it in 1987 as a local Seattle business that sold coffee beans. He envisioned an empire of stores "based on the notion that even though the term 'coffee break' is part of the vernacular, there's traditionally been no place to enjoy one. He sees his coffee houses as, 'An extension of people's front porch,' as he puts it" (Witchel, 1994, p. C1). The firm is now the largest coffee-bar chain in the United States, with a very loyal clientele.

To implement his strategy of having Starbucks stores become an extension of people's front porch, he takes care of employees first so that they will in turn take care of customers: "The customer does not come first, the employee does. It's sort of the corporate version of 'I'm O.K., You're O.K.'" (Schultz as quoted in Witchel, 1994, p. C1). Starbucks was the first company in the United States to grant full health care benefits and stock options to its part-time workers (who comprise 65% of its workforce). As Schultz described his mission (as quoted in Witchel, 1994),

> I always saw myself wanting to be deemed successful and good at the same time.... Service is a lost art in America. I think people want to do a good job, but if they are treated poorly they get beaten down.... We want to provide our people with dignity and self-esteem, and we can't do that with lip service. So we offer tangible benefits. The attrition rate

in retail fast food is between 200% and 400% a year. At Starbucks, it's 60%. (p. C8)

Interviews with the manager and employees at a recently opened store in Cambridge, Massachusetts, illustrated the clear ambitions and satisfaction of Starbucks employees. Serving coffee can be difficult work, but the workers seem satisfied with their positions. Between the medical benefits and the option of a free pound of coffee every week, the employees feel well compensated. There is also the issue of upward mobility: The manager of the store had only worked for Starbucks for 10 months and had no previous experience in the food service industry. A fairly new employee we talked to seemed to be inspired by the manager, commenting, "I hope to be managing my own store in not too many months."

Founder Howard Schultz described the origin of his management philosophy in very personal terms (as quoted in Witchel, 1994):

My father didn't finish high school, and what I remember most was the way he was treated in his adult life, which beat him down. He didn't have the self-esteem to feel worthy of a good job. So, I try to give people hope and self-esteem through a company that respects them. Dad never had that opportunity.... Every one of our actions has to be compatible with the quality of our coffee. It never lets you down. (p. C8)

When asked about the secret of his success, Schultz looked slightly embarrassed and reflected (as quoted in Witchel, 1994, p. C8), "Maybe I wasn't jaded. I always wanted to do something to make a difference. Maybe people gravitated to that." Starbucks's performance seems to be an example of the notion that in business "you can do well by doing good."

This relational approach to career development under the new contract is discussed by Douglas Hall and Associates in their book, *The Career Is Dead—Long Live the Career: A Relational Approach to Careers* (1996). (The meaning of the title is that the organizational career is dead, whereas the protean career is thriving.) In this new environment, the major sources of learning available to the employee will be new work challenges and relationships. The best way to promote adaptability in experienced employees is to provide varied experience through a series of new assignments. A person should not be left to stagnate in one kind of work. (In fact, the good news in today's turbulent corporate environment is that restructuring has eliminated stagnation.) The cheapest, simplest way to provide continuous stimulation and challenge is to continuously provide the person with different assignments that demand different skills. We call this the Mae West rule: She was quoted as saying, "When choosing between two evils, I prefer the one I haven't tried yet."

Like variety, relationships are also in generous supply in the work environment, and they represent a key source of continuous learning. Coworkers, especially if they come from diverse backgrounds (diverse in terms of race, ethnicity, nationality, age, gender, functional training, education, ability, etc.), represent a variety of skills, attitudes, and worldviews that can stretch a person, especially an older employee. Bosses and subordinates and people from different parts of the organization, especially in a team-oriented system, are also good learning sources. Also, customers, in quality-oriented organizations, are excellent inputs for learning. Of course, mentoring, networking, team structures, and coaching are important in promoting growth as well.

Ten Steps to More Rapid Adaptation

One of the most sobering thoughts in our interviews related to the adaptation time in the move to the new contract: It appears that it takes on average approximately 7 years after the start of a major transformation for an organization and its members to arrive at an understanding of the new career contract. This seemed to make sense to people in our feedback discussions, as they thought about how long and difficult the change process had been (i.e., for those in companies that had reached the "sees the forest" stage).

Because it seemed to take approximately 7 years for natural processes to produce the adaptation to the new contract, we argue that with intervention the adaptation process could be accelerated. Because we found that the contract changes were "nondiscussable" in most firms, if there were to be conscious attempts to create dialogue with employees regarding these career contract changes, employees could more quickly understand the environmental forces involved and embrace the degree of autonomy and self-responsibility available to them.

What specific steps should an organization or a manager take to facilitate the career development of employees in this new environment? The notion of what the organization can do is tricky because, as mentioned earlier, the protean career is self-directed. The notion of organizational career management, which was in vogue not too long ago, has become self-contradiction. Thus, the appropriate steps for the organization and manager relate to providing the conditions that will support this career self-direction. Elsewhere (Hall & Associates, 1996), I have proposed the following 10 steps to promoting successful protean careers (these steps are summarized in Table 2.4 on page 43):

1. Start with the recognition that the individual "owns" the career. Employers, even if they wanted to, cannot do meaningful planning for an employee's career, not even for managers and key executives. Instead, like other business processes, development now takes place "closer to the customer" in the form of coaching, 360-degree feedback, mentoring, challenging assignments, and other relational activities. Many of these are spontaneous, everyday activities that are better integrated by the employee, through personal reflection and planning, than by the organization.

2. Create information and support for the individual's own efforts at development. Although the organization cannot do much directly to develop a person's career, it can provide the necessary empowering resources for career development, the most important of which are information about opportunities throughout the organization and support in obtaining information and in taking developmental action.

Information technology is making it possible for employees to learn about the strategic direction of the business, about work opportunities in different areas, about specific position openings, and about upcoming training and development programs. Internet career information and self-assessment sites, company web pages, electronic resumes, and career software (e.g., Career Architect, CareerSearch, PeopleSoft, and SIGI) assist employees in self-assessment and in obtaining company opportunity information. Many corporate and university career centers now have rich offerings available online. For example, the Talent Alliance, a multicompany partnership, provides career information on the Internet for companies seeking employees and for individuals seeking employment. More information on the Talent Alliance is provided in Box 2.2.

BOX 2.2

The Talent Alliance

To illustrate the use of information technology for career growth, consider the Talent Alliance, a U.S.- and Internet-based collaborative coalition of companies, industry and trade associations, professional service firms, academic organizations, and government officials whose mission is to establish best-in-class practices for skills development and employability of the American workforce. The founding companies include AT&T, DuPont, GTE, Johnson & Johnson, Lucent Technologies, NCR, TRW, Unisys, and UPS. These firms contribute time, talent, and financial support to the Alliance, which is organized as a membership-based organization. Activities of the Alliance focus on research, career growth and development, Futures Forum programs, training and education, job/talent matches, industry trends, high-tech careers, displaced employees, and recruitment and academic relationships.

The following are some frequently asked questions from the Alliance's web page to give the reader a better idea of how it will operate:

How will the Talent Alliance accomplish its goals?
- Career growth centers provide online and on-site career planning tools and professional counseling that provide direction and enhance employability.
- Education and training programs enhance skills and employability of member company employees by providing ready access to the best-in-class training and education. Most of these programs will be delivered online.
- A job/talent matching system provides member companies with access to the nation's richest job bank and most qualified talent pool.

Who is eligible to participate in the Talent Alliance?
Currently, member companies determine eligibility criteria for their employees. In the future, the Talent Alliance plans to provide fee-based services to individuals and unaffiliated member companies.

Who pays for Talent Alliance services?
Currently, member companies pay for services.

How can interested companies or individuals join?
They can do so by accessing the "How to Participate" section on the Talent Alliance web site (http://www.talentalliance.com) or by calling 1-888-WorkWays.

In addition, there is a vast array of career self-help resources (books, mentoring programs, seminars, etc.). Professional organizations are becoming increasingly active in providing career services for members. Increasingly, the practice of organizational career development is shifting from being a direct provider to being a career resource and referral agent. This leads us to our next point.

3. Recognize that career development is a relational process in which the organization and career practitioner play a "broker" role. Being a career broker can mean many things. It can mean linking people and assignments in a way that gives more importance to developmental benefits. It can mean facilitating mentoring and other developmental relationships. It can mean creating various kinds of dialogue groups for employees to voice career concerns and interests and to share ideas for action. It can also mean helping work teams and individuals find ways to create settings for reflection and "time out" to work on their own development.

4. Provide expertise on career information and assessment technology, integrated with career coaching and consulting. In the past, organizations often provided specialized career information and assessment assistance, and often this was a different function from that of human resource generalists who may have provided organizational interventions to create organizational career development programs. Now, with fewer human resource staff, career practitioners must be both specialists and generalists. This means being certified on the latest assessment and development instruments, being familiar with the most recent computer software, and knowing how to work with line management to create experience-based career development processes. To accomplish this, personal networking, developing alliances and partnerships, regular participation in professional conferences, keeping current on the professional literature, and the like are all "must dos."

5. Provide excellent communication with employees about career services and the new career contract. All the previous steps are of little value if their existence is not communicated to the employee, who is now required to be more proactive and autonomous. Career professionals, both internal and independent, now publish career newsletters. Company web pages are an excellent vehicle for communicating career resources to employees. Also, external communication (e.g., through the careers column in the *Wall Street Journal*) can also be an excellent way to communicate with one's employees.

6. Promote work planning, not career planning. The key task for the individual in a complex, changing environment is finding a good fit with work that is needed in the world. This means that employees should be encouraged to think in terms of areas of work and projects that they would like to pursue over a time period of, for example, 3 to 5 years. This is not as easy as it sounds. It means providing resources to help employees assess their own identities and values so they can be clear on their own sense of direction to pursue their own path with a heart. It also means being organizationally flexible to enable employees to make changes in their work activities based on their personal interests. Flexibility in the work is a key to work satisfaction (Clark, 2001).

7. Promote learning through relationships and work. The silver lining in the world of corporate turbulence is that the two key resources for learning—relationships and challenging work—are widely available. In the restructured firm, the jobs for the people who remain are more challenging and more team based than were the jobs in the old organization. Successful organizations are becoming learning organizations by encouraging employees to help each other learn the new skills and competencies needed in these more demanding jobs. Although some of this learning comes from formal training programs, we argue that most real training comes from peer-assisted, self-directed learning through such vehicles as project teams, task forces, electronic communication, personal networks, support groups, customer relationships, and boss or subordinate relationships.

8. Provide career-enhancing work and relational interventions. To truly help people learn through relationships and work, managers and career practitioners must be able to influence the kind of work they do and the kinds of people they encounter. This means playing an active role in organi-

Table 2.4   Ten Steps to Promoting Successful Protean Careers

1. Start with the recognition that the individual "owns" the career.
2. Create information and support for the individual's own development efforts.
3. Recognize that career development is a relational process; the organization and career practitioner play a broker role.
4. Integrate career information, assessment technology, career coaching, and consulting.
5. Provide excellent career communication.
6. Promote work planning; discourage career planning.
7. Focus on relationships and work challenges for development.
8. Provide career interventions aimed at work challenge and relationships.
9. Favor the learner identity over job mastery.
10. Develop the mind-set of using "natural resources for development."

zational practices, such as in how job and other work (task forces and projects) assignments are made.

9. Favor the "learner identity" over job mastery. If major sources of career learning are challenging work and helpful coworkers, this implies that continuous learning should be promoted by continuous mobility. The criterion of success in a selection decision should not be limited to mastery of a position; rather, success should be defined as the person's ability to move easily from job to job. We need to promote a culture in which it is just as highly valued to be a learner as it is to be a peak performer. After all, it is good learners who provide an organization with the ultimate competitive advantage: flexibility.

10. Develop the mind-set of using "natural resources for development." Organizations today are seeing that several naturally occurring resources use the everyday work environment as a development tool. The role of the organization, manager, and career practitioner is to help the individual recognize such resources and to find ways to use them. Elements in the natural work environment that can be used to aid career development include assignments (jobs, teams, task forces, and committees), feedback (360 degree and performance review); developmental relationships (such as mentoring), and coaching (skill building, not just remedial). Increasingly, it will be the manager's responsibility to manage the work environment not only to maximize effective performance but also to promote continuous learning and development.

Questions for Further Research

Although the new career contract has been with us for many years now, there is still a need for good research on how people are managing under it. Some of the specific areas of promise for further research include the following:

How do people cope successfully with changes in the career contract? Millions of people have made the transition from the old to the new contract, but these transitions have been largely undocumented. One idea for examining these changes is to focus on settings in which we know the change in the environment has been fundamental: Eastern Europe, the countries of the former Soviet Union, welfare recipients in the United States following welfare reform, and so on. A good model here is the study by Arthur, Inkson, and Pringle (1999) of workers in New Zealand, where the economy quickly changed in the mid-1980s from a welfare economy to a free market.

How do contingent workers manage their learning and adaptation process? As O'Connell (2001) has shown, a successful temporary worker goes through a series of stages in his or her adaptation to a short-term work assignment. Additional studies are needed to test the FAST model. Is the style that the temporary worker employs to navigate movement into, around, and out of an assignment the key to understanding the protean worker?

What is the emerging role of the organization in the new protean career contract? Has the term "organizational career planning" become an oxymoron? What is the appropriate role of the organization in the individual's career if the organization cannot "manage" the career? How can an organization that in the past controlled employees' careers shift to providing resources, support, and autonomy? This new role requires a lighter touch. Where is it being done? What is known about when it works well? More best practice research would be useful in addressing these questions.

Relational and transactional contracts: Can we have both? To date, in the literature relational and transactional contracts have been considered as mutually exclusive. I argue, however, that it is possible to have "neotraditional" contracts— that is, contracts based on the mutual understanding that there are no long-term guarantees but that both parties hope and would prefer to see the relationship continue for a long time, and both parties will conduct themselves accordingly. Thus, both parties would behave as if it were a relational contract while understanding that, legally, it only covers the current transaction. It is a challenge to researchers to determine if there are examples of this sort of relational transaction-based contract. Also, if such a hybrid contract does exist, what are the respective expectations and responsibilities of each party?

What do adaptability and identity growth look like in a successful protean career? What do these career metacompetencies look like in practice? What can an organization do to facilitate identity growth and adaptability in its members? What percentage of the variance in each is accounted for by innate individual differences (such as personality or basic abilities), and what percentage can be explained by the individual's actions, by relational influences, by job challenges, or by formal training and education? Another approach to this question is to conduct holistic studies of individuals who have made fundamental, protean transformations in their careers. These would be people who, by definition, have made major career adaptations and major changes in personal identity. An example of this kind of research is David Krantz's (1977) study of midcareer changers in Santa Fe. Participants in Krantz's study, however, seemed to be rather countercultural, whereas today these major changes are more mainstream. How would these career shifters look today?

Conclusion

This, then, is the new protean career contract. Instead of mourning the passing of the old contract, we are now in a period of implementation of the new contract. For employers that have made this transition from mourning the old to practicing the new, the old contract looks like paternalism, and the new one is described with words such as growing, responsibility, empowering, providing resources and opportunities, and working hard. Reaching the point at which the new contract is "on stream" is a difficult developmental process for employee and employer alike. It takes on the order of 7 years.

Organizations that have had the most success with the new contract are those that have consciously confronted its existence. They have made explicit efforts to identify the new contract. Although they recognize that the new career contract is primarily self-directed, they also realize that there is an important role for the employer to play, by providing information, resources, challenging opportunities, and support.

These "new career companies" have clearly communicated to employees their central business purpose, strategy, and values, from which they have derived clear management development philosophies. In organizations such as Starbucks, employees know what the mission of the organization is and how they fit into that larger enterprise. Also, they derive personal identity and pride from working toward a "good" purpose.

It is also becoming clear that consciously attending to issues of diversity in career and management development provides the organization with a clear competitive advantage in responding to new, diverse markets and rapidly changing technologies. The more diverse and complex the workforce, and the more effective the firm is in using and providing career learning opportunities for all members of that workforce, the more successful it will be in meeting the demands of a complex and turbulent environment.

Finally, organizations that have succeeded in creating a new contract for the new business environment have recognized that the career of the future is a continuous learning process. Also, continuously learning employees are what the organization needs to be a continuously improving business. Successful companies help employees grow.

As James Champy, the "father" of reengineering, mentioned, the success of restructuring depends on the firm's success in developing and enabling its employees. Terry Diamond, of Talon Asset Management investment company, decided to buy shares of Starbucks after hearing Howard Shultz speak in 1991: Diamond stated, "Shultz didn't even mention one financial number. Instead, he talked about how all employees, even temporary employees, got health insurance. After the conference, I walked up to him and told him how much he had impressed me." (The company and its shareholders, in fact, have achieved remarkable financial success since that time.) Mr. Diamond compared the relationship between a firm's top management and its employees to a marriage: "You get out of it what you put into it. If [a leader] cares about his employees, he also cares about customers."

In organizations in which it has worked the best, the new career contract did not represent a discontinuous corporate trauma. Rather, it was simply an intelligent response to a turbulent and unforgiving economic environment. In this contemporary environment, "success" is disguised as an ongoing and difficult struggle, but one with a clear sense of values and vision, an appreciation of the crucial role of employees in achieving that vision, and a lifelong process of continuous learning.

Note

1. A newer case study of Starbucks, written by Aliya Nehal, can be obtained by contacting me at the Executive Development Roundtable at the Boston University School of Management (617-353-2031).

II

Elements of the Career

3 Career Choice
and Decision Making

*I can see now that I started my professional journey on the day at
age 4 when I declared to my parents and to the world, Mom, Dad, I
want to be a fireman. Now this was not some precious instinct towards
civic duty. No, it really wasn't terribly profound. In fact, it was simply
that I loved the color red and I thought black-and-white dogs with
spots were really cool. But when I look back now I see a kid who was
not afraid to commit to a different path through life, and I see parents
who encouraged their child's ambition whatever it was.*

—Carly Fiorina, CEO of Hewlett-Packard (MIT
commencement speech, June 2, 2000)

As Carly Fiorina's experience shows, and as previously stated, under
the "new" career contract, the career is highly *protean*—that is, it
involves pursuing one's own "path with a heart," it is driven by the person, and it can be subject to frequent changes in shape and direction.
This is different from the "old" model, with its view that career choice
was a single event or a terminal process, usually occurring in adolescence or the early twenties, and then the rest of the career years were
spent enacting the career that was chosen earlier. In fact, before 1970,
most of the literature on the psychology of careers focused on the

selection of an occupation or of a college major (which would lead into an occupation).

In this chapter, we take the perspective that a career choice is not just the choice of an occupation (which could occur or recur at any point in one's adolescent or adult life) but any choice affecting one's career. The person makes choices and decisions all the time as the career unfolds, and these choices have effects over time on how the career unfolds. Thus, this chapter is really about getting into and getting along within the world of work, or about what others have called the early career.[1]

Eras of Career Research

As Hall and Mirvis (1995) pointed out, there has been a shift over the decades in the nature of the career choices and thus the models used to study them. In the early years of career research (the 1950s and 1960s), the primary choice studied was what broad occupational field would a person enter (e.g., teacher and engineer). This was perhaps related to the social context in the United States of rapid economic development, in which there was a great need for talent in education and in the sciences (e.g., the "Sputnik era," when the space race between the United States and the Soviet Union was raging) and thus a need to predict who would enter critical fields.

In the 1970s, the focus shifted to specific jobs and to factors that affected job choices and success (Hall, 1976; Schein, 1978; Wanous, 1992). The 1980s were a decade in which the focus moved to the individual in the organization as a system. In an era in which organizations were being fundamentally restructured, downsized, and delayered, there was interest in processes such as career plateauing, career stages, and organizational career ladders and timetables (Hall and Associates, 1986). In their literature review, Chartrand and Camp (1991) indicated, for example, that during the years 1986 to 1990, the most frequently studied career construct in studies published in the *Journal of Vocational Behavior* was organizational commitment.

At the beginning of the 21st century, I argue that the central focus in career research is now the self. As the environment of most organizations has become highly turbulent, complex, and demanding, with organizations able to take less responsibility for employees' career development, individuals have had to adopt the perspective of the career as self-employment. This is what we have termed the *protean career* (Hall & Associates, 1996; Hall & Moss, 1998). This means that if the old career contract was with the employing organization, the new contract is with the self. These changes in focus during the different eras of career research are shown in Table 3.1.

This protean career concept does not invalidate the notion of career choice or even the choice of an organization to enter. It does mean that the person must be more mindful of these choices and of the need to be constantly reviewing choices already made. The career is never on "automatic pilot"; the person must always be alertly operating the controls. In particular, the two most important specific types of career choices the person must think about are (a) the choice of an area of work (or occupational field) and (b) the choice of an organization in which to work. These will be the primary choices on which we focus in this chapter.

There is probably more theory and research dealing with the choice of an occupation than with any other single issue in the field of career development. Occupational choice theories are classified into two categories:

1. Matching theories (or models, in some cases) that describe what kinds of people enter what kinds of occupations based on some measure of compatibility between the person and the chosen occupation
2. Process theories (or models) that describe the manner in which people gradually arrive at a choice of an occupation

In this chapter, we begin by examining these types of theories as means of answering two important questions: How are individuals matched with careers and how is the career choice made? Next, we get more specific and examine how individuals choose to enter particular organizations. Then, based on the theory and research literature, we consider ways in which career choice can be facilitated. Finally, we consider the important issues that arise in the study of career choice.

Matching People and Occupations

As Super (1957, 1990) and others (Brown & Brooks, 1996; Cable & Judge, 1997) have pointed out, career choice and development is basi-

Table 3.1   Eras of Career Research

Era	Desired Match	Example
Stage 1 (1950s →)	Person-occupation	"I am a banker"
Stage 2 (1970s →)	Person-job	"I am a division manager"
Stage 3 (1980s →)	Person-organization	"I work for IBM"
Stage 4 (1990s →)	Person-self	"I do Web design"

cally a *synthesizing process,* a process of achieving compatibility between the person and the chosen occupation. Also, as discussed in the previous chapter, choosing an area of work is a major developmental task in the process of forming an identity and entering the adult world (Levinson, 1996). Because such a large proportion of a person's identity revolves around work, it is not surprising that people try to choose work that will best enable them to fulfill their interests, meet their needs, and express themselves.

Career as Vocation or Calling

At their best, careers provide an individual with a sense of meaning and purpose in life. They are a way of expressing the self. In one classic study, Abraham Maslow (1968) found evidence of this connection between career and personal needs, interests, and identity in a study that indicated that people who were highly self-actualized were also likely to be highly identified with their career. When Maslow asked the people in his study what they would be if they were not in their respective vocations, many hesitated and had difficulty answering. Others responded with comments such as "I can't say. If I weren't a [doctor, scientist, etc.], I just wouldn't be me. I would be someone else."

These comments remind us of a notion from an earlier time of the career as vocation. In fact, the area of psychology that focuses on careers is still called vocational psychology, and one of our most respected career journals is the *Journal of Vocational Behavior*. In a study of Roman Catholic priests, Hall and Schneider (1973) reviewed a vast literature of religious careers that focuses on the notion of a *calling*, the idea that the person was put here in the world to do a certain kind of work. Recently, there has been a resurgence of interest in this spiritual notion of the career as people become more motivated to seek the ultimate purpose of their life and work. For example, there is now an interest group on spirituality in the Academy of Management. The book market is now full of titles covering spirituality, leadership, and business (using the metaphor of Jesus as CEO, many references to the soul and work, etc.). A project organized by Andre Delbecq and James McGee at Santa Clara University is producing scholarly writing and curricular materials integrating spirituality, leadership, and careers (Delbecq & McGee, 2001). A detailed discussion of the differences and commonalities between the concepts of career and the theological concept of calling is provided in a paper by Weiss, Skelley, Hall, and Haughey (2001). All this work on the deep meaning of career serves to remind us of the importance of the process by which the person makes choices about his or her career path.

How Person-Career Fit Is Assessed

How would we know if a person had achieved a sense of calling in his or her work career? How can we know if a person is compatible with a particular occupation? The research on careers indicates that there are four general personal characteristics that determine person-job fit:

1. Interests
2. Self-identity and life stage
3. Personality (e.g., needs, personal orientation, and values)
4. Social background (e.g., socioeconomic status)

Studies in these areas have attempted to determine the degree to which these attributes are possessed by most people in various occupations and the degree to which they are required for effective performance in various occupations or are perceived by the person to be associated with various occupations. Then, by various means (e.g., profiles and peak scores), the researchers identify the occupations that best fit the characteristics of the people being studied. Generally, tests and questionnaires are employed, and the researchers tend to be differential psychologists. In the following sections, we examine each of these four approaches to the study of career selection in more detail.

Interests

According to Super and Bohn (1970, p. 83), "with the exception of intelligence, more is known about interests than about any other single personality variable." Probably one of the most familiar instruments that measure interests is the Strong Interest Inventory (SII), originally developed by Edward K. Strong, Jr., and first published under the name Strong Vocational Interest Blank in 1943. The SII is now published by Stanford University Press and continues to be a commonly used vocational interest inventory. The SII compares the examinee's responses with those of successful practitioners of various professions.

Most of Strong's work involved experimentally identifying relationships between occupations and interest patterns. He defined an interest as a response of liking related to a particular activity; an aversion is a response of disliking. Operationally, Strong measured an interest by asking the respondent to indicate liking (L), indifference (I), or disliking (D) for a particular activity, occupation, or other object (e.g., factory manager, farmer, and florist).

Interests tend to attain a stable pattern at approximately age 21 and remain remarkably consistent over the person's entire lifetime. Test-retest correlations over 20-year periods on the order of .70 are not unusual.

For measurement purposes, Strong defined "vocational interest" as the sum total of many interests that bear in any way on an occupational career. He computed interest scores from each person's responses to the items in the inventory. Strong's basic assumption was that certain occupations involve work activities that best enable a person to pursue a particular range of interests. He reasoned that people in a given occupation, such as management, would hold certain interests similar to other members of that occupation and different from people in other occupations. To test this idea, he examined the likes and dislikes of people in a particular occupation, contrasting them with the likes and dislikes of people in other occupations and also with those of people in general. He searched for interest areas that discriminated between the particular occupational group and the general population. In this way, he was able to obtain scoring weights for each individual occupational scale. A person's interest blank score on each occupational scale was a measure of how much his interest profile was similar to that of members of that occupation.

Psychologist David Campbell, who collaborated on a revised version of the original Strong inventory (which was then called the Strong-Campbell Interest Inventory), has developed another widely used and well-respected interest instrument called the Campbell Interest and Skills Inventory (Campbell, Hyne, & Nilsen, 1992). This instrument uses generally similar methods for measuring interests and for validating results with various norms groups. It goes beyond the Strong and also measures self-reported skills. Rather than use separate scales for men and women, which has generated great controversy, the Campbell measure uses unisex norms. Other well-known interest instruments are the Kuder Occupational Interest Survey (Kuder, 1977) and the Vocational Preference Inventory (Holland, 1997).

Self-Identity and Life Stage: Donald Super's Synthesizing Approach

One of the major theories and programs of research focusing on the impact of self-identity on career choice was created by Donald Super (1957, 1990) and colleagues (Super, Savickas, & Super, 1996). Super began his research in the late 1930s when he was an employment counselor in Cleveland, Ohio. Super saw the career as an ongoing, unfolding synthesis of the person's self-concept and the external realities of the work environment. He saw it as a series of choices and decisions; career choice was not a once-in-a-lifetime event in his view.

It should be noted that because Super's theory is so broad, it is difficult to categorize it under just one of our two major headings in this chapter—content or process. He does talk about career stages and the ways that different life roles interact at different stages, and these are certainly process issues. At the core of Super's thinking, however, is the notion of the career as a *synthesis*, a match between the self-concept of the individual and the requirements and expectations of an occupational role. Obtaining a good match is a matter of content, a good fit between person and environment. Therefore, with this recognition that our conceptual distinction between content and process becomes fuzzy with a broad, eclectic model such as Super's, we proceed with our discussion of his thinking.

Self-Concept. Self-concept is a general term describing a person's image of herself—her abilities, interests, needs, values, past history, aspirations, and so forth. This synthesis develops gradually as the person becomes aware of (a) her self-concept, (b) the opportunities and requirements in particular occupations, and (c) her experiences in implementing her self-concept by working in particular occupations.

Life Span and Life Space. Super's theory is often referred to as a *life span, life space* approach to career development (Super, 1990). He represented the person's life space in terms of the multiple roles in a person's life using the Life-Career Rainbow (see Chapter 4, this volume). The rainbow has two dimensions, time and space (i.e., role), and it illustrates how these life roles emerge and change over time. This model makes a good complement to the life stages and transitions found in the work of Daniel Levinson (1996) and colleagues.

Development in the career consists of passing through a sequence of stages brought about by the interaction between self-concept and occupation. Each of these stages was originally described in a chapter of Super's book, *The Psychology of Careers* (1957), and they appeared in revised form in one of Super's last publications (Super et al., 1996) as follows:

> *Growth (ages 4-13):* This stage includes four major developmental tasks (the italicized developmental tasks for this stage were revised and presented by Savickas & Super, 1993):
>> Developing *concern* about the future
>> Increasing personal *control* over one's own life
>> Developing *conviction* about one's ability to achieve in school and work
>> Acquiring *competence* in work habits and attitudes
>
> *Exploration (ages 14-24):* This stage includes the following major developmental tasks:
>> Crystallizing an occupational choice (going from fantasy to public preference)
>> Specifying a choice (translating it into concrete educational and occupational decisions)
>> Implementing a choice (completing the needed training and obtaining an actual occupational position)
>
> *Establishment (approximately ages 25-44):* This adult stage entails the following tasks:
>> Stabilizing an occupational position (becoming socialized in an organization and performing one's work satisfactorily)
>> Consolidating one's position through positive work attitudes, good performance, and good relationships with coworkers
>> Advancing in one's field, which entails moving to higher levels of responsibility and is not achieved by all individuals
>
> *Maintenance (ages 45-65):* Some people stay in one organization, occupation, or field and go through all of this stage. Others, however, recycle back through the stages of exploration and establishment by switching to other settings

(Williams & Savickas, 1990). Maintenance includes the following career development tasks:

Holding on by sustaining what one has achieved

Keeping up by updating one's skills, knowledge, and perspectives

Innovating by finding new ways of performing or new areas of challenge

Disengagement (over age 65): Although it now seems clear that this stage can come at many different ages, depending on the person, the career field, the economy, the spouse's situation, and many other factors, the basic process here is one of making the transition from a major life/work role and moving into some other life structure. The main development tasks here include

Deceleration, or slowing down, turning over tasks to younger colleagues, and beginning to think about retirement

Retirement planning, a central activity that leads eventually to separation from the work role

Retirement living, which involves organizing and implementing a new life structure

Career Maturity. A central concept in Super's thinking about decision making at various career stages, but especially in the exploration stage, is *career maturity.* This term, borrowed from biology, refers to the readiness of the person to make good decisions at a given point in his or her life.

Because we are talking about careers in terms of development over time, we must consider what development means. When is a person at a more or less "developed" stage in relation to his career compared to someone else? Super and Bohn (1970) defined career maturity as the person's readiness to cope effectively with the developmental tasks of one's life stage in relation to other people in the same life stage. Therefore, career maturity is a relative (rather than absolute) concept in two senses: It involves (a) behaviors related to a particular life stage and (b) an assessment of coping in relation to the person's peers. In this sense, then, we cannot say a person becomes more vocationally mature as she advances in years. Each life stage brings a new set of demands, and the person must "reestablish" her vocational maturity in dealing with them in each stage.

One implication of this is that what constitutes mature behavior at one stage may be considered to be less mature at a different stage. For example, examining various career options is appropriate behavior in the exploratory stage, but it might be seen as less mature during the establishment, maintenance, or decline stages. Similarly, attempting to achieve occupational success is considered mature behavior in the establishment stage, but it may be seen as premature for adolescents. In this sense, then, career maturity is worked for but never finally and permanently attained. It is worked for, attained for a period of time, then challenged, worked for again, and obtained again, and so forth in a series of developmental cycles. Therefore, to assess a person's career maturity, we should examine the process by which he is dealing with career issues, not the outcomes of his career work, such as satisfaction or success.

Most of the work of measuring career maturity has been conducted with adolescents, although there has been more interest recently in adult maturity. Crites (1973) developed a model of career maturity in adolescence, in which maturity is defined in terms of four factors: (a) consistency of career choices, (b) realism of career choices, (c) competencies in career choice tasks, and (d) maturity of career choice attitudes. Given the problems of employees who continue floundering well into their careers and who persist in fields for which they are not well suited, the notion of adult career maturity is of immense value for selection, placement, and career development of personnel.

In one of his last publications, Super and colleagues (1996) discussed career maturity as follows:

> Super (1955) invented the construct of *career maturity* to provide a basis for describing and assessing the stage of career development reached by students of differing ages and grades and their readiness to make educational/vocational decisions. He viewed maturation as the central process in adolescent career development because career choice readiness clearly increases with chronological age and school grade. Having chosen a term from biology forced Super to repeatedly explain that although career maturity increases with age, the impetus is not biological; the impetus is psychosocial in the form of expectations, in the curriculum and in the minds of family and teachers, for students who are approaching the end of their schooling. Once out of school, the psychosocial impetus for individual career development shifts to changes in work and working conditions. (p. 133)

Measures. Several measuring instruments have been developed to aid in the understanding of concepts in Super's theory. The Salience Inventory (SI) is used for mapping a person's life space and to measure work-role importance (Nevill & Super, 1986). The SI examines five roles—school, work, family, community, and leisure. For each role, it assesses the person's participation in the role, commitment to the role (emotional attachment), and the value the person expects to derive from it.

The Adult Career Concerns Inventory (ACCI) (Super, Thompson, & Lindeman, 1988) is a measure of the person's career stage. It measures this by assessing the degree of the person's concerns with developmental tasks associated with a particular career stage. It measures planfulness or concern with tasks related to exploration, establishment, maintenance, and disengagement. Because the instrument taps specific activities within each stage, it is sensitive enough to measure what Super calls "minicycles" involved in adapting to a particular role or recycling and reexploring other options later in life.

To assess resources for working on career development issues, the Career Development Inventory (CDI) is used (Savickas, 1990; Thompson, Lindeman, Super, Jordaan, & Myers, 1984). Two of the variables measured by the CDI are affective, career planfulness and curiosity about career exploration. The other two dimensions are cognitive and tap the person's information about work and occupations as well as one's knowledge about the principles of career decision making. The resultant pattern of the four scores assesses readiness to make good career choices. It also indicates any areas that would be barriers to good decision making.

There are two measures of values that have been used in Super's work. The Values Inventory (VI) (Nevill & Super, 1986) is a comprehensive instrument assessing 21 values that people seek to find in life. The Work Values Inventory (WVI) (Super & Bohn, 1970) focuses just on work roles. It measures 15 values that affect the person's motivation to work. For issues dealing with work/life balance, the VI may be more useful. When the person is trying to do exploration and specification within a set of work roles, the WVI may be more relevant.

Although these instruments were developed originally for use by career counselors, they can also be used for research. For example, Hall (1985), Kram and Hall (1991), and Slocum, Cron, Hansen, and Rawlings (1985) have used the ACCI to address issues of career plateauing. The instrument's psychometric properties are generally quite good (e.g., internal consistency reliability, test-retest reliability, construct validity, and predictive validity), and they are quite clear and amenable to large-sample organizational research studies.

Status of the Theory. Super presents a sweeping set of constructs that explain a wide range of behaviors related to life and career decision making. He described it as a *functional* theory, one in which the emphasis is on the "provisional and tool character of theory" (Marx, 1963, p. 16). He refers to Marx and Hillix (1963), who state that functionalism examines the relationship between an organism and its environment and asks two major questions: What do people do? and Why do they do it? Thus, this kind of research usually focuses on empirical research, it examines relationships among variables, and it does not stress the building of elaborate rational-deductive "superstructures." In other words, Super's theory is more inductive than deductive.

Ironically, despite the major visibility and impact of Super's theorizing, his concepts have not been tested widely, probably because his concepts and propositions are so sweeping that they are difficult to reduce to easily testable hypotheses. For example, a self-concept is difficult to identify and assess in quantitative terms. It is more of a clinical concept, but Super and colleagues did attempt to capture it through multiple forms of measurement—interviews, survey questionnaires, observation of specific educational and occupational decisions, and so on.

To be more specific about the complexity of Super's theorizing, consider some of the summary propositions in one of his final papers (Super et al., 1996). Brown and Brooks (1996) described this paper as "the best description yet advanced of how the theory can be applied by career counselors, a description that will in all likelihood enhance practitioners' views of the theory" (p. 523). As Super et al. (1996) said, there were originally 10 propositions in Super's (1957) original statement of his career development theory, and these were modified and updated several times. There were 14 propositions in the 1996 paper, including the following:

3. Each occupation requires a characteristic pattern of abilities and personality traits, with tolerances wide enough to allow some variety of occupations for each individual as well as some variety of individuals in each occupation.

4. Vocational preferences and competencies, the situations in which people live and work, and hence their self-concepts change with time and experience, although self-concepts as products of social learning are increasingly stable from late adolescence until late maturity, providing some continuity in choice and adjustment.

10. The process of career development is essentially that of developing and implementing occupational self-concepts. It is a synthesizing and com-

promising process in which the self-concept is a product of the interaction of inherited aptitudes, physical makeup, opportunity to observe and play various roles, and evaluations of the extent to which the results of role playing meet with the approval of supervisors and peers. (pp. 122-125)

As Brown and Brooks (1996) pointed out, this is not an especially well-constructed theory in that the concepts are not precisely defined and there is not a carefully developed order among them. Super's conceptualizing is more of a rich description of career and life decision processes made by a keen observer with a very wide-ranging, interdisciplinary understanding of the causal factors in career outcomes. I group Super in the "major thinker" category along with other such giants as Erik Erikson and Peter Drucker. They provide good framing of complex issues; they offer wise, original insights; and not many people would ever really even think about "testing" their ideas empirically. These ideas inform further, more detailed conceptualizing and hypothesizing, and it is these ideas that are tested empirically.

However, I also believe that the field is the poorer for the lack of empirical work on Super's theory. The 14 propositions provide a gold mine for researchers, and I challenge researchers interested in self-concept and identity, as well as life structure and developmental theory, to make the effort to translate these broad concepts and relationships into questions that can be addressed empirically.

Personality Type: John Holland's Theory

The RIASEC Model. A major and well-supported theory relating personality type to career selection has been put forth by John Holland (1985, 1997). Holland, who traces his interest in career theory back to his military work as induction interviewer in World War II, starts with the straightforward assumption that there is an interaction between personality and environment, such that people gravitate toward environments congruent with their personal orientations. He proposed the following six personality types and six matching occupational environments:

1. Realistic: Aggressive behavior, physical activities requiring skill, strength, and coordination (e.g., forestry, farming, and architecture)

2. Investigative: Cognitive (thinking, organizing, and understanding) rather than affective (feeling, acting, or interpersonal and emotional) activities (e.g., biology, mathematics, and oceanography)

3. Social: Interpersonal rather than intellectual or physical activities (e.g., clinical psychology, foreign service, and social work)

4. Conventional: Structural, rule-regulated activities and subordination of personal needs to an organization or person of power and status (e.g., accounting and finance)

5. Enterprising: Verbal activities to influence others and to attain power and status (e.g., management, law, and public relations)

6. Artistic: Self-expression, artistic creation, expression or emotions, and individualistic activities (e.g., art and music education)

Holland's model, showing the relationships among these six dimensions, is shown in Figure 3.1.

Research With the Vocational Preference Inventory. Various occupations were assigned to the previously mentioned six types of occupational environments, largely on an intuitive basis. The individual's personal orientation is assessed with an instrument devised by Holland called the Vocational Preference Inventory (VPI). (A related instrument is the Self-Directed Search [SDS] [Holland, 1997].) The VPI contains a list of 160 occupational titles: The respondent indicates which he likes and which he dislikes. The assumption here is that people reveal or project their own personal orientation in giving their perceptions of those occupational titles. The responses are then scored in terms of the six classifications described previously plus certain other, nonvocational scales.

The central hypothesis in Holland's theory is that the person's VPI score or profile will be a good predictor of his current career aspiration or later career choice. For example, enterprising people will tend to choose careers in enterprising environments, such as management. This hypothesis has been generally well supported in empirical studies.

Research based on Holland's theory has also been used to study the stability of vocational choice. His theory would predict that a college student majoring in a field congruent with his personal orientation would be more likely to remain (or persist) in that major than would a person whose orientation did not match his major. This hypothesis has also received a degree of support from empirical studies, although the

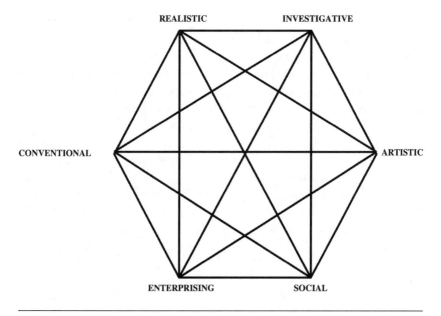

Figure 3.1. Holland's Hexagonal Model for Defining the Psychological Resemblances Among Types and Environments and Their Interactions

nature of the personal orientation alone and the college environment alone also strongly influence stability or change. For example, social people change fields more often than others, whereas intellectuals change less, independent of major field. Furthermore, students in colleges with social environments are more likely to switch majors than are people in nonsocial colleges.

On the basis of factor analysis of VP scores, Holland derived a hexagonal model for describing the relationships between different personal orientations (Figure 3.1). According to Holland's data, the closer two fields or orientations are in this figure, the more compatible they are. Thus, adjacent categories (social-enterprising and realistic-investigative) are quite similar, whereas those diagonally opposite (investigative-enterprising or artistic-conventional) are highly dissimilar. People whose scores fall approximately in the order shown in the hexagon are quite internally consistent, whereas those with high scores in diagonal categories would probably have internal conflicts about their choices.

Like the research in self-concepts and vocational maturity, investigations of Holland's personality and occupational environment categories have not generally been extended to samples of employed people. Holland's typology could be employed usefully in the study of organizational climates, and the VPI seems to have good potential as a predictor of organizational choice in addition to occupational choice. For example, people's images of an organization could be assessed with the VPI, and we could predict that social individuals would enter social organizations, conventional people would enter conventional organizations, and so on. Furthermore, turnover (and floundering) would be lower for those whose self-images provide the best fit with the climate of the organization. Such an analysis would also be helpful in providing a better understanding of why people who are floundering are having difficulty settling into any one organization or career.

Self-Assessment: The SDS. A useful instrument for career guidance is Holland's (1994) SDS, a self-administered, self-scored guide to career selection. The respondent answers questions about personal preferences and then is given instructions about how to score his responses and compute his own profile. He is told the meaning of the various categories and is then directed to a range of occupations that are compatible with his own particular orientation. Research has been conducted that shows that the SDS increases the number of occupations to be considered, increases respondents' satisfaction and certainty about vocational plans, and is rated by respondents as moderately positive in effectiveness (Holland, 1997).

For example, we consider what Holland's theory tells us about the type of person who is oriented toward management. The would-be manager is probably an enterprising person, verbally skilled, who uses this skill to influence and dominate rather than to help and support others and who aspires to power and status. From Holland's hexagonal model, we may infer that the next most likely management candidates would be either social (affiliative) or conventional (rule-oriented conforming) types. These three possibilities fit well with the two dimensions of leadership identified in the Ohio State Leadership studies: consideration (supportive, helpful leader behavior) and initiating structure (task direction, clarifying, instructing, planning, etc.). The enterprising type is high on both dimensions (using social skills to influence and structure the activities of others). The conventional person would be high on structure and low on consideration; the social type would show the opposite pattern. If people who are high on both dimensions are in fact more effective leaders, it would make sense that the person who rates high on both (enterprising) would be the most likely of the three types to become a successful manager.

Gender Issues: Gottfredson's Circumscription and Compromise Theory. Holland's instruments, VPI and SDS, have been criticized because women tend to receive high scores on the social or artistic scales, whereas few receive high scores on the realistic scale. When the instrument was revised by a female graduate student, Linda S. Gottfredson (1978), to remove possible sex bias, however, the results were unchanged. Furthermore, the instrument predicts occupational aspirations equally well for men and women. Holland's position is that all people are subject to strong cultural socializing influences (such as sex, race, and class) that determine one's personal orientation (or type on the SDS). Personal orientation, in turn, affects occupational choice. Therefore, sex affects career choice through sex role socialization and its effects on personal orientation; this seems to be a real social influence, not an artifact of the measuring instrument. (The issue of how sex role socialization occurs is a major problem here and needs a great deal of research and social intervention.)

Gottfredson (1996) presents a wonderful story of her journey to explore the process of sex typing in occupational roles. She started out with the following question:

Why do people of both sexes and of different races and social classes tend to differ, even in childhood, in the kind and quality of jobs they wish for? That is, why do children seem to re-create the social inequalities among their elders long before they themselves experience any barriers to pursuing their dreams? (p. 179)

The result of Gottfredson's work is a complex interaction of self-concept, public and private images of various occupations, and stages of development. She argues that in Stage 1 (ages 3-5), children are oriented to size and power, and they characterize people and occupations in terms of whether they are big and powerful (vs. little). In Stage 2 (ages 6-8) children have progressed to thinking in concrete terms and thinking in dichotomous, evaluative terms (good vs. bad). By this stage, they are beginning to think in sex-typed terms, and they have their own sense of what is a tolerable sex type boundary for classifying occupations. That is, they have begun to rule out certain parts of the occupational world as being the wrong sex type.

In Stage 3 (ages 9-13) they are oriented to social (peer) valuation. They are not only sensitive to male versus female but also to higher versus lower. They begin to see concrete symbols of social class (such as housing, clothing, and possessions), and by age 13 they rank occupations in prestige about the same way that adults do.

By this stage, people also know about occupational hierarchies and see the tight connections between education, occupation, and income. They have also formed concepts of their own abilities and their competitiveness for various occupations. In addition, they begin to form a perception of a tolerable effort boundary, "above which they are not apt to look again unless their self-conceptions of ability and competitiveness change" (Gottfredson, 1996, p. 193).

As a result of these processes, over time people tend to circumscribe or limit the range of occupations that they are willing to consider as realistic for themselves to pursue, and they accordingly make compromises in their occupational strivings. For a full description of this intriguing process, the reader is referred to Gottfredson (1996).

Fortunately, according to Gottfredson (1996), the remedies for such processes are often quite straightforward—and mercifully more simple than the underlying theory. The theory is based on the idea that "circumspection and compromise are often taken for granted and their roots lost to sight" (p. 219). Thus,

> preventing or possibly reversing such constriction requires exposing it and making its bases explicit in the counseling process. This can be as simple as asking why certain options seem to be out of the question or why some compromises are more acceptable or accessible than others. It also involves eliciting information concerning acceptable and preferred selves, both social (social standing, sex role) and psychological (personality). Tolerable level and effort boundaries, perceptions of barriers and opportunity, and the reference groups and family circumstances that influence counselees are all points of inquiry suggested by the theory. (p. 219)

In addition to seeking the previous information from the client, another part of the remedy is helping the person engage in exploration to obtain more realistic information about certain occupations. Using career resource libraries, informational interviews, volunteer work in preferred occupations, studying role models, and internships are all ways of testing the person's assumptions and self-imposed limitations.

Need Theory: Anne Roe

In addition to personal interests, self-concept, and personal orientation, human needs also have a strong bearing on vocational behavior. It seems reasonable to assume that there is a tendency for people to choose careers that will enable them to satisfy their most important needs through their work. Such a theory was proposed by Anne Roe (1957).

The need approach to career choice is based on the assumption that human needs are developed and ordered in a Maslow-style hierarchy, ranging from the lower-order physiological needs through safety, affection, ego concerns, and self-actualization. There is also an assumption of prepotency, meaning that higher needs (e.g., ego needs) would not become important until the needs lower in the hierarchy (physiological, safety, and social affection) had been generally satisfied.

Roe argues that needs satisfied after a very long delay will become unconscious motivators of behavior, and lower-order needs, if rarely satisfied, will become dominant motivators, blocking the emergence of the higher-order needs. She maintains that a major influence on need strength is a person's childhood experiences.

Research has not provided strong support for the theory, perhaps partly because of the problems of obtaining retrospective measures of childhood experiences. Furthermore, most of the difficulties that this writer and others have encountered in testing Maslow's need hierarchy are also present in testing Roe's model. There is also little in the way of practical implications for managers, counselors, or personnel specialists in Roe's model (although it does have much to say to parents). Part of the problem is Roe's stress on childhood experience and her chain of reasoning: Childhood experiences influence personal orientation, which in turn influences career choice. Even if this causal chain is valid, childhood experience should show a weaker relationship to career choice than does personal orientation because its effects are less direct. If childhood experience influences career decisions through its impact on personal orientation, why not just use personal orientation as a predictor? Furthermore, personal orientation is already well-established by the time the person is being studied. Therefore, there would seem to be greater payoff, both in research and in practical terms, in focusing on personal orientation as a more direct predictor, as Holland has done with considerable success, than on the less direct influence of childhood experiences.

Process Models: How Are Career Choices Made?

So far, we have considered various factors in the person and in the social environment that influence the choice of occupations. Although these factors tell us what influences choice, they give us a static view of choice; they do not say much about the dynamics of how and why career choices are made, reconsidered, and revised as the person gains insight, information, experience, and maturity. Therefore, to round out our analysis of choice, we now discuss the process by which career decisions are made.

Ginzberg: Making Choices

According to Ginzberg and associates, the process by which people work on the task of career selection takes place in three stages (Ginzberg, Ginsburg, Axelrad, & Herma, 1951). The first is a fantasy stage, covering the childhood years up to approximately age 11. During this time, the child imagines various things he would like to be when he becomes an adult—a fireman, doctor, policeman, and so on. Here, the person is not really making a choice or even a preference but only beginning to imagine what it will be like to be "grown up."

Next, between the approximate ages of 11 and 16, the person begins to do some career planning, making tentative choices or stating preferences for particular occupations. This tentative career planning is first based on the person's interests. Later, the young person begins to think more about his capabilities and how that would direct or limit him to particular occupations. Even later, the person's values become more crystallized and begin to influence career preferences. Thus, the increasing maturity and development (i.e., identity resolution) of the person manifests itself in the way he or she works on career planning tasks.

The third stage is one of realistic choices, which are more likely to be implemented by the person than are fantasy choices or tentative choices. Starting at approximately age 17, the person has to make specific career decisions, such as whether or not to attend college, what to major in, and what kind of job or training to seek if he does not attend college. There are three substages in the realistic stage: an exploratory period, in which one examines several possible career options; a crystallization substage, in which preferences become more sharply focused; and a specification period, in which the person chooses a particular occupation.

The realistic choice period may continue for many years, long into adulthood, as the person may go through several cycles of exploring-crystallizing-specifying in an attempt to find a career that fits his needs, interests, and abilities.

Thus, the generalization that is stated frequently throughout this book is repeated here: The process of career choice takes place at several different times throughout a person's career. Career choice is not a "one-shot" selection of an occupation in the early twenties. We will expand on this idea later in this chapter.

Once the person has made a choice regarding his or her career, the next task will be to implement or carry out that decision. There is one intervening stage, however, between the selection of an alternative and its implementation, when the person clarifies the choice and dissipates some of the earlier doubts he had about the decision (Tiedeman & O'Hara, 1963). This could also be called a period of *dissonance reduction,* as the term is used in social psychology, in which the person attempts to reduce his internal conflicts regarding (a) the attractive aspects of the unchosen alternatives and (b) the fact that he did not choose them. This process is more likely to be in evidence if the original alternatives were quite similar in attractiveness. For example, assume a student is undecided about whether to take an exciting job in marketing research with General Motors or go to graduate school for a PhD in marketing. Assume that he eventually chooses the GM job after much soul searching. During the period between the time of choice and the time he starts working, he will probably be doing a lot of "cognitive work," building up in his mind all the positive features of the marketing research job and all the negative aspects of the graduate program he rejected. This process of dissonance reduction following job choice has been found in research on MBA students (Vroom, 1966).

If one examines the choice process very closely, as Soelberg (1966) did in an early study of graduating MBA students, it appears that the person has subconsciously made a choice and is performing the clarification tasks even before he is consciously aware of having made it. Soelberg found through intensive interviews at various times in the decision process that the perceived attractiveness of the job eventually chosen became noticeably higher than that of the other job offers weeks before the person consciously decided he was going to accept the offer. It appears that people often make a decision "deep down inside" before they admit to themselves and others that they have done so. What appears to be the process of deciding is therefore often one of clarifying and reducing the dissonance between the preferred alternative and all others.

An important implication of this finding is that once a person knows what his available choices may be, even though he says he is undecided, if he is asked which way he is leaning or what seems most attractive right now, his answer will very likely be his eventual choice. A question that is often useful in counseling students or helping anyone with an important decision is, "If you had to make a decision right now, what would it be?" Very often, the person is surprised to hear his own answer to this question because he had not been consciously aware that he had a preference.

Implementation of Choices:
Schein and Tiedeman and O'Hara

Once a career decision has been made, the next series of tasks involves the execution or implementation of that decision (Tiedeman & O'Hara, 1963). When the decision involves a choice of vocation, implementation means beginning the actual work or the training and education necessary to enter that field of work.

Schein (1971) identified a series of stages in the person's movement into an organization. The first stage is the individual's socialization into the organization. Here, his or her task is to enter and be trained to become a fully functioning member. The new employee learns what is and is not appropriate behavior according to the rules and norms of that organization. The power/influence relationship is tilted in favor of the organization as represented by the person's boss and other supervisors, peers, and often even subordinates (e.g., the seasoned sergeant who has "trained" scores of green lieutenants).

After the person becomes more established in the organization, he or she may then exert efforts toward innovation or change. At this point, the new employee has been accepted and is secure and competent enough to alter the work environment in some way. According to Schein, the person's likelihood of innovating increases as he accumulates seniority, whereas his rate of socialization decreases with time.

If the organization is satisfied with the person's socialization and if the person is satisfied with his or her ability to influence the organization, the person reaches a state of integration with the organization. A satisfactory "psychological contract" (Hall & Moss, 1998; Schein, 1970) has been achieved under which each party understands and honors the expectations of the other. This state of integration is by no means stable and permanent because it is affected by changes in the person or in the work environment (Tiedeman & O'Hara, 1963).

Career Decisions, Psychological
Success, and Identity Development: Hall

If career maturity is a person's effectiveness in coping with the developmental demands of a particular life stage, what then influences this coping effectiveness? In other words, what facilitates the movement of a person through one stage and into the next?

To answer this question, we first assume that people generally strive to increase or maintain their sense of self-esteem. As discussed earlier, one important factor in career choice is self-identity; one important means of achieving a high level of self-esteem is through the development of a competent self-identity or an identity containing a sense of personal competence (Hall & Associates, 1986; White, 1959). As one comes to see oneself as a person who can effectively act on his environment, he values himself more as a total person and thus experiences increased self-esteem.

The person's identity is made up of several subidentities (Hall & Associates, 1986), which represent the various aspects of the person that are engaged when he is behaving in different social roles. (Subidentities will be discussed in more detail in Chapter 6, this volume.) Each social role performed (e.g., worker and mother) presents the social stimuli in the form of behavioral expectations; the corresponding subidentity represents the individual's perceptions of himself as he behaves in response to these role stimuli. The *career subidentity* may be defined as that aspect of the person's identity that is engaged in working in a given career area, and the *career role* is the expectations people hold for individuals in that career. The degree of congruence between the career expectations (role) and one's own perception of his career (subidentity) is defined as *career adjustment*. High career adjustment means that there is little or no conflict between the person's subidentity and his career role. *Career satisfaction* is the extent to which the person values this career adjustment. *Career involvement* may be considered as the importance of the career subidentity relative to other subidentities, the extent to which the person is psychologically identified with the career role.

Occupational selection is the process of choosing a career role in which a high or satisfactory degree of adjustment and satisfaction can be attained. This selection process is not simply a matter of selecting a career role; it is also one of choosing aspects of one's self (skills, interests, etc.) that will be developed through one's career work. Indeed, one reason occupational choice is so difficult is that it means deciding "who I will be" as well as deciding "what I will do." Thus, in terms of the current model, occupational choice could also be called *subidentity selection*.

As the person acquires more competencies and characteristics relevant to his career role, his career subidentity grows. This subidentity extension in the context of the career role is called *career growth*. Specifically, career growth can consist of increases in the individual's knowledge, ability, or motivation related to his career role. Career growth involves personal development, the actual creation of new aspects of the self, in the career area. Thus, the career setting can be highly conducive to self-actualization or self-fulfillment. As the career subidentity expands, proportionately more of the total identity is invested in the career role (i.e., the person becomes more ego involved in his career).

This career involvement is a measure of the strength of one's motivation to work in a chosen career role. Commitment to the entire career field or role is distinguished from commitment to the job (i.e., job involvement) or to one's organization (i.e., organizational identification). These three forms of commitment are often correlated, but they are theoretically distinct and may often have different causes and consequences.

Choice, growth, and involvement can form a spiraling cycle in which each variable feeds back and reinforces the others. As the person sees himself becoming more (or less) competent and successful in an area he has chosen, his satisfaction will increase (or decrease) his involvement in that area, and he will then choose to do more (or less) work in that area, and so on. The term *career development* can be used to describe this spiraling combination of career choice, subidentity growth, and commitment.

A person will experience career subidentity growth when he experiences psychological success in a career-relevant task. Psychological success is defined as the person's feelings of success, as opposed to external measures of success. A sense of psychological success is likely to be achieved under the following conditions:

1. When the person sets a challenging goal for himself (i.e., one representing a high level of aspiration)
2. When the person determines his own means of attaining the goal
3. When the goal is important to his self-concept (i.e., he values the task)
4. When he actually attains the goal (Lewin, 1936)

This sense of personal success will lead, in turn, to an increase in self-esteem.

The basic personality process of developing a competent identity through a perceived personal satisfaction with one's development in career may be illustrated as shown in Figure 3.2.

The need for self-identity as a competent person leads the individual to seek situations in which his self-esteem will be enhanced and to avoid situations in which it will be reduced. Indeed, a person's orientation toward a particular task situation is a function of his current level of self-esteem. If it is high, he will probably be most concerned with seeking success and further developing his competence (i.e., his perceived ability to act effectively on his environment). If his self-esteem is low, on the other hand, he may be more oriented toward avoiding failure and protecting his sense of competence. This idea is supported by aspiration level theory that the person most likely to set a new, higher level of aspiration following a successfully attained goal is the one with a history of previous success. The person accustomed to failure tends to "quit while he is ahead."

Now, we apply this general personality predisposition toward increasing one's self-esteem and competence to the process of occupational selection. The first proposition derives directly from the previous discussion on the determinants of psychological success:

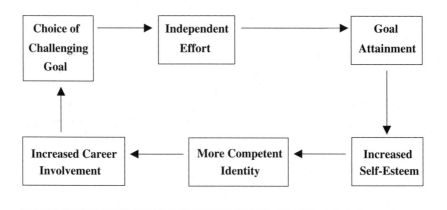

Figure 3.2. Effect of Success on Identity

Proposition 1: In an attempt to experience psychological success in the career, the person will tend to select career roles congruent with current or potential subidentities that are (a) potentially or currently competent and (b) highly valued.

Data relevant to this proposition can be found in the work of Daniel Cable. In one study (Cable & Judge, 1996), it was found that values congruence was positively related to predicted perceptions of person-organization fit, whereas demographic similarity did not. Judge and Cable (1997) further showed how individuals's personality characteristics affected their preferred organizational cultures and how the fit between personality characteristics and organizational culture affected their organizational choices.

Self-esteem is an important factor in determining how successful the person will be in obtaining a good match between subidentity and career role. The more the person searches for information about alternatives, the more effective his choice will be. Examining oneself critically and objectively, however, requires being receptive to "self-data." Because this kind of examination runs the risk of negative discoveries about oneself, the higher one's self-esteem, the lower the likelihood that the person will be threatened by these new insights. Thus, the greater one's level of self-esteem, the more self-aware he will be and the more likely he will be to make a good career selection.

Proposition 2: The higher the individual's level of self-esteem, the more extensive his search will be for information about (a) available career roles, (b) the value he attaches to the relevant subidentities, and (c) his current or potential competence in these areas.

Proposition 3: The more the individual searches for information about available career roles, personal values, and competencies, the more aware he is likely to be of these entities.

Proposition 4: The more aware the person is of her subidentities and available career roles, the closer the match will be between the selected career subidentity and role.

Proposition 5 (derived from Propositions 2-4): The higher the individual's level of self-esteem, the closer the congruence will be between the selected career subidentity and career role.

Support for Proposition 5 derives from research that found self-esteem to be a moderator of the relationship between vocational choice and self-perceived abilities (Bandura, 1986; Brockner, 1988). Other possible moderators of this relationship might be awareness of choice, degree of internal versus external control, or resilience (London & Mone, 1999). Grezda (1999) found that resilience, which he viewed as related to self-esteem and self-efficacy, was positively related to actual career changes involving new duties, skills, and functions.

The individual's level of self-esteem can also affect the degree of risk an individual is willing to take in choosing an occupation (i.e., the level at which the career subidentity-role match occurs). It seems reasonable that people with high self-esteem are more likely to take risks in areas important to them than are those with low self-esteem. This leads to two additional propositions:

Proposition 6: The higher the individual's self-esteem, the greater the likelihood that she would risk committing herself to a career role providing challenge to a highly valued subidentity.

Proposition 7: The higher the individual's self-esteem, the higher will be the difficulty level at which the role-subidentity match occurs.

Proposition 7 is supported by Korman's (1967, 1994) research showing that the ability level of a chosen occupation was higher for people with high self-esteem than for those with low self-esteem. Similarly, Burnstein (1963) found that the following outcomes were associated with fear of failure (which could presumably be an inverse function of self-esteem): (a) lower occupational aspirations, (b) greater willingness to accept lower-prestige occupations, and (c) unrealistically high expectations of achieving high-level occupations.

In contrast to other views of occupational choice, these propositions explain choice in terms of a process of psychological success. Like other theories, the current model is based on person-career fit, but it attempts to show how the discovery of a good fit and the degree of fit are affected by psychological success.

How People Choose Organizations

So far in our discussion, the type of career choice or decision we have considered in most detail has been the choice of an occupation. Career choices can deal with decisions among many different types of alternatives—occupations, job assignments, transfers, promotions, competing job offers, education, approaches to job performance, and so on. Aside from the choice of an occupation or field of work, probably the most important career choice most people make involves deciding for which organization to work.

The theories of person-environment fit that have guided occupational choice research are equally applicable to predicting what organizations people will join. Pervin (1968) was one of the pioneers in this person-environment fit work, and this notion of studying fit took on new energy in the 1990s. Recently, leaders in this area have been Benjamin Schneider (Schneider, Smith, Taylor, & Fleenor, 1998) and Daniel Cable (Cable & Judge, 1996).

As an example of fit models applied to careers that we have discussed so far, the Holland scheme of personal orientation and occupational stereotype could also be extended to include organizational stereotypes. We would predict that realistic-type people would tend to enter realistic organizations, enterprising people would enter active, enterprising organizations, and so forth. Furthermore, turnover would be expected to be lower among people with a good person-organization fit than for those who have less of a match. The degree of fit would be expected to be less strongly related to performance, however, than to satisfaction, attitudes, and affect-related outcomes (such as turnover). In fact, in person-environment fit research in psychology, we do tend to find that the predictions work better for affect-related variables than for performance (Schneider, Kristof-Brown, Goldstein, & Smith, 1997).

The Attraction-Selection-Attrition Model: Schneider

People may choose organizations on the basis of the fit between their needs and the climate of the organization. People with high needs for achievement may choose aggressive, achievement-oriented organizations. Power-oriented people may choose influential, prestigious, power-oriented organizations. Affiliative people may choose warm, friendly, supportive organizations. We know that people whose needs fit with the climate of an organization are rewarded more and are more satisfied than those who fit in less well (Downey, Hellriegel, & Slocum, 1975), so it is natural to reason that fit would also be a factor in one's choice of an organization. Therefore, because the relevant theory and measurement technology are available and fairly well developed, the prediction of organizational choice is a rewarding area for researchers. This is illustrated by research that finds a fit between people's self-concepts and their descriptions of their most preferred organizations (Schneider et al., 1998). Another instrument that could be adapted to the analysis of organizational choice is Holland's (1985) SDS.

This process of people being attracted to certain compatible organizations, which in turn select and reward them, has been expanded on in a process called the Attraction-Selection-Attrition (ASA) model by Benjamin Schneider (Schneider, 1987; Schneider et al., 1997). Schneider et al. (1998) summarized the ASA model as follows:

> The ASA cycle suggests that, first, people are differentially attracted to organizations on the basis of an organization's character and the character's manifestations in organizational structure, strategy, and culture. . . . Thus, the attraction principle suggests that the propensity for organizations to develop a modal personality begins before the organization has the opportunity to formally act in choosing members but is inherent in the preferences held by applicants for particular types of organizations.
>
> Second, through formal and informal selection strategies, organizations choose those individuals who are compatible with the working environment or who fit the character of the organization. Selection further in-

creases homogeneity and the propensity for a modal personality by restricting the type of applicants who enter an organization to those with the competencies, interests, and personality consistent with the goals of the organization. ...[Third, people] who do not fit a working environment tend to leave or "must be relieved." ... Homogeneity is increased by ridding the organization of those people who do not fit and, by implication, leaving those individuals who do. (p. 463)

Schneider et al. (1998) cite several studies that support this model. For example, people with high needs for achievement choose to work for organizations with individual incentive-based reward systems (Turban & Keon, 1993), and people tend to leave organizations they do not fit (O'Reilly, Chatman, & Caldwell, 1991). A study of Roman Catholic priests by Hall and Schneider (1973) found a similar three-step process by which helping-oriented men were drawn to the priesthood, were selected ("called"), and then were socialized into the priesthood. Also, those who did not fit in time left the organization. In a similar vein, Mark Stevens (1981) provides rich descriptions of how these processes work in his inside view of America's most influential accounting firms.

As Schneider et al. (1997) pointed out, this research ties back to Chris Argyris's (1957b) early work reported in his classic book, *Personality and Organization*, describing how organizations create cultures that systematically attract and reward people who are the "right types" for those cultures and equally methodically expel those who are not the right types. Also, as Schneider et al. (1997) note, although this process may have positive effects for individual adjustment (i.e., for employees feeling comfortable and accepted in the organization), the reduction of heterogeneity of thinking in this ASA process can have negative effects on organizational adaptation. That is, if most members think in the same ways, the organization may fail to adapt to changes in the environment that demand new ideas and new ways of thinking. Thus, there may be some optimal level of "misfit" in an organization's membership.

Expectations and Reality Shock

An important aspect of organizational choice is that of expectations. In general, people tend to choose organizations that they view as most instrumental in helping them attain their work goals (Greenhaus &

Callanan, 1994). Studies of the recruitment process (which have generally focused on the university student population) have shown that factors such as familiarity with a specific employer and perceived employer attributes (e.g., company image, rewards, and job challenge) are positively related to applicant attraction and decisions such as acceptance of site visit invitations and job offers (Barber, 1998; Cable & Judge, 1996). In particular, job seekers' perceptions are positively affected by high pay levels, flexible benefits, individual-based pay, and fixed-pay policies. Furthermore, the impact of these rewards is enhanced when there is a strong underlying fit between the individual's personality traits and structural characteristics of the organization (Cable & Judge, 1994).

Where do these early perceptions come from? One study examined the applicant population (general cross sections of students) rather than the specific applicant pool (i.e., students who have applied to that organization) to determine how the applicant population perceived the organization and to evaluate specific recruiting activities as a means of improving these perceptions of the employer (Turban, 2001). Turban found that the firm's image as an employer and the student's familiarity with the firm, as well as the general company image and the work challenge that it would provide, were all positively related to the student's attraction to the firm. Specific recruiting activities, such as whether or not the student had an interview or "wining and dining" activities, did not have a direct impact on perceived attractiveness (when all other variables were controlled), but they seemed to have an indirect effect through the positive image they created in the minds of university personnel, which was related to the student's perceptions. Thus, Turban theorizes that specific recruiting activities serve as signals for unseen organizational attributes (i.e., "If they treat us this well at the interview, this is a preview of how they would treat us on the job."). Thus, to answer our question, the student's expectations are most likely created via experience in the recruiting stage of the employee-employer relationship.

What happens after the student enters the organization with these high expectations? Vroom and Deci (1971) studied MBA students just before and several months after graduation. Both times they were asked to rate the organization they chose and the others they had considered. Vroom and Deci found that the gap between the chosen and unchosen organizations decreased after the person had started work. Given the "reality shock" of actual work experience in the chosen organization, the organization did not look as rosy as it had just after the decision to join. This finding also raises doubts about the permanence of attitude change through dissonance reduction.

Schneider's ASA theory would also help explain why the gap between expectations or aspirations and reality would be greatest at entry, and why the person-organization gap would tend to decrease over time or the person would leave. Over time, the person is socialized and, as Schein's work suggests, also exerts some influence over the organization so that the immediate environment changes slightly to accommodate the person. Both these influences would improve the fit between the person's expectations and the actual organizational experience.

Our final point about organizations concerns the nature of this reality shock versus realistic information as the person enters the organization. From many studies examining lawyers, teachers, doctors, priests, and managers, we know that young people leaving an educational system (college, business school, prison, law school, seminary, etc.) and entering a work organization tend to experience unmet expectations, surprise, disillusionment, anxiety, and other feelings of not being fully prepared for the day-to-day activities and problems of the work environment. This is what we mean by reality shock (Hall & Schneider, 1973).

Additionally, reality shock can happen as the person enters any new assignment. For experienced employees, a common situation in which reality shock is encountered is when an expatriate manager returns to the home country expecting to receive a higher-level job and to use his or her new skills but experiencing an ambiguous role (e.g., a "special project") and a step down in responsibility and authority (Stroh, Gregersen, & Black, 1998; Yan, Hall, & Zhu, 2000). Therefore, anything that would create more alignment in expectations and reduce this reality shock would ease adjustment and help performance in the new assignment.

A factor that undoubtedly contributes to reality shock is the one-sided (positive) view recruiters paint of their organizations. Indeed, some students "psych out" recruiters by determining what features of the organization the recruiter stresses most strongly. This point, they say, is often one the company is most defensive about and reflects an area of greatest weakness.

Several studies, however, have shown that when companies attempt to communicate realistic expectations to recruits, stressing both positive and negative features of the organization, the result is higher satisfaction and retention of the people who are hired (Wanous, 1992). Furthermore, the company's success in recruiting does not seem to be negatively affected by honest information. It is not clear whether these realistic job previews result in a different type of person accepting the offer or if the company gets the same type of person with more reasonable expectations. Either way, the result is a better fit between person and organization at the time of entry.

The issue of expectations and reality shock is especially relevant when we consider diversity in organizations. Research on people who are different from the traditional members of an organization, such as women entering construction organizations (Dainty, Neale, & Bagilhole, 1999), finds that they experience higher reality shock than traditional members as well as slower rates of career progression. This presents a problem for organizations that are attempting to increase the representation of nontraditional employees in their workforce. Even if a firm is successful in attracting and selecting more of what Ann Morrison (1992) calls "nontraditionals" (in terms of the Schneider model), it could still experience high levels of attrition resulting from unmet expectations if the culture and socialization processes are not made more friendly to this more diverse workforce (Kram & Hall, 1996a). Key elements of the organizational culture, such as challenge in assignments, support, visibility, and recognition, must be managed and balanced carefully (not too high and not too low) to maximize the fit for the new nontraditional employee (Dainty et al., 1999; Morrison, 1992).

Relational Influences on Career Choice

An emerging model of how career choices are made is the relational approach (Hall & Associates, 1996). Although this does not negate the importance of the individual and environmental factors discussed previously, it adds another lens for viewing the ways a person obtains and processes information for making career decisions. The relational model describes the role of interpersonal relationships as influences on the development of the person's identity. We know from the work of Levinson, Darrow, Klein, M. Levinson, and McKee (1978), Levinson (1996), Kram (1988), Miller (1986), Fletcher (1996), and others that developmental relationships, such as mentoring, can be useful in helping people work through both career task problems and socioemotional issues as they confront career decision-making situations.

Ironically, although the resources for formal development programs are shrinking in many organizations, the more turbulent the work environment becomes, the more plentiful two major inputs to development become—work challenges and relational support (Kram & Hall, 1991). Another irony is that mentoring is even more important in today's complex, turbulent environments than it was in a more stable environment (Kram & Hall, 1996a). For example, Linehan and Walsh (2001) found that mentoring relationships may be more important for the career success of women managers in international assignments than they are for women managers in home-country positions.

Hall, Briscoe, and Kram (1997) describe the relational model as follows:

> By "relational" we mean the forms of connections the person has with other people, which might occur through work assignments, formal and informal relationships at work, networks of various kinds, as well as social, family, community, and other relationships (Hall & Associates, 1996). Such an approach assumes that relationships are a primary site for learning—both short-term and long-term, both task learning and personal learning. It also assumes that individuals at *all* stages of life and career can benefit from relationships that foster learning; and one of the strengths of such relationships is that they can be reciprocal (Kram, 1988, 1996). (pp. 328-329)

Indeed, because of this reciprocal quality in contemporary developmental relationships, Kram and Hall (1996a) have suggested that a better term than mentoring might be "colearning."

In the current organizational environment, it is clear that developmental relationships occur beyond the bounds of dyadic mentor-protégé pairings. Employees work as members of multiple teams, and they are part of numerous networks that cut across internal and external organizational boundaries (Kram & Hall, 1996a). Monica Higgins (1998) expands on this network concept and discusses how these constellations of relationships can affect career choices and development. Her particular focus is the decision to change careers:

> I name an individual's set of career development relationships a "portfolio," recognizing that an individual's investment in such relationships affects the opportunities and constraints one has with respect to changing careers. . . . Whether or not an individual changes careers depends on the opportunities

and constraints he or she faces at the time. Overall, I expect that the more diverse one's pool of career opportunities, the more likely one is to change careers. The diversity of one's opportunities may be affected by human capital factors, such as the level of education attained, as well as the diversity of one's portfolio of career developmental relationships, defined as the extent to which one's set of career advisors (a) is diverse and so provides access to a variety of social resources, (b) is nonredundant and hence provides a variety of different information to the decision maker, and (c) is heterogeneous and thus provides exposure to different points of view. (pp. 8-9)

In a study of MBA students, Higgins found support for these hypotheses. That is, the greater the diversity of one's developmental relationships, and the greater the amount of career assistance these resources provide, the more likely the person is to make a choice to change careers. One would also presume that this diversity in the relational network would aid in other kinds of career decisions as well.

Given the importance of network governance in contemporary firms (Jones, Hesterly, & Borgatti, 1997), it is critical that we understand more about the role of relational networks in individual career experiences and their impact at the organizational level. In fact, one can argue that a major source of the power of networks lies precisely in the information exchanges and collective learning that they promote. In support of this idea, Meyerson and Fletcher (2000) found that employing such a relational approach, building on the theory of small wins (Weick, 1984), can lead to snowballing and significant organizational change regarding issues such as gender equity in career development. Thus, by learning more about how networks affect individual career decision making, we can also understand more about the more macro phenomena of coordination and safeguarding of exchanges. In this way, career effectiveness and organizational effectiveness are mutually supportive.

Research Issues in Career Choice and Decision Making

As we reflect on the research discussed in this chapter, several important issues emerge for future research on careers. Here, we consider a few questions for future research.

How Do Interests Predict Later-Life Career Decisions, Such as Work/Life Balance Choices? Of all the qualities employed to study career decision processes, interests appear to be the most robust concept. Interests are incredibly stable features of an individual's personality, the tools to assess them are well developed, and they have impressive predictive power in studying career decisions. The vast majority of the research on career interests, however, has examined early career-related decisions, such as the choice of a college major or the initial choice of an occupational field. Much less use of interests has been made to help us understand how people decide to switch fields, to go back to school in midlife, to switch employers, to retire at a certain age, and so on.

Interests could also be potentially very useful in predicting choices that people would make about work/life balance issues, such as who will opt for a reduced work hours schedule, who will stop working outside the home, and who will resume a career that has been on hold. Because we know from the work of Barnett and Brennan (1997) that the levels of distress a person experiences are related to the choices of one's partner, does the couple's pattern of respective interests also have value in predicting life and career outcomes? For example, extending Barnett's findings, one might hypothesize that the extent to which each partner's work environment fits with their interest profiles would predict work satisfaction, a low level of work distress, and a high level of relational satisfaction.

Also, Barnett's research has examined the effects of reduced hours for professional employees, with a focus on the trade-offs involved and the extent to which the schedule fit their own and their partner's work schedules and the needs of family members. Barnett found that fit is a better predictor of career satisfaction than the number of hours worked per se. In one study, however, reduced-hours professionals (physicians) reported lower career satisfaction than their full-time counterparts because the resulting fit was poor and the necessary trade-offs (work activities foregone due to the reduced hours) were difficult (Barnett & Gareis, 2001). It would be interesting to determine how other types of fit, such as person-role fit on interests (à la Holland), correlate with the outcomes of these kinds of work/life balance decisions.

How Can Super's Self-Concept Ideas on Career Development Be Translated Into Midrange Theory to Make It More Accessible for Empirical Research? As discussed previously, there is much potential in the ideas of this seminal thinker. It is my impression that people who currently do research in career psychology view Super's theory as dated and are not too interested in using it in their work. Also, for many people the gap between the level of abstraction of his concepts and the level required for operationalization is too wide. Super's ideas, however, concern many of the subtle dynamics that could be extremely useful in making progress on old, nagging problems.

For example, there are many unresolved questions about interrole conflict in the field of work/life dynamics (see Chapter 8, this volume), and Super's ideas on the interaction of life stage and life role have never been empirically examined. Sekaran and Hall (1989) presented a theoretical discussion of role synchronicity and stage, but there is a great need for good empirical work here.

How Does Personal Orientation (as Measured by Holland's Instruments) Develop? We discussed the gender links found with some of the Holland scales, and Holland argues that these result from early gender socialization. This raises the question of just how these personal orientations arise in a person. As described earlier, Gottfredson (1996) developed and tested a sophisticated theoretical model showing that these self-limiting perceptions of self and occupation develop at different stages in a child's life. We need more research on the "how" of the basic processes involved.

It would be very helpful to inquire more into some of the everyday "micro" transactions between child and environment that in fact produce these perceptions. Careful observational research with infants might be employed to determine just how early these personal preferences can be found. Much of this kind of research is already available in the literature on child development, and it might not be too difficult to "translate" some of these finding into career theory and link them to concepts such as personal orientation.

It could also be possible to examine early childhood education experiences to determine how various kinds of social influence relate to the growth of these orientations. For example, using Bandura's (1997) model of self-efficacy, how does task success in grade school relate to the development of orientations? How does social persuasion by teachers and coaches predict their development? What about modeling by peers and adult role models? In view of the predictive power of these personal orientations, it would be useful to know more about how they develop. The next research question is, what kinds of interventions have the most impact on the development of personal orientations?

How Might the Process Models of Career Choice Be Employed to Help Us Understand the Later Life Process of Protean Career Changing and Learning Cycles? What leads a person who is successfully and happily engaged in a given line of activity to begin exploring new areas of activity? As early work by Ginzberg, Super, and Tiedeman shows, we have a good sense that people progress from fantasy to tentative to realistic choices. We also know that the person has to do "identity work" to integrate the new activities into the overall self-system or sense of identity. Also, we know that there are predictable stages by which these decisions and identity changes happen over time.

Again, as noted earlier, there is not much research that focuses on how these career decision and implementation processes play out in the lives of employed adults. Hall (1986) proposed a theoretical model of trigger events that initiate a change cycle in midcareer and later, and this could provide some leads for ways that formal models of career choice and decision making might be employed to study midcareer change processes.

What Is the Role of Psychological Success in Satisfactory Career Decision Making? Although research has been carried out on specific components of the psychological success spiral, we still do not have much understanding of how the whole process operates. What initiates an experience of psychological success? What is the difference between a success experience that leads to important career decisions and one that does not have career consequences? When does a person see a certain task as having career relevance? We know that increased self-confidence results from task success, but when does self-confidence in turn lead to future success? That change probably entails a longer chain of intervening experiences.

How Does the ASA Model Relate to More Career-Specific Models? Can ASA Help Us Produce a More Integrated Career Model? An interesting feature of career choice models and the ASA model is that they both show how people find increasing degrees of person-environment fit. Both describe decreasing degrees of heterogeneity that occur over time as a person interacts with an organization. The ASA model, however, is a general or umbrella model asserting that this growing fit does take place, whereas the career models provide specific content to explain how the growing fit actually happens.

It could be useful, as a way of integrating career theory, to use ASA as an overarching framework to tie together various career models. For example, attraction could encompass the content theories of career choice, such as Holland's work on personal orientation and Campbell's work on career interests and skills that predict occupational environments that provide good fit. The process models, such as Ginzberg's and Super's models of stages in career decision making, involve exploratory and trial interactions with an organization that also involve successive selection processes by the organization. The content models, again, could help us understand which individuals might represent systematic attrition by the organization.

What Are the Various Ways That Developmental Networks Influence Career Choice and Decision Making? The theoretical model provided by Higgins and Kram (2001) provides excellent fodder for future research, particularly their two dimensions of the diversity of the network and strength of the developmental relationships in the network. Although their model relates more to the processes of development, it appears that because the network provides both information and influence, it can have great potential for affecting the way basic career choices and other decisions are made. For example, the model contains the prediction that people whose networks are more entrepreneurial are more likely to make changes in their careers than those whose networks are more traditional, opportunistic, or receptive (Higgins, 1998).

Conclusion

Although the process of career choice is one of the oldest in the careers field, it is still one of the most relevant to what is happening today. Even though the original view of the career as being largely determined by one's initial choice of occupation has been replaced with the more emergent, protean perspective, there is a fresh need to understand how choices are made on an ongoing basis. We have moved a focus on what we might call "big C" career choices (i.e., big choices and once-in-a-lifetime choices) to "little c" career choices (everyday, continuous learning decisions).

Because we now need to think about choice as more of an ongoing activity, the original distinction between content models and process models should be reduced. If the process is becoming more continuous, the content becomes less critical. The important thing is for the person to remain adaptive and to be able to gather self-assessment identity information as part of everyday life.

This view of the career as a work in progress leads us naturally to consideration of how the identity evolves naturally and how the person can maintain a constant state of adaptability. These questions provide the basis of the next two chapters.

Note

1. I am grateful to Michael Arthur for this observation and this phrasing.

 **4** Life, Career,
and Learning Stages

Once I was listening to a group of children trying to deal with a member who was being quite obstinate about not permitting anyone else to play with his toys. As the hostility level was increasing, peace was restored by a wise old 10-year-old who said, "He's not usually like this; it's just a phrase he's going through."

If she was a bit off in her jargon, our young neighborhood sage was correct in her understanding of human development. People do go through phases and stages when they experience changes in their passion and purpose, needs, aspirations, values, skills, motivations, and other important human characteristics. We have all heard comments such as "He's a new man since he started working" and "She isn't the same person I married 20 years ago." People do change over the course of their lives and work careers, and they do so in some fairly predictable ways. In this chapter, we examine some of these stages.

Are Career and Life Stages Still Relevant Today?

First, we consider whether the basic notion of life and career stages is still relevant in this era of extreme turbulence, complexity, and rapid change. Maybe the concept of regular, predictable stages or phases is an anachronism. My answer to this question is clear and definitive: yes and no.

When I say "yes," I mean that things are not as regular and predictable as they were 25 years ago. If regular stages still exist, they are probably not as clearly defined as they once were. Also, I have argued, as discussed later, that we now have a new way of looking at careers over time: careers as learning stages. As discussed later, the career is a process of continuous learning, and over a lifetime of work a person goes through many career role transitions. Each role transition requires a sequence that looks like miniaturized versions of more traditional career stages: exploration of the new role, establishment in the new role, mastery, and then exploration of different roles and exit into something new. These ministages are often superimposed over longer, more traditional phases or seasons in a person's life and career, as Daniel Levinson (1996) called them. So, yes, there is a new way of looking at career and life stages.

We have not lost the experience of regular, predictable changes in our roles, expectations, concerns, and self-images that come packaged as life and career stages, however. We are still adult human beings who go through a regular series of life experiences and tasks that lead to regular phases of adult development. During our adult careers, even though we may make many shifts of occupational field, organization, and institutional context and moves from performer to learner and back, our adult careers still have a beginning and an ending (even if that ending occurs at a much more advanced age). Also, if the careers have beginnings and endings, by definition this means that they have middles—a point at which we become aware of being more senior and of seeing the end coming closer. Thus, we can still talk about early adult life and early career, midlife and midcareer, and later life and late career.

One factor that makes these life and career stages appear so different today is the greater asynchronicity between various life and work roles.[1] That is, the stages of our career and our life stages do not line up together as neatly as they did before. It used to be, with the one-life, one-career imperative (as Seymour Sarason, 1977, described it), that early adulthood and the early stage of a lifelong career occurred at the same time. Now, however, a person is as likely to be starting a new career at age 35 or 45 or 55 as at age 18 or 20 or 25. Also, because the cycles of the work and life stages interact in different ways now, the experiences often feel different. This notion of asynchronicity was first discussed in comparing women's and men's careers in the context of a dual-career relationship (Sekaran & Hall, 1989).

Thus, I argue that career and life stages are still relevant to modern careers, but they have more complex interactions and overlays, like harmonic overtones in music. Also, as in music, if the life is composed well, the melody is sweet; if not, it can be very discordant.

Life Stages

We may view a person's life cycle as a series of stages characterized by changing patterns of developmental tasks, career concerns, activities, values, and needs, which emerge as he ages and passes through various age ranges (Hall & Associates, 1986; Hall & Mirvis, 1995; Levinson, 1986, 1996; Levinson, Darrow, Klein, Levinson, & McKee, 1978). We should remember, however, as Cain (1964) observes, that

> in spite of the observed ambiguity of age status and of the abundance of descriptive data on the subject, supplied by historians, anthropologists, demographers, researchers in social welfare, and others, sociologists have yet to devote more than passing attention to these data and to their implications for the total social structure. (p. 272)

This is applicable to psychologists as well as to sociologists.

Unlike the life stages of childhood and youth, which are well defined by age and institutional role transitions (e.g., the start of grade school, high school graduation, driving age, university graduation, legal age, and marriage), the important changes in the adult years are more difficult to delineate. This "fuzziness" of adult life stages has increased in recent years, as life's boundaries have become more permeable in contemporary society (Sheehy, 1995). Marriage and parenthood are often the last institutionalized status passages experienced until retirement; thus, a person tends to pace his own life cycle in terms of the life cycle of his children and the total family unit. In fact, a person's social behavior is probably related more to his stage in the family life cycle than to his age (Levinson, 1986). Cain (1964) said, "To be the father of a teen-age daughter elicits certain behavior patterns, whether the father be 30 or 70 years of age" (p. 289). As previously mentioned, however, it is different to be an older father of a teenage daughter than it is to be a younger father. (I had that experience first in my 30s and then in my 60s, and I can personally attest to the similarities and the differences.)

The person's stage in his or her work career is another factor that can strongly affect (and is likewise affected by) social behavior and attitudes; this variable may not be closely tied to age either. A lawyer or manager who is on the first permanent job following professional training (law school or business school) will probably be concerned about advancement and establishing a reputation among colleagues, whether he or she is 25 or 45 years old. (The 45-year-old who started a career in that occupation at 25, however, will probably have quite a different set of concerns, which are described later.)

Erikson's Theory of Life Stages

From clinical psychology, part of Erik Erikson's theory of the eight stages of the life cycle can be logically applied to the study of working careers. (The first four of these stages—oral, anal, genital, and latency—describe childhood and therefore are not relevant here.) Erikson believes that each stage is characterized by a particular developmental task that the person must work through before advancing fully into the following stage.

In the first stage of youth, adolescence, the central developmental task is achieving a sense of ego identity (Erikson, 1963):

> The growing and developing youths, faced with this physiological revolution within them, and with tangible adult tasks ahead of them are now primarily concerned with what they appear to be in the eyes of others as compared with what they feel they are, and with the question of how to connect the roles and skills cultivated earlier with the occupational prototypes of the day. (p. 261)

The next stage is young adulthood, during which the developmental task is to develop intimacy and involvement. This includes, but is not limited to, interpersonal intimacy; it entails learning how to let oneself become ego involved with another person, group, organization, or cause (Erikson, 1963):

Thus, the young adult, emerging from the search for and the insistence on identity, is eager and willing to fuse his identity with that of others. He is ready for intimacy, that is, the capacity to commit himself to concrete affiliations and partnerships and to develop the ethical strength to abide by such commitments, even though they may call for significant sacrifices and compromises. (p. 263)

The danger at this stage is that the person may be so afraid of losing or compromising his newfound sense of identity and autonomy that he shuns involvements and develops a deep sense of isolation and self-absorption. To describe these issues further, Erikson (1963) referred to Freud's famous reply when asked what he thought a normal person should be able to do well—"Lieben und arbeiten" (love and work):

It pays to ponder on this simple formula; it gets deeper as you think about it. For ... when he [Freud] said love *and* work, he meant a general work-productiveness which would not preoccupy the individual to the extent that he loses his right or capacity to be a genital and a loving being. (p. 265)

The seventh stage described by Erikson (1963) is adulthood, during which the person deals with issues concerned with the generation of that which is of lasting value to other people—his contributions to following generations, and thus in a sense his antidote to mortality:

Generativity, then, is primarily the concern in establishing and guiding the next generation, although there are individuals who, through misfortune because of special and genuine gifts in other directions, do not apply the drive to their own offspring. And, indeed, the concept of generativity is meant to include such more popular synonyms as *productivity* and *creativity*, which, however, cannot replace I. (p. 267)

In the work setting, generativity may be achieved through such things as building organizations; developing creative theories, discoveries, or products that will endure; coaching and sponsoring the development of younger colleagues; and teaching and guiding students. Generativity is really an outgrowth of the preceding stages (as is the case for any other stage): Once the person has developed a sense of identity and has committed it to a cause, person, or organization, the next stage is to accomplish or produce something as a result of that commitment. The opposite of generativity is what Erikson calls *stagnation*, which means standing still, producing nothing. Stagnation also carries the connotation of decay, not just the absence of growth.

The eighth and final stage of development is maturity, during which the fully developed person acquires a sense of ego integrity (versus despair). This is the feeling that the person is satisfied with his life, with his choices and actions. He sees it as meaningful and is willing to leave it as it is (Erikson, 1963):

> [Ego integrity] is the ego's accrued assurance of its proclivity for order and meaning. It is a post-narcissistic love of the human ego—not of the self—an experience which conveys some world order and spiritual sense, no matter how dearly paid for. It is the acceptance of one's one and only life cycle as something that had to be and that, by necessity, permitted of no substitutions.... In such final consolidation, death loses its sting. The lack or loss of this accrued ego integration is signified by fear of death: The one and only life cycle is not accepted as the ultimate of life. Despair expresses the feeling that the time is now short, too short for the attempt to start another life and to try out alternate roads to integrity. (pp. 268-269)

One characteristic of a cycle is that it has no beginning or end, in a sense; the completion of one cycle feeds into the beginning of the next. Erikson (1963) ends his discussion of the eight stages by showing strikingly the connection between the end and the beginning of life:

> Webster's Dictionary is kind enough to help us complete this outline in a circular fashion. Trust (the first of our ego values) is here defined as "the assured reliance on another's integrity," the last of our values. I suspect that Webster had business in mind rather than babies, credit rather than faith. But, the formulation stands. And, it seems possible to further paraphrase the relation of adult integrity and infantile trust by saying that healthy children will not fear life if their elders have integrity enough not to fear death. (p. 269)

A person must achieve a satisfactory resolution of the issues in one stage before he can deal competently with the issues at the next stage. Thus, it is possible for a person's development to become arrested, in a sense, at any given stage. If a person were "hung up" at the identity level, for example, he may remain plagued with doubts about his career choice, shifting from job to job and perhaps career to career, long after his contemporaries, who had settled on a career and an employer, were advancing within their firms. According to this theory, a person cannot achieve a full, deep commitment (intimacy) to an organization, person, or cause until his identity is pretty well defined; similarly, he cannot attain higher-stage experience, such as creative production (generativity) or ego fulfillment (integrity).

The work of Erikson is based on his clinical, anthropological, and historical observations, and it has not really been tested with experimental and statistical methods. The theory has received considerable support from clinicians, however, and has a great deal of face validity. It has been extremely useful in understanding specific developmental problems, such as identity confusion and midlife career crises. For example, it has been found that students who had made well-adjusted vocational choices and had developed mature career attitudes had also been most successful in moving through the first six stages identified by Erikson (Munley, 1975).

There may be sex differences in the course of the life stages. One study (Douvan & Adelson, 1966) found that adolescent girls often achieve a sense of identity only after they have established a sense of intimacy (generally heterosexual) in their relationships. Thus, the intimacy stage may precede the identity stage for girls. Adolescent boys, on the other hand, are seen by these researchers to be able to achieve intimacy after they have attained a sense of identity, which fits with Erikson's model (Douvan & Adelson, 1966). Also, Miller (1991) reports that the formation of the sense of self differs for girls and boys. Girls develop their sense of self through relationships with other people, whereas boys' sense of self comes from autonomy and mastery. In adult life, these differences show up as men placing greater value than women on independence and mastery. Thus, relational activities, which are critical to the performance of most tasks that require collaboration and teamwork, and on which many women are strong, tend to be systematically undervalued and they "get disappeared," in the words of Joyce Fletcher (1994a, 1994b, 1996, 1999).

Super's Model of Life and Career Stages

Other theories also correspond, in part, to Erikson's conception of life stages. In the realm of vocational behavior, as in Chapter 3, Super and associates employed a model of five developmental stages: (a) childhood, (b) adolescence, (c) young adulthood, (d) maturity, and (e) old age (Super, 1992; Super & Bohn, 1970). The main task in the childhood stage (up to age 14) is growth. In this stage, the person begins to fantasize about careers and develops vocational interests and capacities. During adolescence, the person begins to explore his own interests and different specific career opportunities. This corresponds to Erikson's identity stage. In young adulthood (approximately ages 25-44), the person may initially flounder a bit (as seen in the high initial turnover of recent college graduates) and eventually establish himself in a particular field. This corresponds to Erikson's intimacy stage, with some hints of generativity later. In maturity (approximately ages 45-64), the person continues to hold his own in a sort of career plateau. This stage is probably when generativity concerns would be most important. Old age (65 and older) is a period of disengagement. This is the time during which ego integrity is achieved if the person has resolved all the earlier stages. Super's model has been supported in research on organizational careers (Hall & Mansfield, 1975; Ornstein, Cron, & Slocum, 1989), although not as well for women as for men (Ornstein & Isabella, 1990). (The vocational stages defined by Super were discussed in detail in Chapter 3 as they relate to career choice and decision making.)

Levinson's Theory of Adult Life Stages

Psychologist Daniel Levinson and colleagues (1978, 1986, 1996) developed a theory of life stages and transitions based on in-depth clinical case studies of a sample of men and a sample of women. They employ the concept of the life structure, which is formed by the following:

- The individual's sociocultural world (the societal context in which the person lives—class, religion, ethnicity, family, occupational structure, etc.)
- Aspects of the self that are played out and those that are inhibited or neglected (complex pattern of motivations, conflicts, values, talents, character traits, modes of feeling, thought, and action)[2]
- The person's participation in the world (transactions between self and the world through relationships and roles such as citizen, worker, boss, friend, parent, lover, and member of various groups)

Levinson and colleagues viewed the person's choices as the key to understanding the person's life structure. It is necessary to understand the meanings and functions of each choice the person makes (Levinson et al., 1978):

To choose something means to have a *relationship* with it. The relationship becomes a vehicle for living out certain aspects of the self and for engaging in certain modes of participation in the world.... In characterizing each choice ... it is necessary to understand the nature of the [person's] relationship with it, to place it within the life structure, and to see how it is connected to both self and world.

One or two components (rarely as many as three) have a central place in the structure. Others, though important, are more peripheral, and still others are quite marginal or detached from the center.... The life structure may change in various ways. A component may shift from center to periphery or vice versa, as when a man who has been totally committed to work starts detaching himself from it and involves himself more in family life. A formerly important component may be eliminated altogether. (p. 44)

Levinson found that the components that were most often central are career, marriage and family, friendship and peer relationships, ethnicity, and religion. Furthermore, career and marriage and family are usually most important.

In the two major studies (one of men and one of women) conducted by Levinson and colleagues, they found that "the life structure evolves through a relatively orderly sequence during the adult years" (Levinson et al., 1978, p. 49). It is composed of a series of stable, structure-building periods called *stages*, separated by a series of structure-changing periods called *transitions*. A transition serves a dual purpose—terminating the existing life structure and introducing the new one. Thus, a transition is a bridge or boundary zone between two time periods of greater stability. For example, the midlife transition is the bridge between two great "eras" in life, early adulthood and middle adulthood.

In the Levinson et al. (1978) model of adult life stages, the authors claim that the ages are accurate to within approximately 2 years. Thus, ages 17 to 22 are the early adult transition during which childhood and adolescence end and early adulthood begins. From ages 22 to 28, one is entering the adult world, which is the initial creation of an adult life structure. This might be the initial job, the first committed love relationship, one's first home away from parents, and so on. The person is both exploring a range of new possibilities as an adult and creating a stable life structure. Finding a balance between these two tasks is not easy because they represent opposites—expanding out versus settling down. Managing these polarities or paradoxes, however, is a major way that development occurs.

The ages 28 to 33 are the age 30 transition. At this point, the person reexamines the choices made in the 20s and has the feeling that if he or she wants to make a change, it should be done soon. Otherwise, it seems as if it would be "too late." The result of this transition is that the person could either make a renewed commitment to the initial life structure or make a significant change of structure. Then, during ages 33 to 40, the person forms a second adult life structure, which is called the settling down stage. During this period, the person tries to establish a niche in society and to achieve success.

Then, from ages 40 to 45 there is another questioning of the previous structure, the midlife transition. This is a serious reexamination of previous choices, with a stronger sense of time urgency than in the 30s. In this transition, the previously neglected parts of the self "urgently seek expression and stimulate the modification of the existing structure" (Levinson et al., 1978, p. 61). This transition marks the move to the next great era in adult life, middle adulthood. Then, ages 60 to 65 represent the late adult transition, which begins the move into late adulthood, which is the third great adult era.

An interesting feature of the Levinson model becomes apparent if we add the years spent in each of these types of periods, stages, and transitions. Before age 65, which is considered normal retirement age in North American culture, the total time spent in adult transitions is 24 years, and the total time spent in adult life stages is 27 years. Thus, almost half of an adult worker's lifetime is spent in a period of change. This is in contrast to the view that most young people hold that once they become adults, their life will settle down and they will feel "grown up." In fact, we spend our adult lives doing the work of "growing up." Growth is a process, not a destination.

Gender and Life Stage

There has been much debate throughout the years about whether Levinson's life stage developmental model, which was developed from his male sample, adequately describes the lives of women. Levinson's much-awaited book, *The Seasons of a Woman's Life* (1996), did in fact find that for his sample of 45 women academics, homemakers, and business professionals in the 35 to 45 age range, the same age-related stages described their life experiences. He did report, however, that they had to deal with more conflicts regarding the way they enacted their life roles. Also, it appears that the age 30 transition relates to choices over life roles more for women than for men, whereas these choices over life roles assume more importance for men in the midlife transition. In a similar vein, Roberts and Newton (1987) reported that the age 30 transition for women involved choices about switching from a career focus to a family focus or vice versa. In an earlier, more conceptual work, Bardwick (1980) had hypothesized similar differences.

It also appears that women, compared to men, are more likely to have "split dreams," as Roberts and Newton (1987) described it. That is, their dreams are more likely to involve combinations of or balance between different life roles, as opposed to a desire to develop within a particular role domain, such as career or family. Perhaps a better term to describe this pattern for women is "integrated." (Although I am not a deconstructionist, this terminology is interesting here: "Split" implies that the life focus contains two incomplete entities, whereas "integrated" implies a positive, holistic orientation.) For example, Candida Brush (1992, 1999), in her comparison of male and female entrepreneurs, found that women had an integrated orientation, in which their business and their family were interconnected. For men, their focus was much more single-minded—on the business.

There also appear to be differences in the ways women and men make developmental progress in their lives. As Jean Baker Miller (1991) pointed out, men have learned in childhood to deal with problems with a focus on independent mastery. Women, on the other hand, have learned in childhood to grow in connection (i.e., through their relationships with others). In a similar vein, Bardwick (1980) used the terms *egocentric* and interdependent to describe men's and women's sense of self, respectively. By egocentric, she meant having an orientation toward autonomy and taskmaster, and by interdependent she meant being relationship oriented, working with and helping others, and defining self in terms of the other people in one's life. Thus, women come to view development more as a mutual, interdependent process than do men. These relational ideas have been applied to adult and career development by Joyce Fletcher (1996, 1999). Fletcher's research found that the following features characterize growth-fostering relational interactions:

- Interdependence—a belief that interdependence versus autonomy, which includes vulnerability, need, and inadequacy, is the ideal state in which to grow and develop
- Mutuality—both parties approach the relationship expecting that each will grow and benefit from it
- Reciprocity—the expectation that both parties will have the skills to use this two-directional model of growth and will be motivated to use them

I suggest that these relational qualities have become critical factors to facilitating development for all people, not just women (Hall & Associates, 1996). Indeed, as organizational resources become more limited and less available to individuals for career development, relational resources are becoming increasingly important and used (Kram & Hall, 1996b).

Hall and Nougaim's Three Stages of Organizational Career Development

Most research on organizational career stages uses a three-stage model of career development: establishment, advancement, and maintenance. This scheme was first identified by Douglas Hall and Khalil Nougaim in a study of young AT&T managers and is discussed here.

Establishment

In their study, Hall and Nougaim (1968) found that in the first year of employment, there were strong concerns for safety-gaining recognition and establishing oneself in the organization. In Year 1, this need was second in importance only to the need for achievement and esteem, which was clearly of paramount importance to this group of executive hopefuls. By the fifth year, however, the need for safety had declined significantly and was the least important of the four needs measured. Furthermore, the managers who eventually attained the greatest success in the company were those with the lowest need for safety in the first year. This result was consistent with other findings that tolerance of uncertainty was correlated with managerial success (Berlew & Hall, 1966). It seems that becoming established is a central concern when the young manager first enters an organization, and those who can feel the most comfortable with the insecurity and uncertainty involved can cope most effectively. Hall and Nougaim described this stage as follows:

The beginning of the career is a new experience, and here the person is mainly concerned with defining the structure of his position and with feeling secure in it. At this point he is at the boundary of his organization, a very stressful location, and he is searching for means integrating himself into the system. Being new, he does not have a strong identity relevant to his particular organization, and he is struggling to define more clearly his environment and his relationship to it. (pp. 26-27)

Advancement

The next stage seemed to reflect concerns for advancement: promotion and achievement. At this point, the person is not so concerned with fitting into the organization (moving inside) as he is with moving upward and mastering it (Harquail, 1991). The young managers in the Hall and Nougaim study showed a significant increase in the importance of the needs for achievement and esteem between the first and fifth years of the career. Furthermore, the most successful managers experience increased satisfaction in this need area, whereas those who were less successful showed less satisfaction. This was the only need area in which there were differences in satisfaction levels between successful managers in either the first or the fifth year. Other studies have also shown increased concerns for achievement and autonomy between the first and eighth years of employment (Bray, Campbell, & Grant, 1974; Howard & Bray, 1988). Promotion was found to be a dominant intermediate career concern of scientists (Glaser, 1964).

Maintenance

Later research by Hall and colleagues found evidence for a later maintenance stage, also speculated about by Hall and Nougaim (1968) as follows:

Our subjective impression is that once the incumbent had cues that he was nearing the limit of his advancement, his career would start to level off, and the need—or opportunity—to compete would decrease. If he felt successful, he might become concerned with helping younger men—his successors— grow, in order to strengthen the organization and perpetuate his work. If he felt unsuccessful, he might still define his mission as helping these young men, or he might use his power to block their progress and thus punish them for his failure. Whatever the specific behavior at this later stage, the period does represent the onset of a ... plateau. (p. 28)

Data supporting the existence of such a maintenance stage were, in fact, observed by Hall and Schneider (1972) in samples of Roman Catholic priests, professional foresters in the U.S. Forest Service, and engineers and scientists in 22 research and development firms. Hall and Mansfield (1975) also found evidence for this maintenance stage, as did Hall (1986) and Hall and Louis (1988) in a downsizing manufacturing organization.

Other empirical evidence of this three-stage model of organizational careers was reported by Gould and Hawkins (1978), Morrow and McElroy (1987), Raelin (1985), Slocum and Cron (1985), Stumpf and Rabinowitz (1981), and Lynn, Cao, and Horn (1996). As Lynn et al. (1996) pointed out, some of these studies used organizational tenure as their measure of time, whereas others used the individual's age. For careers with regularized status passages, such as professional accountants, lawyers, and professors, there may be natural development stages based on professional tenure. Thus, in these cases, time in the profession might be a better operational measure of career stage than time in a particular organization.

An Integrative View of Career Stages

With the exception of the Erikson model, which deals with general life stages rather than work career stages, the models resemble general biological growth and decay curves: early period of exploration and trial, then growth, a stable period in the middle (maintenance), and a stage of decline and withdrawal from the work environment. Daniel Levinson et al. (1978) refer to the exploration stage as "entering the adult world," the growth stage as "settling down," and the middle years as "becoming one's own person."

These different models can be synthesized graphically as shown in Figure 4.1. The dashed lines and question marks in Figure 4.1 reflect an unresolved question regarding the midcareer period. This appears to be a time when individual differences may be extremely noticeable. Why do some people continue to grow in midcareer while others enter the maintenance plateau and still others begin to decline? This issue will be examined in more detail later.

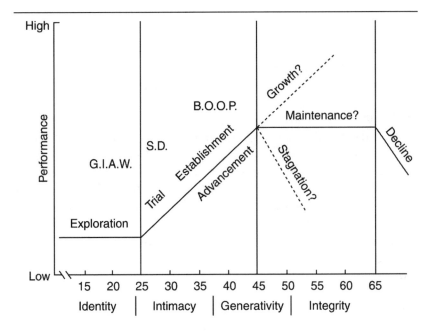

Figure 4.1. Hall's integrated model of life and career stages. B.O.O.P., becoming one's own person; G.I.A.W., getting in the adult world; S.D., settling down (reproduced with permission from Hall, 1976, p. 57).

Comparisons With Organizational and Other Career Stage Models

The safety and establishment concerns identified in the three-stage Hall model are clearly part of Super's establishment stage, representing an attempt at stabilization. The second Hall organizational career stage, advancement, does not emerge clearly in the Super model, but it is probably part of the process of becoming established in an organizational career context. The maintenance stage described by Hall and others fits well with the maintenance stage described by Super. It appears, however, that stabilization occurs earlier in managerial careers than for careers in general as described by Super, with advancement taking up the remainder of the years Super lists under stabilization.

Gender and Organizational Career Stage

Many of the studies of organizational career stages have been conducted with male samples or predominantly male samples. One study
that did examine gender and career stage, however, found that the
correlates of career stage were not as strong for women as for men (Lynn
et al., 1996). These authors, as well as Ornstein and Isabella (1990),
suggested that these findings might have been due to the functioning of
the glass ceiling and of interrupted career patterns for women, which
meant that promotions did not occur in a continuous manner for
women. That is, because of a combination of individual career and life
choices and organizational variables (such as discriminatory delays in
promotions), women's promotions tend to occur later in the career
than for men. Thus, one implication for research is that different career
stage cutoff points might need to be used for men and women.

Schein's Model of the Organizational Career

To be complete, a model of career development in organizations needs
to describe the career from two separate but related perspectives—the
career as described by the characteristics and experiences of the person
who moves through the organization and the career as defined by the
organization (which involves policies and expectations about what
people will move into what positions and how quickly, in relation to the
organization's overall staffing needs).

A useful approach to understanding this relationship between the
individual and the organization "sides" of career development has been
proposed by Schein (1971), who views the organization as a three-
dimensional space like a cone (or in some cases, a cylinder) in which the
external boundary is essentially round and in which a core or inner
center exists. This model is illustrated in Figure 4.2.

The three dimensions represent the following three types of moves a
person may make in the organization:

Vertical: moving up or down, representing one's changing rank or level in the
    organization

Radial: moving more (or less) "inside" in the system, becoming more (or less) cen-
    tral, part of the "inner circle" acquiring increased (or decreased) influence in
    the system

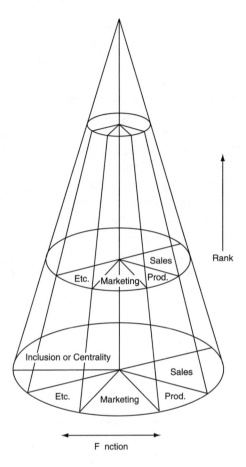

Figure 4.2. Schein's Three-Dimensional Model of the Organization as a Career Space (reproduced with permission from Schein, 1971)

Circumferential: transferring laterally to a different function, program, or product in the organization

Three types of boundaries correspond to each type of movement:

Hierarchical boundaries: These separate the hierarchical levels from each other.

Inclusion boundaries: These separate individuals or groups who differ in the degree of their centrality.

Functional or departmental boundaries: These separate departments or different functional groupings from each other.

Boundaries can vary in terms of the number of each type that exist in an organization, their permeability (ease of movement from, for example, production assignments to sales), and the type of filtering process (i.e., criteria for deciding who is transferred or promoted). All these factors have bearing on both the functioning of the organization and the course of the person's career. Other critical factors are the size of the organization and its shape. If it is more like a cylinder than a cone, there are more promotion opportunities for lower-level people. A steep cone means more competition for promotions, whereas a flat cone means few promotions will occur, with probably less competition.

The individual is viewed as having (a) basic personality characteristics, which are probably unchangeable, and (b) constructed social selves that represent the differences in the way people present themselves in different social situations. These social selves are largely a result of socialization and are subject to change through resocialization, such as that which occurs when a person joins an organization. As Schein describes the process:

> The changes that occur in a person during the course of a career, as a result of adult socialization or acculturation, are changes in the nature and integration of his social selves. It is highly unlikely that he will change substantially in his basic character structure and his pattern of psychological defenses, but he may change drastically in his social selves in the sense of developing new attitudes and values, new competencies, new images of himself, and new ways of entering and conducting himself in social situations. As he faces new roles that bring new demands, it is from his repertory of attributes and skills that he constructs or reconstructs himself to meet these demands.
>
> When we think of organizations infringing on the private lives of their members, we think of a more extensive socialization process that involves changes in more stable social selves. Clearly, it is possible for such "deeper" influence to occur, but in assessing depth of influence in any given individual-organization relationships, we must be careful not to overlook adaptational patterns that look like deep influence but are only the activation of and changes in relatively more labile social selves. (Schein, 1971, pp. 308-309)

It is important to note that the organizational career (the part of the person's career that is spent in one organization) is not the same as the person's career. Most organizational careers are much shorter than the person's total work career, especially with today's short learning cycles.

For example, careers in many organizations are either "early-leaving" careers (e.g., professional athletes) or "late-entry" careers (judges, university administrators, and physicians). Also, we may think of a person's experiences in any kind of system through which he or she moves in regularized status passages as constituting an organizational career. Thus, students go through their "college career"; the 6-month volunteer has a "military career." In general, in those systems in which people enter, move through, and leave in large numbers and through fairly regular transitions, the stages in the organizational career can be identified.

Contrary to most early views of organizational careers, which focused on the organization's influence on the person (socialization), Schein was a pioneer in viewing the career as a two-way influence relationship between the person and the organization: The person influences the organization (innovates) and is influenced himself. This is an especially critical point, considering the great importance that today's economic environment places on organizational and individual adaptation and renewal.

Given the importance of socialization and innovation, we now examine in depth the two periods in the person's career during which each process is most likely to be clearly shown. As Schein hypothesized, socialization is most likely to occur early (i.e., during early adulthood and in the establishment and advancement stages of the career). Innovation is more likely to occur in the later advancement stage and in the maintenance stage. We conclude this chapter with an examination of the preretirement or disengagement period.

The Early Career Years: Becoming Established

Consider a person who has just completed her formal education and is about to enter the world of work. Perhaps the reader is at or near this career stage. It would probably be helpful for you to relate your own experiences to the issues we consider here.

Training and Expectations

What happens during one's education and training for a profession? First, one acquires a body of specialized knowledge (e.g., business law and organizational psychology) and some technical skills (e.g., linear programming, accounting, and marketing). According to research on law students, student teachers, and medical students, the person probably also acquires a certain set of professional values and attitudes imparted by her peers and faculty (Hall, 1968). Finally, one develops a set of aspirations and expectations about what one will encounter in one's work. As previously discussed, however, the career is a mutual-influence process, and the organization also holds certain expectations of the new recruit.

What are the expectations of the person as she enters her first job? Perhaps most important, the young person usually expects challenging work—work that is meaningful and ability stretching. She wants to be able to apply the knowledge and skills that it took so many difficult years to acquire. She wants to be able to test herself, to experience psychological success and a sense of competence. This need for competence, the need to have an impact on one's personal environment, is an important basic human need (White, 1959) and is especially important for young people.

Related to the desire for challenge is the need for psychological involvement in one's work. Young graduates tend to place increasing stress on intrinsic rather than extrinsic rewards for their work. Dissatisfaction with intrinsic work challenge seems to be especially strong in the first year of work, as discussed later. The return of many young people today to craftwork is one reflection of this interest (and of the assumption that intrinsic involvement is difficult to find in large organizations).

At this stage, the young person also has a strong need for feedback in his performance. Without valid information on how one is performing, it is difficult to improve and grow. As an extreme example, a person would not think of driving his car for even one block blindfolded, even if the block were straight and the car headed initially in the right direction. Outside factors, such as children playing, bumps in the road, other cars approaching, and unforeseen deviations from the original course, all call for periodic braking, steering, and accelerating. Steering one's own career is far more complex than driving a car for one block, but feedback is far more difficult to obtain.

Related to feedback, which often comes from the supervisor, is coaching and psychological support from the boss. There is a fine line between the supervisor controlling and directing his subordinate's work and coaching him when he (the subordinate) requests it. Most supervisors either provide too much help or direction and are perceived as over-controlling or they provide too little, letting the person "sink or swim."

A second aspect of the supervisor-subordinate relationship the young graduate probably desires is a collaborative authority relationship. He wants some say in making important decisions that affect his job and his career. He expects the boss to listen to his ideas and to apply them when they are good. He expects the boss to respect his opinion regardless of his age or seniority.

Finally, he expects a good salary and good promotion prospects. He expects to have these rewards contingent on good performance on his part, but he does not want to see them blocked by factors beyond his control.

So much for the individual's expectations. What does the organization expect to see in the new recruit?

Competence to get a job done—to identify the problem and see it through to solution

Ability to accept organizational "realities"— to grasp those values that deal with non-technical factors, such as the need for stability and survival, recognition of group loyalties, informal power arrangements, and office politics

Ability to generate and sell ideas—to have in effect a whole range of skills, such as

> The ability to translate technical solutions into practical, understandable terms
>
> The ability to diagnose and overcome sources of resistance to change
>
> Patience and perseverance in gaining acceptance for new ideas
>
> The ability to work through or around organizational "realities"
>
> Interpersonal skills or the ability to influence others

Loyalty and commitment—to place the goals and values of the organization ahead of his own selfish motives and, if necessary, to sacrifice some parts of his personal life

High personal integrity and strength—to stick to his own point of view without, however, being a deviant or a rebel (must know how to compromise when necessary)

Capacity to grow—to learn from his experiences (mistakes are expected, but the repetition of mistakes is not tolerated); to demonstrate the ability to take on increasing responsibility and maturity in the handling of interpersonal relationships (Schein, 1964, p. 70)

The Recruit and Her Goals:
The Need for Career Planning

Unfortunately, these mutual expectations are often not realized, and the psychological contract all too often comes apart. With better long-term planning by the organization, however, the chances for a successful contract can be enhanced. Perhaps most important is the creation of an employee-centered work planning program, as recommended by Hall and Richter (1990). The purpose of such a program is to establish collaborative goal settings and more self-directed careers. The organization and the individual, however, must be aware of and avoid the tendency for such programs to "vanish" in the sense used previously. Such a program should allow for individual differences in administrative and interpersonal skills, which have been found to be related to career success (Howard & Bray, 1988). Its focus should be on developing these skills in terms of specific day-to-day behaviors that can be measured and changed by the person and his supervisor.

Another useful exercise is for the new recruit and his supervisor to examine the company's goals (or the department's or work group's goals) in relation to the recruit's personal goals and desires. One issue is the attractiveness or "valence" of the organization's goals to the recruit. Can he identify with them? Are they important to him? How can they be made more important? The other issue is their instrumentality. Does he see his efforts toward the organization's goals as also leading to his own satisfaction? If not, how could this connection be better established?

The organization must be aware of the emotional development taking place in the recruit in his early career years. Organizations, like universities, have tended to view personal growth as being independent of or irrelevant to the "really important" career development changes (i.e., skills, abilities, and knowledge). The bulk of a person's career changes, however, are in the motivational and attitudinal area (Campbell, 1968; Howard & Bray, 1988). Because motivation and attitudes are related to performance and success (Hall, 1971; Hall & Foster, 1977), it is clear that organizations should view these personal changes as relevant to their interests. In particular, one never knows when, how, and what attitudes may be acquired by a new employee. The change may result as much from the climate of the organization as from the work. Much personal stress may result from the need to achieve and the relative lack of security in the first year with a new organization. It would also be useful to be alert for turning points that may help mark important career transitions—the first performance appraisal, the first completed project, or a particular transfer or promotion. Certain events may have symbolic value, which makes them far more important to the recruit than the organization or the supervisor may realize, and it is important to attempt to view the recruit's career from the recruit's perspective.

Family Changes

Along with recognizing the career as emotional change and identity development, it is also important to recognize the impact of another important contributor to these changes—the family. Family changes, such as marriage, children, relocation, or the death of a relative, often have profound effects on a person's identity, attitudes, and motivation. If these family changes happen to be congruent with career changes, the mutually reinforcing effects could be far more potent than the sum of the separate influences. An example of congruent family and career effects might be the way marriage and a significant promotion could contribute to both increased career involvement and personal responsibility. On the other hand, a problem in a critical family transition could greatly disrupt a person's adjustment to an important career change. An example might be in-law problems in a new marriage and problems with the supervisor in a recent promotion; both might conceivably center on the issue of competence in relationships with older people or authority figures. The combination of similar problems regarding the same issues in two central areas of one's life could greatly compound any feeling of incompetence or low esteem that might result from either problem separately. This interaction of family and career issues has been widely discussed during the past 20 years (Googins, 1991; Hall & Associates, 1996; Hall & Hall, 1979; Levinson et al., 1978, 1996; Sekaran, 1986). (See Chapter 8 for a more detailed discussion of work and family roles.)

Midlife and Midcareer: Maintenance and Reexamination

Once a person has become established in his or her career, the next stage, from the forties to retirement, is often called a maintenance period. In contrast to the fierce strivings and achievements of the trial and establishment periods, the maintenance period is more like a plateau;

holding your own, maintaining what has already been achieved. As Super notes, it is not a time for breaking new ground.

Does this maintenance stage sound like a fairly tranquil period, one of reaping the fruits of earlier labors and achievements? There is a growing body of evidence indicating that the transition into this stage is not at all smooth sailing in many cases (Levinson et al., 1978, 1996). Furthermore, for many people this is a period for embarking on a new career rather than maintaining the old one (Hall, 1986). In many ways, it appears that the transition into midcareer is perhaps more stressful than the move from the educational institution in early career years.

In a classic paper, Elliott Jacques (1965) referred to this stage as the *midlife crisis.* He noted that 37 seemed to be a critical age in the lives of creative artists. In a random sample of 310 great painters, composers, poets, writers, and sculptors, Jacques found a sudden surge in the death rate between ages 35 and 39 that was far higher than the normal rate. Then he found a decrease in the death rate between ages 40 and 44, followed by a return to the normal rate. It appeared that the greater the artists' genius, the more pronounced was the peak in death rate. These data are compatible with the peaks found in the scientific contributions of scientists in the late 1930s and early 1940s (Lehman, 1953; Pelz & Andrews, 1966). For scientists, the peaking is also more pronounced for more major achievements, and the time of the peaking is later in life for less abstract fields. This indicates that the peak performance/crisis would occur for managers and other more applied professionals in the 40s rather than the 30s.

Midcareer changes are not restricted to great artistic and scientific geniuses. It is becoming clear that as people move into the maintenance stage of their careers, they experience a variety of physiological, attitudinal, occupational, and family changes:

- Awareness of advancing age and awareness of death: At age 40, many people report the sudden feeling that "life is half over"—that they now have as much or more time behind them than ahead of them. They are now symbolically "middle-aged." Time now feels like a scarcer resource.
- Awareness of physical aging: The person becomes aware that his endurance in sports is decreasing while his recovery time is increasing. Aches and pains become more frequent, and physical performance (e.g., reaction time and running speed) drops off. One review of the literature on aging (Kutner, 1971) cited a depressing list of physical changes that occur in the 40s and 50s:

There is a change in pituitary secretions so that body fat doubles.

There is a decline in metabolic rate.

There is a decline in secretion of dominant sex hormones, allowing opposite-sexed hormones to have more influence.

Energy decreases: Lungs have less capacity and heart pumps less blood.

There is a decrease in muscle tone.

There is a rapid increase in disability and invalidism.

Arteries harden, blood pressure increases, and coronary problems occur.

Visual efficiency declines rapidly after age 40.

Hearing gradually diminishes, starting with higher frequencies.

Skin loses its elasticity, becomes coarser, and shows wrinkling, resulting in "flabby skin hanging in loose folds."

Skin shows discoloration (pale or yellow), dark circles appear under eyes, and varicose veins appear.

Men's hairlines recede, stiff hair appears in nose and ears, and women develop more facial hair and men less.

Weight shifts downward from the chest to the abdomen, so the torso looks pear-shaped. (As a wag once said, "Middle age is like the stock exchange in bad times—it's all still there, but lower.")

- The person has a clearer sense of how many of his career goals he has or will attain: By the time a person reaches his forties in a managerial or professional career, he has a pretty good idea of how far he will advance in the organization, profession, or industry. This may be more true for men than for women because women's career stages do not seem to be as strongly tied to age as are men's (Lynn et al., 1996). Even in midcareer, managers find themselves confronted with unrealistic expectations regarding promotions and career advancement (Buchanan, 1974; Hall, 1986; Levinson et al., 1978; Osherson, 1980). Ironically, the stress may be greater if he has achieved his career goals; then he may wonder, in the words of Peggy Lee's classic song, "Is that all there is?" In either case, the goals that have formerly guided the person's work life are no longer operative. Even Catholic priests are not immune to this midcareer letdown (Hall & Schneider, 1972, 1973).

- There is a search for meaning and new life goals: Spirituality is becoming increasingly important, especially for people in midlife. With the former goals now viewed in a different perspective, and with time seeming suddenly shorter, the person may begin to search for new values, goals, and meaning in life. There is more concern to produce something lasting and worthwhile. Often, people make complete breaks with their old lives and careers and embark on totally different courses. One marriage counselor quoted a statement often heard among his colleagues: "Between the ages of 40 and 50, a man changes jobs or changes wives." The result of this search, of course, could be a reaffirmation of one's current goals. An example of these changes is found in David Krantz's (1977) report of "The Santa Fe Experience," which focuses on people who made radical career changes in midlife and moved to Santa Fe.

- There is a marked change in family relationships: Children are now teenagers, in need of authority figures to rebel against. The person's spouse is not quite the dashing young thing he or she was 20 years ago, physically or emotionally. People's values, needs, and interests change as they mature, and what was a good match in 1975 may have become a mismatch. Women in general have experienced greater freedom as a result of the women's movement, and this can also put strain on the marriage contract. The apparent weakening of these family bonds may cause the person to ask what life is all about.

- There is a change in work relationships: The person is no longer a "bright young man/woman" on the way up. He or she may now have advanced to a position of influence, with authority over younger people who are competing for promotion and perhaps for the person's job. These young subordinates may be questioning the person's authority, much like the kids are at home. Not only does this make a person feel older but also it leads one to occasionally question one's own competence and purpose.

- There is a growing sense of obsolescence: The bright young subordinates and their recent technical knowledge and skills may present a sharp contrast with the middle-aged manager, who may not have learned much of today's technology and has perhaps forgotten a great deal of what he did learn. With all the increased administrative demands on the person in midcareer, he has little opportunity to bring himself up to date. This contributes to the gnawing anxiety that someday he will be "found out." As Satchel Paige once said, "Never look back; someone might be gaining on you."

  Kaufman (1974), in an impressive review of the literature, defines obsolescence as "the degree to which organization professionals lack the up-to-date knowledge or skills necessary to maintain effective performance in either their current or future work roles" (p. 23). Someone recently described the condition as follows: "There's been an alarming increase recently in the number of things I know nothing about."

- The person feels less mobile and attractive in the job market and therefore more concerned about security: Many companies are reluctant to lure a manager in his forties or older for various reasons—they believe he is untrainable, obsolete, has too little time left, is too expensive, and so on. Furthermore, in the recent recessions, many firms found they could achieve great savings by cutting back in their middle-management ranks. Therefore, the middle manager may feel more dependent on (or perhaps trapped in) his current organization.

Referring to Erikson's model of life stages, in theory the midcareer person should be in the generativity stage, concerned about what he is producing of lasting value for future generations. The changes reported previously indicate that this is the case for many people in midlife. They are experiencing a generativity crisis, directly analogous to the identity crisis experienced by many adolescents. Although the midlife phenomenon may appear to be an identity crisis, with concerns about goals and questions such as "Where am I headed?," it has more to do with leaving one's mark on future generations as well as an awareness of limited time.

One way in which all these problems show up is in physical indexes of health. One study indicated a sharp increase in specific symptoms, such as extreme fatigue, chest pains, and indigestion, in young executives on their way into top management. Only one third of these symptoms among managers aged 31 to 40 could be linked to organic causes (Levinson, 1969). It appears instead that many of the symptoms are caused by depression associated with midcareer changes.

Changes in the Work Environment

What are some of the changes in the work environment that contribute to the midlife crisis? Harry Levinson (1969) identified seven factors. Although Levinson's analysis was conducted many decades ago, it appears that the same factors are present today—in fact, perhaps even more strongly so in this youth-oriented economy. Similar themes can be found in the recent work of Daniel Levinson (1996) on women's lives and in his earlier, classic research on men (Levinson et al., 1978). In fact, if anything, these environmental pressures regarding age and career stage have been heightened during the era of the information economy for the following reasons:

1. Increasing contraction of the hard-work period: The average age at which people become company presidents is decreasing, whereas people start their careers later owing to increased training (e.g., MBA programs). What we saw during the "dot.com" era was perhaps an extreme illustration of this phenomenon, but in today's entrepreneurial climate major success can still happen very early in life. Therefore, people have less time to "make it."

2. Inseparability of life and career: For many young professionals, their careers are their lives, and they live on a self-made time schedule. Time spent in each level is

critical, and each passing year is a milepost. Again, the experiences of young Internet entrepreneurs illustrate this idea in the extreme, but the same level of extreme work involvement occurs for young workers in other industries as well.

3. Continuous threat of defeat: With the pressures, competition, and need for success so intense, the thought of defeat (psychological failure) can be devastating.

4. Increase in dependency: To remain successfully competitive, the professional, especially the technical specialist, must come to depend increasingly on subordinates and support personnel. He may not fully understand the data, the subordinate, or the process by which the data were generated, however. "He is therefore often left to shudder at the specter of catastrophe beyond his control" (Levinson, 1969, p. 52).

5. Denial of feelings: The executive career involves self-demand, self-sacrifice, guilt about making decisions affecting others' decisions, and anger at himself and the organization for the other life goals he must sacrifice. A person with leadership responsibilities often believes that he or she cannot allow himself or herself to get close to superiors, subordinates, or peers (competitors) and to experience human feelings about work (such as laying people off or forming close relationships at work). Therefore, the person must repress these feelings, which drains energy.

6. Constant state of defensiveness: As in the child's game, King of the Hill, the person is busy either fighting his way to the top or defending it. There is no respite, which means being constantly in a state of emergency, a very stressful condition.

7. Shift in prime-of-life concept: Because society now values youth more than in the past, the attainment of success is partially offset by the loss of youth. Levinson (1969) noted that "since only rarely can one have youth and achievement at the same time, there is something anticlimactic about middle-age success" (pp. 52-53).

A New Stage Model for the Middle and Later Career Years and Beyond: Learning Cycles

The New Career Metacompetencies: Identity and Adaptability

One of the keys to understanding the new contract is the fact that the employee's needs and career concerns change during the course of the career, in a much more dynamic way than in the past. Continuous learning is required for continued success. As suggested earlier, I argue that career stages do not operate exactly the way they did in a more stable organizational environment, as described by Hall (1976) and Super et al. (1967), when midcareer was viewed as a period of mastery and maintenance.

An issue for women and men in midlife and later is how to learn continuously and be adaptable after establishing an initial life structure that "works" and yields psychological success. Hall (1986) discussed how early adult success can reinforce a stable routine of behavior and lifestyle, which can put the person at risk later in the career of being closed to necessary new learning. In short, although success breeds success (Hall, 1971; Hall & Foster, 1977) over a period of, for example, 5 years, over the longer run success may lead to failure if the previously successful behaviors are unexamined and unchanged. McCall (1998) discussed in detail how this overuse of skills can lead to later career derailment.

The keys to career success at all stages are identity and adaptability (Hall, 1986; Howard & Bray, 1988; London, 1983, 1998; London & Mone, 1987). If the older person has the ability to self-reflect, to continue assessing and learning about herself or himself, and to change behaviors and attitudes, the chances are much better for a successful midcareer transition and a good fit with the new work environment.

Changing Career Routines: Learning Stages

Hall (1986) presented a model of how a career routine in middle or later career can be interrupted by various triggers in the person and in the environment, leading to conscious exploration of alternative ways of being, "routine-busting," and new cycles of learning. If this exploration leads to experimental changes in behavior that lead to success, these are likely to be integrated into the identity and may thus encourage future explorations and adaptations. External conditions, such as autonomy, feedback, and support, can greatly facilitate this midcareer identity change process.

Because of the greatly increased variety in the work environment (Handy, 1989, 1994), based on the concept of equifinality, there is an equally great potential variety in the range of individual responses to changes in this environment. I argue that what we are seeing now, instead of one set of career stages spanning a life span (as the Super model posits), is a series of many shorter learning cycles over the span of a person's work life (Hall, 1994; Mirvis & Hall, 1994). Careers will be increasingly driven by the core competencies of the fields in which a person works (Quinn, 1992). Because the life cycle of technologies and products is so shortened (Handy, 1989), so too are personal mastery cycles. As a result, people's careers will increasingly become a succession of "ministages" (or short-cycle learning stages) of exploration-trial-mastery-exit, as they move in and out of various product areas, technologies, functions, organizations, and other work environments. The key issue determining a learning stage will not be chronological age (in which the 40s and 50s were "midcareer") but career age, where perhaps 5 years in a given specialty may be "midlife" for that area. Thus, the half-life of a career stage would be driven by the half-life of the competency field of that career work. This model is shown in Figure 4.3.

This model of career learning ministages provides a more specific view of the functioning of the protean career as the person grows older. As the person acquires career experience, his or her protean qualities are usually not random or capricious changes. They are not something negative, and proteanism should not be confused with career indecision. It is a process of doing identity exploration and development, becoming more complex and mature, as one learns from experience (Kegan, 1982, 1994).

This point is especially crucial in appreciating the potential of later career stages. The more psychologically mature the person is (and most developmental models posit that maturity increases with age), the freer the person is to be a protean self-learner. If we can remove the bases of insecurity that plague older workers (e.g., job insecurity, health insecurity, and physical insecurity), we can free up these positive self-direction and growth drives and tap into a rich supply of experienced human talent.

Interestingly, this focus on lifelong learner for the older employee can produce a gender benefit as well. The more we come to view continuous learning as part of the new career contract and not just as a type of career pattern for a certain type of person (i.e., "spiral" or "transitory" people in Cox and Driver's [1994] typology of career concepts), the more we can value both female and male patterns of development. By this, I mean that the protean form involves more horizontal growth, expanding one's range of competencies and ways of connecting to work and other people, as opposed to the more traditional vertical model of success (upward mobility). In the protean form of growth, the goal is learning, psychological success, and expansion of the identity. In the more traditional vertical form, the goal was advancement, success and esteem in the eyes of others, and power. Thus, the protean form can

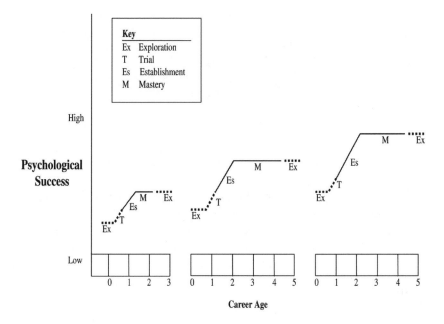

Figure 4.3. A Model of the Career as Learning Cycles (reproduced with permission from Hall, 1993)

embrace both mastery and relational growth—that is, both "male" and "female" ways of developing (Fletcher, 1999; Miller, 1991).

What this means is that careers unfold in erratic episodes. They move in fits and starts. They take sudden left turns. They are not nearly as orderly as our traditional theories of career and adult development stages might suggest. In fact, contemporary careers might properly be viewed as a series of learning cycles over the person's life (Hall 1994; Hall & Mirvis, 1995). Thus, instead of the career being one long cycle containing stages such as exploration, trial, and establishment, as I described careers in an earlier era (Hall, 1976), the career today is composed of many short cycles or episodes lasting perhaps 2 to 4 years, during which the person learns about and masters a new area of work. Each episode might have an exploratory phase, a trial or testing period, and a period of getting established or mastering the work. Then, whether for external reasons, such as new technology and market changes, or for internal reasons, such as personal or family needs and values, the person might "get itchy" and start to explore some other terrain. For example, when dot-coms boomed, many people surfed into the new business platform. In the wake of the dot-com tailspin, information technology professionals are jumping back to traditional companies.

Later Career and Adjustment Into Retirement

The third critical adjustment for most workers (after the early career years and the midcareer crisis) is the later career stage and the transition from the status of working person to retired person. Because work is such an important part of one's identity, especially for highly job-involved people such as managers and professionals, the loss of one's work role (and therefore one's work subidentity) feels like part of one's self being removed. Also, there are many difficulties in the work environment that contribute to the difficulties older workers experience with adaptation and identity changes.

External Environment Issues

As companies undergo continuous restructuring, they will rely increasingly on employees at all levels to redefine corporate strategy and to adapt it to changing conditions in the marketplace. Firms will also depend more on multiskilled workers, who will be moved from job to job, from unit to unit, and even across organizational boundaries to respond to pressing organizational needs and to continuously learn new skills. A variety of barriers must be overcome, however, for this vision to become reality. Even enlightened managers may doubt the cost-effectiveness of investing in older employees, and undoubtedly many managers in companies today think older workers are too inflexible to accommodate rapidly changing employment options and too set in their ways to learn complex new skills. As Hall and Mirvis (1994a, 1994b, 1995) argued, however, there are many options for more creative and effective deployment of older workers, and there is far more capacity for adaptation among older workers than is currently recognized in the ageist cultures of many organizations.

Internal Identity Issues

One manifestation of the importance of work in a person's life is the fantasy of many workers that they would soon die following retirement; this is one of the "distressing feelings" described previously. The following interview illustrates the connection between employees' perceptions of retirement and fear of death:

Question (to a 64-year-old stock marker): Why should you want to keep on working?

Answer: Why? I'll tell you, last year a man I know reached 65. Then, they had to retire, even the big shots. But, he told the foreman he wanted to go on working. The foreman told him: "Why the hell should you go on working? You have the house, the car, the family, the money—Why don't you want to quit?" He answered: "Sure I have the money and the car, but I'm used to working. If I quit, I'll die in a little while." The foreman told him he had to quit anyway, and 3 months later he was dead. When a man's used to exercise and work, he can't just quit and do nothing. The only way to stay alive is to keep working. (Friedman & Havighurst as quoted in Sofer, 1970, p. 95)

This man and others interviewed in a study by Friedman seemed to have "equated 'keeping busy' with 'keeping alive' and feared that their failure to keep busy would result in death" (Friedman & Havighurst as quoted in Sofer, 1970, p. 95). On the other hand, having a variety of roles and being highly involved in one role are strongly related to happiness in old age (Sofer, 1970).

In theory, this stage should be one of decline (Super & Bohn, 1970), both in physical capability and in work involvement. Job involvement, however, continues to increase in late career for research and development professionals (Hall & Mansfield, 1975). Research on aging also casts doubt on the decline (Baltes & Schaie, 1975). Among Catholic priests, the career years involved a "mixed bag" of fairly stable work activities, increasing satisfaction, and declines in skill utilization and self-image (Hall & Schneider, 1973). Moving into late career and retirement involves a similar mix of positive and negative reactions during the move into retirement (Hall & Mirvis, 1994b). The extent to which late career is a period of growth, maintenance, or decline may depend on the individual and the organization, as Hall and Mirvis (1993, 1994a,

1994b) report based on a national survey of corporate human resource management practices regarding older workers. It is clear that, with the population (particularly the bellwether baby boom cohort) aging and entering late career, many questions about career development process at this stage are in need of future empirical work.

The difficulty of the transition into retirement may be eased in various ways: part-time work, hobbies, and preparation for retirement. Because we seem to be entering an era of multicareer lives (Hall & Mirvis, 1993), the person at retirement age (which has been decreasing in recent years) may simply switch to a different employer or a different type of work. Indeed, the greater amount of leisure time people enjoy now, with increased holiday benefits and 4-day weeks, is forcing people to plan more creatively the use of leisure time; this could be a good form of preparation for retirement.

There appears to be a trend toward earlier retirement as both a benefit to older employees and an opportunity to provide faster advancement for younger, lower-level employees. This means that adjustment to retirement will become more of a problem: If a person retires at age 50 (a possibility in some occupations today), he or she could have another 25 years (50% of present age) still ahead. In some way, a sense of meaning and purpose will have to be found. If multiple careers or frequent career learning cycles, as discussed earlier, become a concomitant of early retirement, however, then the concept of retirement changes. In this case, we would not be talking about retirement from work but retirement from a particular occupation as a prelude to a career shift, much as professional athletes "retire." If multiple careers become more widespread, retirement as we know it today and its concomitant role-removal problems may become a novel experience.

Summary of Developmental
Needs in Early, Middle, and Late Career

As a way of tying together our discussion of early, middle, and late career, consider the practical question of how organizations can facilitate the person's development in different stages. Table 4.1 summarizes the previous discussion about the developmental needs that arise at each stage. Early career is a time when the person needs to develop action skills so that he or she can apply the concepts and competencies that were acquired in school. These are good years for creativity and innovation, qualities that should be developed. Also, in a world in which work gets done in team settings, the person needs to develop his or her helping and team learning skills.

The person should also be encouraged to go into depth in one area and develop a specialty. This specialty, however, could easily become a trap if the person comes to be seen as too indispensable in this area. Therefore, it is also important to become a generalist at the same time, to enable one to play, for example, the marketing specialist on a team if there is no marketing expert on the team. Also, the person should rotate to a new specialty after a few years to avoid becoming too narrow, or even obsolete, as the specialty changes.

The socioemotional needs in early career call for a combination of support and freedom (supportive autonomy)—freedom to make mistakes, learn, and develop confidence that one's successes are one's own, but help and support should be provided when needed. Feelings of rivalry and competition toward other fast-moving young colleagues must also be managed. This is also an important time to develop emotional intelligence because it is easy to focus solely on technical skills.

In midcareer, the person needs to redefine his or her task role. First, there is a need to move from "player" to "coach" and to develop a broader view of the organization and one's identification with it. Second, the person needs to update and develop new skills, ideally through new job assignments that require him or her to learn continually. If this job rotation continues in midcareer, obsolescence may be preventable. More generally, this is when the person has to master learning how to learn. (Developing a clear sense of identity and adaptability skills are key here.) On the socioemotional side, the person needs to have developmental opportunities to express feelings about midlife, gradually rework his or her self-image, and engage in mutual problem solving for coping with midcareer stress. Having access to settings in which one has a connection with peers in midlife can provide an important context for working on these socioemotional needs.

In late career, the person's task and socioemotional needs both revolve around his or her gradual withdrawal from the work organization into some other setting—another type of work, retirement, volunteer work, and so on. This is a time when the person's experiences can be a useful source of wisdom and guidance to younger people, and a person often needs support to be able to see this. The central emotional need is to

Table 4.1 Developmental Needs in Early, Middle, and Late Career

Stage	Task needs	Socioemotional needs
Early career	• Develop action skills • Develop specialty and general skills • Develop creativity, innovation • Develop helping and team skills • Rotate into new area after 3-5 years (new learning cycle)	• Support • Autonomy • Develop emotional intelligence • Deal with feelings of rivalry, competition
Middle career	• Develop skills in developing and mentoring others • Master learning how to learn • Develop broader perspective on own work • Rotation into new area of work, requiring new skills	• Opportunity, support for expressing feelings about midlife • Revise sense of personal identity (regarding work, family, personal life, values, mortality, etc.) • Reduce self-indulgence and competitiveness • Connection with midlife peers
Late career	• Shift from power role to consultation, guidance, wisdom • Explore, begin to establish identity in activities outside current work role	• Gradual detachment from current work role and organization • Support to help see purpose, legacy in one's work • Acceptance of one's one and only life cycle • Support to help see own integrated life experiences as a platform for others

develop what Erikson calls a sense of integrity, an awareness of the integration and value of one's life.

Research Issues

The issue of stages in life, career, and learning provides fascinating ground for creative research. Because the developmental processes involved are elusive, there are many contributions to be made at both the methodological and the content levels. The following is a sampling for the adventurous investigator:

- Starting at the beginning, what is the relationship between the three types of stages (life, career, and learning)? Following the appearance of early work by Levinson et al.(1978), there was a string of studies that investigated the relationship between adult life stages and career stages. Perhaps because both models were so amenable to empirical cross-sectional examination (even though the concepts call for longitudinal research)—the life stages model and the career stages model both had handy age ranges to define stages—it was easy to send out a survey, identify stage groups, and then run some multivariate statistical comparisons. Most of the questions posed, however, were fairly simplistic, such as the following: Are the models valid? and What explains the data better, the life stage model or the career stage model?

  We can now use research that goes beyond these basic validation designs and examines the more subtle interplay of the different cycles involved. Assume that the basic Levinsonian model of adult life stages is valid, which I am willing to do. Are there still career stages in the current economy? My observation (based on anecdotal data) is that we still see systematic differences between people in early career (e.g., younger than age 35), midcareer (ages 35-55), and late career (age 55 and older). Perhaps it is the impact of life stages on the ways people think about their work and career, but these age differences still seem connected to career experience.

- Superimposed on these career stages, do we find evidence of the learning cycles posed in Figure 4.3? This is where it can get interesting. What is the difference between the operation of the learning cycle in different career stages? I hypothesize that people are more open to learning (i.e., have higher adaptive motivation) in early career than in midcareer. In midcareer, when people may be feeling stressed by performance pressures, work/home conflicts, and nagging concerns about possible obsolescence, they may be feeling more threatened by learning and less willing to put themselves in the learner role. Then in later career, in which performance pressures and work/life stresses are lower, people may be more hungry for the stimulation of learning, and we may see more self-initiated exploratory behavior leading to new learning cycles.

- What triggers learning cycles and development? In Chapter 7, I present a model of adaptation proposed by Morrison and Hall that identifies factors in the person and in the environment that are hypothesized to stimulate adaptation and adaptability. Although there has been considerable research on the basic process of adaptation, there has been little research on adaptation and change in the context of the career. This is ironic in view of the fact that the past quarter century contained much career turbulence (and undoubtedly this century will also). We simply need more research to help us understand what gets people into these learning episodes.

- How do we define and measure development? We have developmental models such as Super's, Levinson's, and Kegan's, but their writings are complex, and they do not give us handy operational definitions to determine when a person has just "developed." We need more specific indicators of what development looks like. It is easier to measure learning (the growth of skills and competencies) than changes in identity and stage changes.

- What interventions aid development? Aside from the issue of definition and measurement, we know little about interventions by organizations and helping professionals that actually cause developmental change. Change is difficult to measure, and establishing causality about change is even more difficult. My recommendation is to start with interventions that we know from years of experience and observation have an impact on personal development, such as taking an international expatriate assignment. We can use qualitative methods after repatriation to probe and identify the types of development that have occurred. This can help us develop a profile of what development looks like. Then, we can probe the expatriate assignment retrospectively to determine what kinds of factors were associated with that development. Other examples of settings in which there is a high likelihood of development include a major career or personal failure (such as business demise or a divorce), becoming a parent for the first time, or surviving a major increase in job scope.

- We need more research on peer coaching and other relational sources of development. My hunch is that when people have undergone major personal development, it was often associated with the aid of a significant other in a strong helping relationship. We know from a body of research that traditional senior-junior mentoring promotes development, and it even helps people cope with the stresses of downsizing and other corporate traumas (Hall & Kram, 1991). In the contemporary work setting, the rapid change may make the help of a peer more relevant than that of someone more senior because the senior's experience was in an environment that may no longer exist. Also, having access to an entire network of relationships (e.g., professional associations, current and past coworkers, and support and learning communities) may now also have more of an impact than traditional mentoring.

- We need more research on identity, particularly about how identity changes. Although we are jumping ahead of ourselves a bit (because we do not discuss identity until Chapter 6), we cannot study development without studying identity. If we want to understand better the whole person at work and how the whole person grows, we need to understand the concept of identity at work better. Work by Ashforth (2000) and Whetten and Godfrey (1998) provides wonderful guidance for this work, and we need to build on their descriptions of identity processes to learn more about how identity can change and grow.

- Can a protean career be developed? If so, how do the metacompetencies (identity and adaptability) relate to the protean career? Is the protean career something that a person either has or does not have? Is this career orientation a stable individual difference variable, or can careers develop from traditional to protean? My observation is that both may be true. Some people have protean careers from the beginning. Others start with traditional organizational or professional careers and then become more autonomous and creative. For the lifelong protean career, what early life experiences or personality factors might be at play? Also, for the evolved protean career, what life or work experience or what inner qualities were associated with this development?
- Finally, the most important question: How and when do adaptation and identity come into alignment? That is, when does the protean careerist develop a congruent identity that values being protean? In my observation, one of the problems of the protean career is that it is difficult for the person to value being protean. Although the person may be doing what he or she loves to do and is following his or her own path with a heart, the outside world may not value this. As a result, the person might experience low self-esteem in relation to this work. Even in today's environment, when the person does not have the traditional "trappings" of success, such as organizational status, wealth, or power, the person may have a nagging feeling that questions his or her success. The objective and the subjective career may not be in alignment. Under what conditions does the protean careerist feel self-confident, self-respecting, and respected by others? One simple idea here is to identity protean careerists who have high self-esteem and high job satisfaction, as well as high regard from others, and then study these people and their role senders and determine what makes them different from protean careerists with less self-esteem and job satisfaction. Better yet, see if we can catch protean careerists in the process of having experiences that boost their self-confidence and document those experiences. The research question is what work experiences, relational experiences, and learning experiences lead to a growth in self-confidence for protean careerists?

Conclusion

The central point of this chapter is that people experience changes in their needs, expectations, abilities, and behavior as they go through different stages of their careers. Therefore, the career stage is a critical individual characteristic that can explain differences in behavior and attitudes among different people in organizations, although the concept has not been widely used in organizational research. For example, the response of a 60-year-old employee to increased responsibility and challenge may be less positive than that of a 25-year-old, even though each of them might benefit. Administrators seem to have been more aware of the impact of age and career stages than have researchers.

Because age and career stage influence the person's responses to the job and organization, employees have different needs regarding career development. Programs for career development should obviously be designed to provide different experiences for people in different career stages. Some possible differential development experiences for people in different career stages have been proposed by Hall and Mansfield (1975) based on a study of the career stages of research and development professionals:

> If the younger person is in fact in a trial period, he or she should be hired for jobs in which turnover may be desirable—for example, specific time-bounded projects, experimental programs, or visiting positions. These ad hoc activities may be sufficiently exciting to test his or her creativity and meet some self-fulfillment needs, without obligating the person or the organization to a long-term commitment. Once hired, the early career person will be motivated more by challenge and variety than by security and long-term benefits. Investments such as training and development should be made carefully because of the employee's high mobility at this stage.
>
> The midcareer [person] is ready to settle down and advance in a more stable, long-term relationship with an organization. The prospects of long-term development and advancement will be strong inducements in hiring, rather than the excitement of the immediate assignment. Organizational recognition and esteem for the [employee's] accomplishments will be powerful motivators.
>
> The late-career [employee] is motivated by a steady, secure position. Job offers are few and far between at this point, and the person becomes increasingly involved in his or her present job and organization. Good job security, recognition of the person's continuing value to the organization, and health and pension benefits would be effective inducements in hiring and motivators on the job.
>
> It would also be wise to seek people at each stage who have qualities not normally found at that stage—for example, a "settled down" young [employee] or a late-career person who is still oriented toward growth. Such individuals would probably embody the best qualities of several stages. Another way to combine the strengths of different stages is to assign people at different stages to the same project. The younger [professional] would bring his or her new ideas, energy, and growth drive while the older person would bring maturity, stability, more concern for the organization's goals,

and an established "track record." Such a combination could aid performance as well as each person's career development, as the young person learns maturity and how to work within the organization from the older professional, and the older absorbs some of the new ideas, techniques, and zeal of the younger. (pp. 209-210)

Now that we have discussed the general and common experiences that are found in most careers, we return to individual differences in career experiences. In Chapter 5, we examine the factors that account for differences in a critical career outcome, the degree of success the person achieves as the organizational career progresses. Here, however, the important predictors are not solely characteristics of the individual alone. Success and performance are also largely determined by features of the organization and work environment as well as by the interaction of personal and environmental characteristics.

Notes

1. I am grateful to my friend and colleague, Jack McCarthy, for pointing this out.

2. The ways in which these developmental changes manifest themselves in the person's emerging identity, or sense of self, are discussed in Chapter 6.

5 Predicting Career Effectiveness

PERFORMANCE

Now that we have explored common stages in organizational careers as they develop over time, we turn to the issue of individual differences in this career process. Related to these questions is the matter of performance: How can knowledge about these career-affecting factors be applied to facilitate the development of careers in organizations? To help answer this question, we examine many points in the unfolding of a person's career in which attempts at development have been—or could be—made and then draw conclusions about what seems to work best.

What Is Career Effectiveness?

Before discussing the factors that influence career effectiveness, we discuss our criterion: What exactly do we mean by career effectiveness?

Generally, in the research literature, career effectiveness has been defined in terms of performance and the popular symbols of success—money and position. Position has been employed in the following ways: rank or level in an organizational hierarchy, number of promotions received over a given time period (i.e., rate of advancement), or, conversely, length of time in current position. Typical financial indicators are current salary, average yearly salary increases (often expressed as average percentage increases), or salary in relation to other people with equivalent length of service or of similar age. Other measures of effectiveness in this category are supervisory ratings of performance, success, or contributions; the number of employees for whom the person is responsible; size of the budget for which the person is responsible; revenue accounted for by the organization unit that the person manages; and so forth. Another important measure of career effectiveness is the way the career is perceived and evaluated by the individual himself or herself. This personal evaluation is part of a broader class of outcomes called career attitudes, which will be discussed in Chapter 6.

A third criterion seldom employed in the past, but becoming increasingly crucial to the protean career, is adaptability. As job mobility and technological and social change continue to increase, obsolescence in midlife becomes ever more threatening. For a person to provide for long-term performance, he must learn the skills of adaptability. We examine adaptability in Chapter 7.

The fourth measure of career effectiveness is the person's sense of identity. Identity has two important components. First, it entails the person's awareness of her values, interests, abilities, and plans. The clearer and more internally consistent this is, the clearer is her self-concept and the greater her identity resolution. If her values, interests, abilities, and plans seem undefined or unclear, or if she has internal conflict about them, we would say she is experiencing identity confusion. The second important facet of identity is the degree of integration between past, present, and future concepts of self—the person's sense of continuity and sameness. A person may see that her values and interests have changed quite drastically over the years, but if she sees how the "old self" relates to and helped create the "new self," her sense of identity will remain strong. If, on the other hand, she sees her current values and interests as being totally distinct from those of a previous age, she may feel alienated from her past, and her identity will be weakened since she is now essentially two people—the one she used to be and the one she is now.

Identity, then, is a measure of wholeness—of how well integrated the person's life is. It tells how well the pieces (values, interests, etc.) fit together in the present and how well the current fit is linked to that of the past and the future. We examine identity in-depth in Chapter 6.

The reader may have noticed that these four dimensions of career effectiveness combine together in certain ways. Career performance and career attitudes are similar in that they are both measures of current or short-term phenomena. Attitudes are by nature fleeting, having to do with what the person is feeling about her career in the present. Similarly, what matters in performance is how the person is doing right now as opposed to what last year's results were or what they might be 5 years hence.

On the other hand, career identity and adaptability both involve a longer time span. One aspect of identity is the extent to which the person feels integrated over time—that is, whether the person's current self-image is integrated with who he was 10 years ago and is connected with where he hopes to be 10 years from now. Similarly, adaptability by definition relates to the person's capacity to meet the demands of an environment that is yet to be. Thus, on the time dimension, identity and adaptability have a long-term time orientation, whereas performance and attitudes deal with short-term phenomena.

There is another way that we can sort these four effectiveness dimensions—the task versus personal axis. Two of the dimensions describe the way the person works on task challenges (performance and adaptability), and two relate to how the person deals with issues of self and personal development (attitudes and identity).

Thus, we can think of these four dimensions of career effectiveness as representing a 2 X 2 grid, as shown in Table 5.1. When *Careers in Organizations* was published in 1976, most research on careers was in quadrant I, performance. The main variable of interest in careers was how successful the person was, with success usually defined in terms of salary and position. There was also much empirical research on career attitudes (e.g., satisfaction and commitment) mainly because attitudes were good predictors of turnover. There is even more empirical work now on performance and attitudes (so much that I will not attempt to cover it all here).

Table 5.1   Four Types of Career Effectiveness

	Time Span	
Focus	Short Term	Long Term
Task	Performance	Attitudes
Self	Attitudes	Identity

There was very little research in the 1970s on the longer term aspects of career effectiveness, identity, and adaptability. As shown here and in later chapters, this situation has been remedied.

Understanding How the Process of the Career Affects Performance

Because there is such a large amount of literature related to career performance for the full range of occupations, we attempt to narrow our focus in two ways. First, we will not attempt to cover all occupations but will look at either studies of multiple occupations or studies of managers. Because this book was prepared for an audience that is primarily in the areas of organizational behavior and industrial-organizational psychology, managers constitute a population of interest. Second, we examine only those studies that attempt to understand the overall process of the career. This is in contrast to examining specific individual differences that might predict success, such as needs, interests, and values. For this research, the reader is referred to Betz, Fitzgerald, and Hill (1989) and to Brown and Brooks (1996).

Clinical Assessment Data Versus Performance

In understanding the multiple dimensions of career performance, it is desirable to obtain a holistic view of the person's career and work. During the past 40 years, assessment data have proved very effective in this regard for predicting management performance and success (Howard & Bray, 1988; Moses, 2001). The advantage of the assessment approach is that it uses multiple methods of measurement and thus can benefit from the best of the variety of methods and instruments available in the literature. Typically, many situational performances, background data, questionnaires, projective tests, and ability measures are used to obtain a file of data on each person. Using these data as inputs, a staff of assessors who could be clinical psychologists or line managers rate the person on his potential for managerial success.

A classic program of applied research was the American Telephone and Telegraph Company's (AT&T) two landmark longitudinal studies, the Management Progress Study (MPS), directed by Douglas W. Bray, and the later Management Continuity Study (MCS), conducted by Bray, Ann Howard, and colleagues (Howard, 1992; Howard & Bray, 1988). The MPS, started in 1956, was composed solely of men (who represented the dominant gender in the AT&T management ranks at that time). The study was described by Campbell, Dunnette, Lawler, and Weick (1970) as "the largest and most comprehensive study of managerial career development ever undertaken" (p. 232). Bray and Grant (1966) described the three unique features of the MPS as follows:

1. There is no contamination of the criterion data by the assessment results. The data are held in strict confidence and not reported to management. The assessment ratings therefore have no effect on the careers of the 442 people studied.
2. The subjects have been or will be reassessed; therefore, growth in the assessed characteristics can be taken into account.
3. Because the study is longitudinal and includes many types of data, there are limitless analyses that can be conducted.

The MCS was started in the 1970s and is composed of baby boom generation managers. It also contains a significant number of women.

In both studies, the following techniques were used to generate data on which to rate people for the previously mentioned qualities: interview; in-basket exercise; manufacturing problem; leadership group discussion; projective tests; ability tests; questionnaire measures of needs, values, and attitudes; personal history questionnaire; autobiographical essay; and self-descriptive measures. Groups of 12 subjects spent several days at the assessment center. At the end of this time, the staff compiled all the data, discussed each assessee in detail, and arrived at ratings of each person on each of 25 dimensions.

The results indicate that the assessment ratings are effective predictors of future middle-managerial attainments. As one would expect, such global ratings predict success better than any single measure alone.

Combined results show that 51% of those who were predicted to make middle management have made it, whereas only 14% of those predicted not to make middle management have reached that level (Bray, Campbell, & Grant, 1974). As one would expect, the two samples having the longest service in management since being assessed show the strongest predictions: Of the 55 men achieving middle management, 78% were correctly predicted, whereas of the 73 men who have not advanced beyond the first level, the assessment staffs predicted 95% would not reach middle management within 10 years (Bray & Grant, 1966). Campbell and Bray (1967) report that those managers who were assessed as unacceptable but were nevertheless promoted beyond the first level tended to be below-average performers. There was also a tendency for participation in the assessment center to produce a modest but significant improvement in performance at the first level. The AT&T researchers stress that a key factor in the success of the MPS has been the support and involvement of the line managers in the Bell system.

Many studies reviewed by Campbell et al. (1970) have similarly shown that clinical assessments resulted in better predictions of later performance than interest, intelligence, or personality tests (correlations ranging in the .40s and .50s). Clinical assessments appear more promising than what Campbell et al. term "actuarial methods," in which scores from multiple predictors are combined in some objectively determined, statistical manner such as multiple regression.

One indicator of the popularity of assessment methods is the growing list of companies that employ assessment centers for the identification of managerial talent. Unfortunately, few companies are conducting the kind of research on these programs that was used in the former Bell system.

Career Experiences Versus Performance

We now discuss the experiences in the career as a source of data for career performance—the process approach to the study of careers. The assumption is that the interaction between the person and the work environment produces opportunities, learning, attitudes, achievements, and other outcomes that affect the future course of a person's work life. Thus, in contrast to the background approach, the personality approach, and the assessment approach, which primarily examine the person for clues about future success, the career experience approach examines the work environment and the situations encountered therein as major influences of later performance. Like most environmental approaches, it assumes that management success can be learned; the three person-oriented approaches carry more of an implicit assumption that managers are "born, not made."

One of the classic studies of career processes is White's *Lives in Progress* (1952). White's intention was to contribute to our knowledge of the growth of human personality in an area largely unexplored by his psychologist colleagues: "The gap at that point where it becomes necessary to consider the continuous development of personality over periods of time and amid natural circumstances" (p. 22). White's book is based on extensive study of three case studies—people he knew originally as college students and whom he studied again later in their careers.

Although it is not possible to capture the richness of White's (1952) insights in a short discussion, he highlights the following key features of adult development (p. 328):

1. The person undergoes more or less continuous change.
2. The person is acted on by a multiplicity of influences to which he necessarily makes a selective response.
3. The person not only receives influence but also takes action on the environment. People are not static, nor are they passive and helpless.
4. Because our examples of growth include the years of young adulthood, it is also necessary to consider seriously the nature of the reality in which adult development occurs.

White concluded with a discussion of four general trends in the process of growth. First, there is a strengthening of ego identity. Ego identity refers to the "self or the person one feels oneself to be" (p. 332). Growth here entails developing a clearer concept of what are one's strengths and weaknesses, interests, aspirations, memories, commitments, and other personal characteristics. With growth, the person's ego identity develops clearer definition and continuity. Second, there is a freeing of personal relationships, a movement toward relationships that are "less anxious, less defensive, less burdened by inappropriate past reactions, more friendly, more spontaneous, more warm, and more respectful" (p. 343). The person becomes both more autonomous and more capable of concern for others.

The third growth trend is a deepening of interests. This does not mean developing more and varied interests but becoming deeply absorbed and involved in perhaps just one or two so that the person carries them through to some end result, with its accompanying sense of fulfillment. The fourth growth trend is a humanizing of values. White uses the term *humanizing* to indicate that (a) the person's values become increasingly a reflection of his own experiences and motives, and (b) the person increasingly discovers the human meaning of values and of their correlation to the achievement of social purposes.

It is interesting to consider the four growth trends in the light of the midcareer changes (described in Chapter 4, this volume), which often involve the reexamination and subsequent reaffirmation of one's identity, with an increased sense of stability as one important outcome. Often, the change is precipitated by a deepening of one's interests and an increased tendency to apply one's own values to one's own life experiences. In summary, we might hypothesize that following a successful midcareer transition, a person would rate higher on White's growth trends than before the changes began, even though that prechange period may have appeared more stable, successful, and "well developed" in terms of more popular definitions of career success.

Job Design and Socialization

Undoubtedly, the major source of stimulation and reinforcement for the personal development of the individual (i.e., the major source of inputs in systems terms) is his or her job. The relationship between the person-job environment interchange and the person's growth is described by Elliot Jacques (1973) as follows:

> Working for a living is one of the basic activities in a man's [sic] life. By forcing him to come to grips with his environment, with his livelihood at stake, it confronts him with the actuality of his personal capacity—to exercise judgment, to achieve concrete and specific results. It gives him a continuous account of his correspondence between outside reality and the inner perception of that reality, as well as an account of the accuracy of his appraisal of himself. (p. 6)

One of the underlying assumptions of this book is that careers develop or that people develop during the course of their careers. Development involves growth and learning over time. The person's stage of development today is very much a product of the stimulation, reinforcement, and learning he experienced yesterday. Therefore, it is not only the person's job that influences his or her career development but also the job history—the total history of influences in the work environment.

By extending this reasoning to its logical extreme, one can see that the person's initial job experiences and earlier socialization can have a long-range effect on his career. Likening the first year of the person's work life with his first year of life, with its "blank-slate" quality, it appears that this is a critical period for learning. The importance of initial job experiences is described by Berlew and Hall (1966) as follows:

> Of particular interest is the early development of performance standards and job attitudes. From the moment he enters the organization, a new manager is given cues about the quality of performance that is expected and rewarded. The probability that these expectations or standards will be internalized is probably higher when the individual has just joined the organization and is searching for some definition of the reality of his new environment. In terms of Lewin's field theory, when the new manager first enters an organization, that portion of his life-space corresponding to the organization is blank. He will feel a strong need to define this area and develop constructs relating himself to it. As a new member, he is standing at the boundary of the organization, a very stressful location, and he is motivated to reduce this stress by becoming incorporated into the "interior" of the company. Being thus motivated to be accepted by this new social system and to make sense of the ambiguity surrounding him, he is more receptive to cues from his environment than he will ever be again, and what he learns at the beginning will become the core of his organizational identity. In terms of Lewin's model of attitude change, the new manager is unfrozen and is searching for information and identification models on the basis of which he can change in the direction he feels the organization expects him to change. (p. 210)

Using data from two operating telephone companies in AT&T's MPS, Berlew and Hall predicted and found that the level of challenge in the initial jobs of young managers is related to performance and success 6 and 7 years later. One possible alternative explanation for these results is that the better managers may have been put in the better jobs. Examination of assessment data, however, indicated little relationship between personal characteristics and initial job assignment, which was consistent with the system's policy of considering all new employees equal until their performance proves otherwise.

A second alternative explanation of the results is that a challenging initial job may give a person high visibility, and that visibility, not performance, may lead to success. Initial challenge, however, correlated very highly with performance during the first few years of the person's career. Also, when the person's performance over 6 or 7 years was held constant (by partial correlation analysis), the correlation between initial challenge and later success became nonsignificant. This indicates that initial challenge is important because it stimulates a person to perform well in subsequent years. Also, it is this increased performance, not the initial challenge or resulting visibility per se, that leads to success.

The positive impact of initial job challenge on later performance has also been documented in other AT&T companies (Campbell, 1968) and in the General Electric Company (Peres, 1966) and the Roman Catholic Church (Hall & Schneider, 1973). On a more macrolevel, Lipsett and Malm (1955) found that the occupational level of the first job, over a number of different occupational groups, was a good predictor of the occupational level the person would attain later in his career.

Some companies have applied these findings by upgrading initial jobs in an attempt to facilitate the career development of new employees (Hall, 1999). It appears that improved first jobs reduce the high turnover of the first years. Unfortunately, none of these companies has systematically related improvements in initial job challenge to later performance. This would be a fruitful area for controlled field experiments. There also appear to be two unintended consequences of giving high-quality initial jobs. First, the supervisors of these jobs must be carefully selected and trained because they are the ones who largely define the job for the employee. Second, when the person advances from his enriched initial job to a "regular" second job, the contrast often results in frustration and dissatisfaction; in fact, the high turnover experienced among second-year employees in one firm suggests that it had succeeded in simply postponing turnover from the first year to the second. Thus, it was necessary to improve second-level jobs to retain the new employees. In time, a wide range of jobs in the company were reviewed. The company found that a program of career development in fact entails a commitment to organization development, a systematic effort to increase the effectiveness of the entire organization through behavioral science methods. It is difficult to change one component of one employee's work environment without affecting another employee's environment; such is the interconnected, interdependent nature of social systems.

Relational Influences and Socialization

Socialization is a learning and development process in which new members of an organization make the role transition from outsider to insider (Brim & Wheeler, 1966; Major, 1999; Wanous, 1992). From the organization's perspective, socialization serves the function of transmitting and perpetuating the culture by inculcating it into new members. From the employee's perspective, socialization serves the process of helping the new member learn the expectations and required behaviors of the new role. Thus, by definition, socialization has a positive effect on role and job performance.

The traditional view of new-employee socialization is that a newcomer enters, engages in interactions with a network of "insiders" (i.e., long-term employees who are centrally involved in the organization), and is influenced by these interactions. The newcomer's values may change to conform to those of the insider, role performance may change to fit with the insiders' expectations, and the person's sense of identity may change so that he or she feels like more of a part of the organization (i.e., more identified with it) (Hall, 1976). From the organization's perspective, socialization is said to be complete when the newcomer has come to understand and accept the critical values, goals, and activities of the organization (Schneider & Rentsch, 1988).

As Major (1999) suggests, however, this one-way influence model from insiders to newcomer is not consistent with the realities of today's organizations. Increasingly, it is the newcomer who has access to the new technology, the new cultural values, or the international arena; thus, it is often the newcomer who is helping the insider to learn and adapt to new ways of working. We already discussed ways that relational influences have become a major source of learning for employees in modern work settings (Hall & Associates, 1996), and learning from newcomers is just one way that this relational development can occur.

Mentoring

Another important form of relational learning that has a powerful impact on performance and career development is mentoring (Kram, 1985). Kram describes two basic types of mentoring functions, through which mentoring has its effects. One, which is probably most familiar to most people, is the *career functions*, which cover instrumental, career-enhancing helping activities (such as sponsoring and coaching). The other type of mentoring, perhaps even more important, is the *psychosocial functions*, which provide the emotional support that a learner needs (such as acceptance and confirmation).

To illustrate these functions, Box 5.1 presents material developed by Lisa Cheraskin at Eli Lilly & Company as part of a mentoring program she developed in collaboration with Kathy Kram and David Thomas. Many of the concrete examples of the mentoring activities are quotes from Lilly managers describing their own experiences with mentoring.

BOX 5.1

Developmental Functions in Mentoring Relationships

Lisa Cheraskin
Eli Lilly & Company

The following table highlights a range of developmental functions that may be found in a mentoring relationship. Research suggests that relationships most beneficial to a mentor and mentee alike involve both career-related functions and those labeled psychosocial (interpersonal). To assist you in finding creative ways to enrich your mentoring relationship, we have included examples of how each of the functions might be fulfilled. Many of these examples are taken from the actual experiences of mentors and mentees participating in the Eli Lilly Executive Mentoring pilot (indicated by *). Although written from the mentor's perspective, most of the behaviors could also be appropriately initiated by the protégé.

Career functions

Sponsorship/exposure

Definition	Opening doors; making connections that will support the mentee's career advancement; creating opportunities for the mentee to demonstrate competence and learn.
Examples	• Recommend mentee for participation on relevant special projects, task forces, etc. (ideally when the mentor is also a member of the group).

- Introduce mentee to external local/regional community leaders.
- Recommend mentee for membership or a leadership role in professional organizations, external boards, community organizations, interest groups, etc.
- Recommend attendance at relevant external conferences that will provide key networking opportunities.
- Personally introduce mentee to other potential internal and external mentors.
- Send a letter of introduction/background to other senior management to provide context for career option interviews being conducted by the mentee.*
- Identify areas where work/research by the mentee can be appropriately and usefully applied to or replicated in another area of the business.
- Identify connections between the mentee's business goals/issues and the goals/issues of other parts of the business and arrange for the two to discuss these.*

Challenging work

Definition
Supporting assignments that stretch the mentee's knowledge and skills in order to stimulate growth and preparation to move ahead.

Examples
- During staffing discussions, recommend mentee for appropriate and challenging assignments.
- Appoint mentee to appropriate special projects/task groups in your area of the business.
- Ask mentee to review/react to your area strategy, business plan, project plan, etc.*
- Arrange appropriate training/coaching to support skill building in the mentee's new assignment.*

Coaching

Definition
Teaching the "ropes"; giving relevant positive and negative feedback to improve the mentee's performance and potential; directing mentee toward relevant resources and experiences.

Examples
- Conduct an informal "live" 360° assessment by gathering feedback on the mentee from various management (with mentee's permission) and discuss the implications for further development.*
- Share your senior management perspective and insights into the rationale of various corporate decisions, organizational changes, etc.*
- Review a presentation and advise on how to position key messages to gain upper management buy-in.*
- Advise on the informal network necessary to accomplish a specific goal.
- Ask mentee to reflect on the issues/barriers to success in his/her area/role and collaborate on possible actions to address these.*
- Describe a recent business issue/problem you have faced and ask the mentee to "resolve" it. Then give feedback on mentee's problem-solving process and thinking.
- Recommend internal/external experts, etc. on a topic of interest or relevant business issue.

- Send books, articles, etc. relevant to the mentee's interests and development needs.*
- Walk around your business area/plant site/lab with the mentee and describe how work gets done.*
- Review the mentee's development plan and advise on relevant resources to meet identified needs, etc.*

Counseling

Definition   Providing a helpful and confidential forum for exploring personal and professional dilemmas; acting as a sounding board; demonstrating excellent listening, trust, and rapport which enable both individuals to address central development concerns.

Examples   - Inform mentee of how some action or decision is likely to be interpreted by the larger organization and/or senior management.*
- Share dual family-work issues and dilemmas.*
- Challenge mentee to actively make hard decisions about his/her career.*
- Share the "human side" of your career history, including the necessary choices and any values/personal issues surrounding them.*
- Describe from your perspective the developmental learning opportunities and other pros and cons of job assignments/career options the mentee is considering.*
- Discuss how a mentee's new role might require her/him to operate differently.
- Reflect on key messages you believe are important foundations for understanding and look for opportunities to appropriately include these in conversations with your mentee (e.g., Lilly values, Operations Committee Beliefs, and new organizational structure rationale).*

Psycholsocial functions

Role modeling

Definition   Demonstrating valued behavior, attitudes, and/or skills that aid the mentee in achieving competence, confidence, and a clear professional identity.

Examples   - Invite mentee to observe or participate in meetings that reveal the nature of work and decision making in your area of the business.*
- Invite mentee to observe you and/or other senior executives at relevant external meetings.*
- Point out the actions and choices of others who you admire.
- Point out what you are trying to do and why as you describe some of your personal and professional actions and decisions.

Protection

Definition   Providing support in difficult situations; taking responsibility for mistakes that are outside the mentee's control; acting as a buffer when necessary.

Examples	• Represent the mentee's perspective/rationale in relevant meetings/forums.
	• Intervene when consequences are disproportionate to mistakes.
	• Warn the mentee about the risks and potential consequences of a behavior, decision, action, etc.
	• Help the mentee identify and strategize upcoming risks he or she will face.
	• Help the mentee prepare well, get wise counsel, then trust his or her own decisions and actions.

Acceptance and confirmation

Definition	Providing ongoing support, respect, and admiration that strengthen self-confidence and self-image.
Examples	• Describe current business issues you are excited or concerned about and invite reaction (or even help) from mentee.*
	• Share your experience with a business issue/problem when you might describe yourself as having "failed."*
	• Invite the mentee to spontaneously call you to discuss some issue or dilemma the mentee finds himself/herself faced with.
	• If one or two scheduled meetings are canceled by mentee, express your concern and commitment to the mentoring relationship and attempt to reschedule a meeting ASAP.
	• Share the Operations Committee Beliefs and ask your mentee to give you feedback if he/she observes you operating inconsistently with these.*
	• Share with the mentee any positive feedback you hear about his/her performance, potential, integrity, etc.*
	• Send the mentee an encouraging e-mail or voice mail message when you know he or she is approaching a challenging decision or action.
	• Let the mentee know how any of his or her suggestions, insights, etc. have been useful to you.

Friendship

Definition	Mutual caring and intimacy that extends beyond the requirements of daily work tasks; sharing of experience outside the immediate work setting.
Examples	• Find and discuss a topic of mutual personal rather than professional interest (e.g., food, music, sports, etc.).*
	• Invite mentee to accompany you as you run errands, go shopping, or engage in other ordinary daily activities.*
	• Invite mentee and his/her family to dinner with your family or at your home.*
	• Invite mentee to accompany you to a sports event or some type of shared recreational interest.*
	• Send the mentee a book, video, etc. that relates to his/her personal rather than professional interests.

The New Mentoring: Developmental Relationships

Like socialization, mentoring is a concept that has traditionally assumed a unilateral, top-down influence process. That is, the "senior"
person was the mentor, who was older, more experienced, and at a
higher level than the learner or protégé (the "junior" member). As is the
case with socialization, however, mentoring has now been stood on its
head, and it is often the senior who learns the most from the junior. This
learning agenda can include new technology, current customer expectations, new work methods, new perspectives on work/life balance, and
new ways of learning (seeking and using feedback, redefining the self,
and adaptability).

Furthermore, the "new mentoring" can occur in a wider range of
relationships than the traditional junior-senior dyadic pairing. The
mentoring can occur among peers, in which fellow newcomers help one
another "learn the ropes" (which, in fact, is very similar to the process of
peer socialization, which has a long history in the socialization literature). Also, the mentoring can take place in settings beyond dyadic relationships, in environments such as professional association meetings,
task forces, and project teams. The work environment has become
increasingly turbulent, collaborative, and interdependent (Howard, 1995),
and although this can increase time pressures and other stresses at
work, the relationships can provide important positive benefits, such as
mutual learning and emotional support (Kram & Hall, 1996b). Thus,
processes such as socialization and mentoring have changed from being
unilateral, authority-based influence processes to processes of colearning.

A description of these different kinds of naturally occurring relationships that can be used explicitly to foster development has been developed by Hall and Kahn (2001), and it is shown in Table 5.2.

The nature of mentoring and other developmental relationships has
been fundamentally transformed by this new turbulent context. These
twin forces of turbulence and diversity require us to rethink what
mentoring and other developmental relationships look like and could look
like in the contemporary work environment. Environmental turbulence
and increasing workforce diversity require everyone to be a learner. The
new "career contract" has substituted psychological success for vertical or
promotional success (Hall, 1994). Career paths are no longer clearly defined, and lateral movement or redefinition of one's current job may be

Table 5.2   Types of Developmental Relationships

Type	Definition	Primary Functions	Characteristics	Impacts
Mentor/ protégé	Intentional relationship focused on developing self of relatively un-seasoned protégé through dialogue and reflection; implicit focus on development of next generation in context of interper-sonal relationships	Develop protégé's capacities for learning about tasks and self; transmit information, knowledge, culture, and wisdom; enable mentors and protégés to meet appropriate adult developmental needs	Relatively intimate cross-generation relationships marked by transmission of stories, lessons, and perspectives in response to protégé's needs to learn about self, role, and organi-zation; focus on whole person of protégé	Anchors protégés, enabling them to reflect on and learn from their experiences at work; enhanced functioning based on learning about self in role
Coach/ sponsor	Intentional relationship focused on developing specific developmental objectives in regard to relatively junior organization member	Increase member's capacity to assume increased responsibil-ity for identified role and tasks; enable coach to delegate, support, and provide resources rather than control	Interactions marked by coach's increasing movement toward posing questions rather than providing answers, thus building other's capacities for autonomous thinking, acting, and reflecting on specific tasks	Enhanced capacity of junior member in thought, action, and reflection in regard to specific types of roles and tasks; coaches move from control to coordination
Support group/ network	Formal or informal group of individuals who join around common characteris-tics, interests, goals, or visions and provide meaningful personal and professional support to its members	Emotional support in the form of encouragement, reinforcement, and acknowledgment; instrumental support through network of connections and information	Focus on maintaining support group through regular meetings, group and subgroup communi-cation efforts, and personal relationships that provide members with sense of shared identity and meaning	Enables members to feel connected to, supported by, and joined with like-minded others at work; offers sense of identity, meaning, and confidence
Supervisor/ coworker	Naturally occurring work relationships centered around given tasks and roles; development of person is incidental rather than intentional	Completion of work tasks and goals through various forms of coordination and collaboration; development of skills and knowledge necessary to perform work	Relatively frequent, often intense contact determined by task requirements and organizational structures and processes	Completion of given tasks, supported by growth in person's task-related capacities

Table 5.2 (Continued)

Type	Definition	Primary Functions	Characteristics	Impacts
Project team/ task force	Formally structured work group focused on completion of shared goals, requiring intense collaboration	Completion of work tasks and goals through cross-boundary collaboration; development of skills and knowledge related to collaboration	Relatively frequent, often intense contact determined by project requirements and organizational structures and processes	Completion of given tasks, supported by growth in person's task-related capacities
Training workshop/ program	Formally structured learning experiences that emphasize transmission of information from experts to learners	Increase learner's knowledge, skills, and capacities for effective thought and action in specific areas and types of situations	Academic- or practitioner-based courses and programs that transmit knowledge and information, with varying degree of relatedness to actual work experiences	Learning of concepts, ideas, techniques, and perspectives that vary in terms of relevance and applicability to work situations
Role model	Non-reciprocal relationship between person observing admired other in order to learn desired traits and behaviors	Provide model of desirable traits and behaviors to emulate—an embodiment of a desired set of skills and knowledge	Relatively distant relationship marked by observation, study, and comparisons between self and others	Learning through observation and reflection, to the extent possible without dialogue with other; offers sense of hope

SOURCE: Hall and Kahn (2001).

needed to grow new skills and competencies. Also, individuals can no longer expect to have a lifelong career in one organization; security is now based on one's skills, identity, and adaptability (Hall, 1993).

The major mentoring-related development concerns of diverse segments of today's workforce can be summarized in several identity group categories as follows:

1. Young white males: worried about their own development
2. Senior white males: besieged yet responsible
3. The senior pioneers: stuck in midlevel and midlife
4. Women and people of color: bailing out

Less Value Attached to Seniors' Career Advice?

Mentoring theory and research are rooted in a world that no longer exists—a world of more stable and homogeneous organizational environments. From early studies, we learned that significant relationships between juniors and seniors had the potential to serve career functions and psychosocial functions; the former were aimed primarily at advancing the junior's career, and the latter were aimed primarily at enhancing self-esteem, identity, and self-worth (Dalton, 1989; Dalton & Thompson, 1986; Dalton, Thompson, & Price, 1977; Kram, 1985; Levinson, Darrow, Klein, Levinson, & McKee, 1978).

The pervasive instability of careers—and the associated uncertainty about what opportunities the future holds—can render certain advice and coaching obsolete and misleading. In contrast, it seems clear that regardless of specific environmental conditions, simply being in a mentoring relationship and receiving emotional support (for both junior and senior party) may be the most important form of career assistance in today's uncertain, high-stress work environment (Kram & Hall, 1991).

Mentors as Colearners

With the transformation of context, it seems clear that seniors are necessarily becoming learners as well. First, they are no longer experts on career strategy; what worked for seniors in more stable periods will not work now for juniors in organizations in which the "rules" have changed. Although seniors may have some insight on the question of survival (given their wisdom of experience and their proximity to decision makers), they are novices under the new rules, new products, new services, and new technologies. Thus, they are most likely to find themselves coinquirers in the search for work meaning and career growth in the midst of turbulence.

Heterogeneous Relationships

In the past, in naturally occurring mentoring relationships mentors and protégés usually gravitated toward partners who were similar in race and gender. Now, however, many organizations have implemented formal mentoring programs to support diversity objectives. Usually, senior white men are matched as mentors with junior women and people of color who are viewed as having high potential.

It is clear that the one-on-one hierarchical dyad is not the only vehicle for mentoring in the new workplace. Peer relationships are equally valuable for aiding development at every career stage (Kram & Isabella, 1985). At the same time, as organizations have downsized and become flatter and structured around teams, there is a growing recognition that individuals can mentor and learn from various members of their work teams in addition to the boss (Handy, 1989, 1994).

Shorter Term and Multiple Relationships

In the context of teams (project teams, task forces, and committees), task-related peer mentoring can flourish, particularly if the team leader supports such mutual learning. Also, two additional types of developmental groups have come into existence: core groups (also called dialogue groups), developed originally by Barbara Walker at the former Digital Equipment Corporation (now part of Compaq) (Walker & Hanson, 1992), and mentoring circles (e.g., originally Bell Atlantic and now Verizon). Core groups bring together individuals of diverse backgrounds who want to learn how to more effectively build supportive relationships with those who come from different gender, racial, or cultural backgrounds or all three. Mentoring circles bring together one or several senior managers with junior or midlevel professionals/managers for the purpose of supporting the latter's development.

Greater Availability of Coaching

Finally, internal and external coaches are increasingly viewed as key resources in helping managers and executives learn, particularly when time is very limited and developing new competencies and perspectives is essential (Hall, Otazo, & Hollenbeck, 1999). Coaching might be thought of as a short-term form of mentoring, which has heavy stress on the career functions. Often used in conjunction with a management development program or a 360-degree feedback process, a coach will help an individual to reflect on his or her own experience, interpret data about his or her impact on the organization, and develop strategies for building a wider repertoire of effective behavioral responses to current challenges.

Basic human resource functions need to be revised to reflect these new mentoring realities—processes such as formal mentoring programs, education and training activities, performance appraisal and reward systems, succession planning, dialogue and organizational learning, and work teams. This is an ideal time for creative action research on these real-time learning processes. Also, given the sensitivity of the issues involved—a potent brew involving power, sex, and race—this is also a necessary time for conviction and courage on the part of human resource researchers and practitioners.

An intriguing model has been developed by Higgins (1999) to describe some of the specific mechanisms by which these relational mechanisms might contribute to career learning. Combining the fields of mentoring and network theory, Higgins focuses on what she calls the *career portfolio,* the person's set of career advisers. She examines both the content of the portfolio (the potential learning content that the network contains, both psychosocial learning and career task learning) and its structure (the density and range of relationships). Higgins found some support for the idea that the portfolio of relationships has a positive effect on career learning (defined in her research as making career changes), and these relationships have effects through the creation of confidence, competence, and career opportunities for the learner. Specifically, portfolio content qualities such as psychological assistance and career assistance enhance the person's confidence and competence as well as career opportunities. In addition, if the structure of the portfolio contains a high range of connections, with low density (i.e., weak ties), these qualities also boost confidence, competence, and career opportunities. It seems reasonable to hypothesize that these intervening factors would also lead to enhanced performance within a role and to changes in the role.

The Psychological Success Cycle

In another examination of the early career socialization process, Hall and Nougaim (1968) identified a system of interrelated changes in work attitudes and performance that occur during the first few years of a young manager's career. This phenomenon, which they termed the *success syndrome,* was hypothesized to occur as follows:

1. For all managers, the need for achievement and esteem increases over the years that they are with the company.

2. Managers who have met high standards of performance will be rewarded with promotions and pay increases, or, in more global terms, with success (Berlew & Hall, 1966).

3. These successful managers have achieved a great deal and have been given additional managerial responsibility. Therefore, their satisfaction with achievement and esteem increases and becomes significantly greater than that of their less successful colleagues in the fifth year.

4. Possibly as a result of their greater satisfaction with achievement and esteem, they become more involved in their jobs. By the fifth year, their work is significantly more central to their overall need satisfaction than is the work of the less successful group.

5. With increased job involvement, they are more likely to be successful in future assignments than other managers scoring lower on these dimensions. Thus, they are caught in an upward spiral of success.

The converse of this syndrome does not seem to occur for the less successful managers; although their satisfaction with achievement and esteem does decrease, the average work centrality score increases slightly. If this score had decreased, we could then say slightly that these people were becoming alienated and withdrawing emotionally from their work. But they seem to remain at about the same level of work centrality, their higher needs increasing at about the same rates as the successful group and with their higher-order satisfactions not increasing. (Hall & Nougaim, 1968, p. 30)

I have described the relationship between challenge, success, and career involvement in a model of career development. The model is based on the experimental work of Lewin and associates on goal setting and levels of aspiration (Lewin, 1936; Lewin, Dembo, Festinger, & Sears, 1944). Lewin found that goal-directed behavior was likely to lead to psychological (or self-perceived, intrinsic) success under the following conditions:

1. The goal represents a challenging but attainable level of aspiration.
2. The goal is defined by the person.
3. The goal is central to the person's self-concept.
4. The person works independently to achieve the goal.

When these conditions are present, goal attainment should result in a feeling of psychological success. Other people (bosses, peers, parents, etc.) may or may not perceive the attainment as "success," but the person should, according to the theory. For example, for a 5-year-old girl who is just learning to swim, being able to swim 5 yards unaided in the deep end of the pool results in a great flush of psychological success; some other 5-year-olds, old hands at swimming, may tolerate her glee but would not define her feat as an objective success. On the other hand, an Olympic swimmer may set a new record (an objective success to most observers), but he may not feel psychological success for one of several reasons: (a) He may have aspired for an even faster time, (b) he may not have set any particular goal for himself in that race, (c) he may have viewed his feat more as his trainer's and coach's success than his own (an unlikely prospect, to be sure), or (d) setting new records may no longer be important to his self-concept. For many reasons, self-defined and externally defined success can often be quite unrelated. The research has indicated, however, that self-perceived success has greater impact on future goal setting and task involvement than externally defined success.

What follows the experience of psychological success? First, the person experiences a sense of increased competence and self-esteem relative to that task area. Furthermore, the person is likely to engage in additional goal-directed behavior in that task area, often with an increased level of aspiration (i.e., more difficult goals). Livingston (1976) compared this upward spiral, driven by challenging goals and high expectations of others, to the self-fulfilling prophecy or "pygmalion effect."

Although Lewin's work dealt with well-defined, specific tasks, his concepts can be logically applied to more complex, inclusive domains of task activity, such as work careers. If a person sets a goal for himself in his work that meets the four theoretical conditions listed previously, the attainment of that goal will probably result in feelings of psychological success. Because the goal pushes him to reach some new level of competence, his self-esteem and self-confidence in that area will increase. Furthermore, his increased self-esteem will probably generalize by association to a sense of satisfaction with work in that task area. Thus, his involvement in his job may increase. Because of his increased commitment and confidence, he may now be more likely than before to set additional goals for himself in this area. This cycle of events can be self-reinforcing and continuing. When it occurs, the person shows great enthusiasm for the relevant career area and may describe himself as "really finding himself" or being "really turned on" by his work. In other words, this is the process by which "success breeds success."

The conditions for psychological success can be translated into requisite conditions in the job environment. To be able to work on difficult goals, the job must have a certain degree of objective challenge. What a person experiences as challenge is obviously a function of individual differences in ability and interests, but some jobs, such as stuffing envelopes, would probably be viewed as challenging by very few people, whereas other jobs, such as supervising 1,000 employees, would have more potential for challenging people. Autonomy is necessary to enable the person to set work goals and to work independently. If he is closely supervised in pursuit of a goal, then he may believe that his goal performance reflects more the success of his supervisor than of himself. Some degree of support, help, and coaching from the supervisor is useful in aiding the person to attain his objectives. Feedback is necessary both to improve performance and to help the person evaluate his or her performance.

Perhaps an example may help explain this process of career development. Consider a manager about to create a new management information system. Perhaps his training is in accounting; working with management information systems is a completely new type of behavior to him. He chooses to install the new system, however. If the system is successful, the manager may realize that he possesses skills in designing and implementing information systems—skills he never considered as being part of him before. He may also recognize that his general managerial and administrative skills are higher than he realized since managing such an innovative system affecting the work of so many people is a good test of these abilities. Thus, his self-esteem as a manager may grow. His satisfaction with and involvement in his job may also increase. With this success behind him, he may now be more likely to try some other new career behavior at a future date.

Supervisory Behavior

As discussed previously, it appears that a person's supervisors may have a strong impact on the development of his career. The person's boss has a great deal of influence over the objective challenge available in his job. The boss also controls to a great extent the amount of autonomy, feedback, and support the person will receive. All these relational factors are critical to career development, according to my model (Hall, 1976; Hall & Associates, 1996).

The supervisor can also be important as a sponsor, opening crucial doors to the person, bringing him along with promotions as he (the boss) is promoted (Dalton, 1959; Jennings, 1971). This sponsorship function has been examined more by sociologists than by psychologists.

Although sponsorship does occur in particular cases, of which the reader is undoubtedly aware of some examples, it is not clear that sponsorship is as frequently a factor in aiding a subordinate's career as are the less dramatic functions of job autonomy, support, feedback, and challenge.

Work Climate

Work climate is often used as an "umbrella" concept, encompassing the array of situational demands and opportunities present in a work assignment. In the organizational behavior literature, climate often covers at least four general features of the work environment: (a) leadership or supervisory style, (b) interpersonal relationships, (c) intrinsic meaning in work, and (d) extrinsic reward characteristics.

Hall and Schneider (1973) viewed climate as an intervening variable— that is, one that intervenes in the relationship between independent variables (such as personal or organizational characteristics) and outcome variables (such as performance or satisfaction). In this view, the person gradually forms an impression of the climate of the work setting based on numerous interactions and experiences at work. Thus, climate seems to be more an attitude the person holds toward the job or organization than an objective characteristic of either.

Work climate is related to the performance of employees (Pelz & Andrews, 1966; Steiner, 1965). Because climate does seem strongly related to the career development of employees, it would seem to be a useful concept to apply in facilitating careers. Because it is an intervening variable, however, climate cannot be manipulated directly. For example, a climate of high trust cannot be achieved directly through a manager's actions; he must take other actions, such as increased openness or new reward practices, which may or may not lead to changes in the trust level of the climate. Therefore, manipulations of the work climate are probably less feasible than more direct manipulation of the factors that create the climate—supervisory practices, job characteristics, interpersonal relationships, the reward system, and so on.

Climate may be more easily applied in the case of an individual selecting an organization. There is evidence that individuals select organizations on the basis of their apparent climate. Furthermore, organizations tend to reward people who do what the climate values (e.g., power-oriented organizations reward people with a high need for power, and achievement-oriented organizations reward people who are high achievers) (Andrews, 1967). Therefore, a person interested in strong work performance and achievement should choose an achievement-oriented organization; the climate will help him develop those aspects of himself that he most values.

Organizational Characteristics

There is evidence that the type of organization for which a person works, especially early in his career, can influence later developments in his career. This seems to be a logical analogy to the role of the initial job in career facilitation. In academic careers, it appears that the quality of the university at which the person did graduate study and the quality of the organization when he held his first job are both strong correlates of later career performance (Crane, 1966). This result could be due to the challenge of the work, the quality of one's learning, and the contacts one develops.

Unfortunately, there is little research on the impact of organization characteristics on career development, although there is plenty of folklore available. Should a person start with a large firm to learn as much as he can in its training program and then move to a smaller firm? Should he start with a small firm to acquire early responsibility and more of an overall picture of how the organization operates? Should he go with a company that trains specialists or generalists? Everyone has his or her own set views on the type of organization that trains people best for later success, but there is little research to distinguish wives' tales from wisdom.

Person-Organization Fit Versus Performance

In addition to characteristics of the organization influencing the development of the person, it might also be argued that the interaction or congruence between the person and his organization could affect his career outcomes. Support for this has already been cited briefly in a study by Andrews (1967) of two firms in Mexico. One firm was characterized by an extremely high level of achievement motivation in its managers, whereas the other was characterized by high needs for power. In the former, the people most likely to receive promotions were those who had high needs for achievement, and in the latter it was employees with high needs for power. In other words, people whose personal needs best fit the climate of the organization were most likely to succeed.

In a classic study of a bank, Argyris (1954) found that the bank was characterized by what he called a "right-type" person. The right-type person was quiet, unaggressive, polite, disliked giving orders, and liked receiving orders. Right types tended to be promoted, whereas non-right tended to leave. An analogous phenomenon was observed in the United States Forest Service by Hall, Schneider, and Nygren (1970). The Forest Service's primary goal is public service, and the researchers found that the people who identified most strongly with the Forest Service were those who viewed themselves as supportive and involved, two characteristics quite relevant to public service. People who viewed themselves as intellectual showed no tendency to have either high or low organizational identification. People who identified highly with the Forest Service, in turn, tended to be highly satisfied in their jobs. Thus, the right types tend to be rewarded here, too, although the rewards studied were intrinsic rather than extrinsic.

The work of Pervin and of Schneider focused explicitly on the fit between the person and the organization and his organization. Pervin's (1968) research examined college students in relation to their university environments. He found that the fit between their self-images and their perceptions of the college was a good predictor of satisfaction with college but a weaker predictor of academic performance.

Schneider's (1972) early research focused on recently hired life insurance agents. Schneider predicted that the closer the new agent's expectations matched the actual climate of the agency, the higher his production would be. To date, it appears that this relationship does not occur for individuals, but it does for agencies. That is, the better the person-agency fit, averaged for the agency as a whole, the higher the production in that agency. Unfortunately, it does not appear that we can predict individual performance with this fit measure. Pervin's (1968) results suggest that fit at the individual level might better predict individual satisfaction.

Schneider, Smith, Taylor, and Fleenor (1998) examined person-organization fit in terms of personality type, as measured by the Myers-Briggs Personality Type Indicator. Using a large database of managers who had completed leadership development programs at the Center for Creative Leadership, Schneider found strong positive relationships between personality type and organizational culture. Also, the better the fit between the manager's personality and the culture of his or her organization, the higher the person's satisfaction and performance (Schneider et al., 1998).

Competencies

Closely related to motives, skills, and abilities is the concept of competencies. Whereas skills and abilities refer to specific capabilities to perform particular tasks, a competency is a more global quality of the person that enables him or her to be effective in a larger area of functioning, such as a job role (Boyatzis, 1982; Briscoe & Hall, 1999; Evers, Rush, & Berdrow, 1998).

To measure competencies, in a classic and perhaps most methodologically rigorous approach to competency development (popularized by the late psychologist, David McClelland, and the Hay/McBer consulting practice), executives are nominated who are perceived to be top performers. These executives are interviewed and asked to give behavioral examples or "critical incidents" that exemplify the keys to their success. Such behaviors are systematically analyzed and validated as consistent with top performers (as distinguished from good but not superior performers) (Boyatzis, 1982). This process is usually labeled "behavioral event interviewing." A less rigorous approach is to simply interview or survey executives or human resource professionals familiar with executive skills needed in their current performance (Briscoe & Hall, 1999).

Once a competency "model" (i.e., a profile of competencies) has been identified for a particular role, it is possible to predict that managers who score high on those competencies will be more successful than those who do not score high. This analysis is usually done with cross-sectional data (i.e., where the measure of competencies and the measure of performance are collected at the same point in time), but in some companies it has also been done more rigorously with longitudinal data (where competency data are collected at one point in time and the performance data are collected at a later date) to provide stronger inferences about causality (Boyatzis, 1982).

Competency models have become a widely used method for predicting successful performance in professional and managerial roles (Briscoe & Hall, 1999; Spencer, McClelland, & Spencer, 1996). Like the assessment technology, which has similar historical roots, it is based on some well-established psychological principles. One is that behavior-to-behavior correlations are stronger than attitude-to-behavior correlations (and competencies are essentially measures of specific incidents of demonstrated behavior). The other key principle here is that one of the best predictors of future behavior is past behavior; again, the behavioral event interview is a method of tapping demonstrated behaviors that support the existence of a specific competency.

Emotional Intelligence and "Metacompetencies." Daniel Goleman (1995, 1998) identified the concept of *emotional intelligence* (EI) as contrasted with technical competence or IQ. Emotional intelligence has to do with a person's ability to understand himself or herself and to relate effectively with others. There are five dimensions of emotional intelligence. The first three describe *personal competence* (how we manage ourselves):

- Self-awareness (knowing one's internal states, preferences, resources, and intuitions)
- Self-regulation (managing one's internal states, impulses, and resources)
- Motivation (emotional tendencies that guide or facilitate reaching goals)

The other two dimensions of EI describe *social competence*, which determine how we handle relationships:

- Empathy (awareness of others' feelings, needs, and concerns)
- Social skills (adeptness at inducing desirable responses in others)

An emotional competence is "a learned capability based on emotional intelligence that results in outstanding performance at work" (Goleman, 1998, p. 24). Emotional intelligence indicates a person's potential for learning the practical personal and social skills related to the five dimensions, whereas emotional competence describes how much of that potential the person has actually converted into capabilities on the job. Goleman identifies 25 emotional competencies, which he groups under the five intelligence dimensions.

Goleman (1998) presents a variety of types of data showing a relationship between emotional competencies and effective performance in a variety of work roles. Using two different ways of analyzing many companies' competency models (covering all types of competencies, not just emotional competencies), he found that approximately two thirds of the corporate competencies used were emotional competencies. Thus, he concludes that "emotional competencies were found to be *twice* as important in contributing to excellence as pure intellect and expertise" (p. 31).

Criticisms of the Competency Approach. Despite the popularity of competencies in predicting and developing career performance, there have been criticisms of this method. One is that, as an artifact of the research method (using current top performers to represent "success"), organizations are not necessarily identifying those candidates who will be top performers in the future. In fact, this method may be actively creating a "hardening of the arteries" in the living system that is the organization (Briscoe & Hall, 1999). Another issue is that the method of identifying competencies has deviated from its research roots in many organizations so that the resulting competency models are derived from either the cultural values of the organization or its business strategy. In fact, as Briscoe and Hall observed, the values-based and strategy-based approaches may be more effective in creating leaders for the future, but these methods cannot claim to be empirically based.

Another criticism, articulated by Morgan McCall (1998), is that a competency, as measured by the behavioral event interview, is essentially an "end-state" variable—that is, it is a measure of the actual performance that is demanded in the focal role. Thus, a competency is not really a predictor of future behavior but, rather, a current demonstration of the required role behavior. Thus, the competency approach is not measuring potential but actual performance.

Adaptability and Identity as
Key Learning Metacompetencies[1]

An alternative to the competency approach, and a way of dealing with the need to develop different competencies in leaders of the future, is to assess the individual's ability to be a continuous learner, without worrying about his or her mastery of specific competencies at any one point in time (London, 1998). What would this continuous learning approach to competency development look like in practice? Hall (1986) proposed the concept of a *metacompetency*—a competency that is so powerful that it affects the person's ability to acquire other competencies. An analogy is reading: Once a person has the ability to read, all sorts of other learning that is communicated through the written word become accessible to that person.

In particular, Hall (1986) proposed that two key metacompetencies related to career development are identity and adaptability. If a person has adaptability, he or she is able to identify for himself or herself those qualities that are critical for future performance and is also able to make personal changes necessary to meet these needs. Adaptability alone is not enough, however. The person also has to change his or her awareness of self so that he or she internalizes and values that change. Thus, the second metacompetency is identity learning—the ability to gather self-related feedback, to form accurate self-perceptions, and to change one's self-concept as appropriate.

Adaptability without identity can be mindless reaction to the environment with no self-direction. Identity changes without adaptability would be very self-aware inaction. With adaptability and identity change, the person has learned how to learn.

How would one define and develop these two metacompetencies? Adaptability learning competencies include behaviors that would demonstrate the following:

- Flexibility
- Exploration
- Openness to new and diverse people and ideas
- Dialogue skills and eagerness to accept new challenges in unexplored territory
- Comfort with turbulent change

There are many things that companies do to provide adaptability experiences for their managers, and simply reframing them in this way would be helpful. For example, diversity training can heighten adaptability, as can international assignments. Managing a major change process, leading a turnaround, or launching a start-up venture are business assignments that demand and develop adaptability.

Identity learning competencies involve behaviors related to the following:

- Self-assessment
- Seeking, hearing, and acting on personal feedback
- Exploring, communicating, and acting on personal values
- Engaging in a variety of personal development activities and being willing to model this personal development activity

- Rewarding subordinates for personal development work
- Being open to diverse people and ideas
- Actively seeking out relationships with people one considers as different, in which one is being challenged to learn
- Being willing to modify self-perceptions as one's abilities, roles, and other personal qualities and situations change

What drives identity changes? As an executive moves to higher levels of responsibility, he or she must learn to change the basis of his or her self-identity away from individual contributions as the basis for self-esteem and toward defining personal value and esteem through the accomplishments of subordinates. This change in the basis of personal identity is an incredibly difficult form of identity learning, especially in professionally based organizations (e.g., technology-based businesses and financial services). It is essential for personal and corporate growth and adaptability, however. A certain "hardiness" of personality is undoubtedly helpful as well (Kobasa, 1982). Self-assessment and personal development programs, such as the Leadership Development Program or Leadership at the Peak at the Center for Creative Leadership, provide significant identity learning. Executive coaching and 360-degree feedback are other popular ways that companies are providing identity learning for their managers and executives.

One company that we studied has already taken a bold step toward this in one of their divisions. They report that in that division, the managers designed their new competency system around two skills: (a) the ability to learn from experience and (b) potential for long-term growth. For another, more specific example of how an early adopter of metacompetencies is defining and envisioning them, see the discussion of AT&T in Box 5.2.

BOX 5.2

An "Early Adopter" of Metacompetencies: AT&T

Although the notion of metacompetencies is still largely theoretical, one firm, AT&T, has begun to put them into practice. According to Laurie Hutton-Corr, then-Director, Human Resources-Strategic Executive Development & Staffing,

In our leadership system approach, we have embedded the metacompetencies in our Performance Management process, our People Planning process (including development, career management and succession) and our hiring. Multi-source feedback and supervisor observation are the source of input for internal employees, while the interview process attempts to get at those areas for external candidates.

In the AT&T Leadership Model, identity is called self-awareness and adaptability is called openness to learning. These metacompetencies are framed as "personal competencies," which form the foundation for specific business and technical skills and knowledge, as well as management and leadership skills. These more specific skills, in turn, show up in the form of workplace behavior (e.g., performance). This leadership model is envisioned at AT&T as a pyramid, as shown in Figure 5.1.

Self-awareness is defined as follows: "Has mature insight into own skills, beliefs, and motives resulting in confident, wise, and courageous behavior." This metacompetency is defined operationally through such descriptors as:

- Has a realistic and accurate self-view
- Is willing to speak the truth and advocate positions even when unpopular
- Responds genuinely and consistently to people and situations without hidden motives or artificial tactics
- Recognizes and uses own ability to affect complex business problems and difficult people issues
- Remains focused on the most important needs of the business in times of stress and hardship

Openness to learning is defined as follows: "Recognizes and uses the lessons of experience and personal interaction as opportunities to grow." Sample descriptions include:

- Seeks feedback from others that leads to changes in own behavior
- Keeps current in areas important to the business
- Is open to and invites ideas, new information, and diverse perspectives
- Responds to criticism and negative results by seeking to understand the lessons to be learned
- Reflects on own experience in ways that create insight and improve effectiveness

Some of the key experiences that are seen as developing self-awareness include supporting people, developing international or cross-cultural awareness, and leading organizational change. Openness to learning (adaptability) is seen as enhanced through experiences such as growing a business, collaborating across functions or organizations, working in teams, leading organizational change, and developing international or cross-cultural awareness.

Emotional Well-Being

As early as the classic Hawthorne studies, we have heard the expression, "A happy worker is a productive worker" (Roethlisberger & Dickson, 1939). Unfortunately, subsequent research did not support that positive proposition (Porter & Lawler, 1968). Recently, however, with interest in organizational citizenship (Organ, 1988; Organ & Konovsky, 1989) and human capital theory (Pfeffer, 1998), and with a realization that employee loyalty can be linked empirically to customer loyalty and retention (Reichheld, 1996; Schneider & Bowen, 1995), research on employees' emotional states has received more attention.

One intriguing stream of research is that of Barry Staw and colleagues, who explored the longitudinal relationships between an employee's emotional well-being and his or her later performance on the job (Staw & Barsade, 1993). This research has made clear the distinction between emotional well-being and job satisfaction: Well-being is positively related to performance, even with satisfaction held constant, whereas satisfaction is not related to performance when well-being is held constant (Wright & Cropanzano, 1997).

Thus, it appears that the many studies of job attitudes and satisfaction to test the original Roethlisberger-Dickson hypothesis may have been using inadequate operational measures of the happy worker. When happiness is measured not as job satisfaction but as emotional well-being, it does seem to be related to job performance.

These conclusions from the Staw-based research also support Goleman's (1998) findings on the importance of EI and competencies. One could argue that an individual with strong EI and emotional competencies may be likely to select and enter a work environment that is a good fit for him or her (i.e., one in which he or she will be happy) and

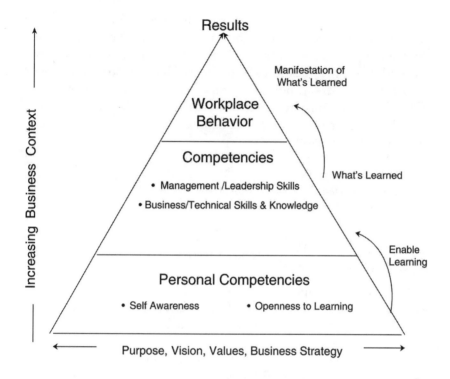

Figure 5.1. AT&T's Leadership Model (Developed by Laurie Hutton-Corr. Reproduced with permission from Briscoe & Hall, 1999, p. 47)

will also be able to construct relationships that will make him or her, as well as coworkers, happy. Thus, emotional well-being may be a function not only of the way the person is (read: personality) but also of the person's emotional skills that he or she has developed at work.

Summary

To summarize the relationship between capabilities and performance, we turn to the work of Morgan McCall (McCall, 1998; McCall, Lombardo, & Morrison, 1988). In his book *High Flyers* (1998), he made the point that the qualities we look for in high-flying talent, those performance capabilities that we call the "right stuff" (from Tom Wolfe's description of the original U.S. astronauts), are not inborn traits. On the contrary, what we call the right stuff is the result of experiences that have developed a person's natural talents. Thus, in the area of executive leadership, on the question of whether leaders are born or made he argues that "leaders are both born and made but mostly made, based on a significant amount of research showing that executives do learn, grow, and change over time" (p. 4). McCall expresses this relationship, in simplified form, as follows:

Talent + experiences = "the right stuff"

Research Issues

We have now completed our survey of factors associated with work performance, which is the first of our four general criteria of career effectiveness. We now consider a few issues for future research.

- What seems to work best for identifying future high performers? If you were responsible for personnel development of an organization, what factors would you use in the early identification and development of management potential?

  Unfortunately, we do not have anything so handy as average predictive validities of the many variables we have considered here. From the great volume of research on the managerial personality, we know this variable can give us statistically significant, but not especially strong, predictions of success. When personality data are combined with situational exercises, ability tests, and other measures from an assessment center, predictions of success can be markedly improved. The assessment center has been an extremely useful but expensive means of identifying managerial talent. Because it provides information one cannot obtain elsewhere, however, the expense is often justified by the benefits.

  Therefore, the question is how can one capture the kind of rich information that an assessment center provides in a more efficient way? Tools such as CCL's Benchmarks and Lominger's Career Architect have been widely applied in industry, but they have not received much empirical research attention. During the past 10 years or more, vast amounts of data must have been collected on these instruments and are just waiting for some enterprising soul to seek them out.

- Perhaps the most useful predicting method of predicting career success is the process of the career. The early AT&T work and the later CCL research make the importance of the career process as a predictor abundantly clear. To paraphrase Morgan McCall (1998), the right stuff is developable. The person's early job experiences in the organization are especially good predictors here. In addition to its predictive power, the career process is also attractive to organizations because job experiences can be controlled and changed to aid career development. Therefore, we need research on how career process affects career outcomes. Higgins's work on career networks is one example, but this examines relationships and not the intrinsic content of jobs. More research on the impacts of various sequences of job assignments would be useful.

- A useful way to examine the effects of job experiences would be to measure the intervening variable between job characteristics and career performance: learning. The theory of the effects of job challenge is that it "stretches" the person to learn and to develop new skills. To date, however, there have been no attempts to measure this learning directly. We have examined "human capital" through surrogates such as education, where we assume that if the person has attained a certain level of formal education he or she has developed certain skills. We know how to measure these skills directly, however, and we should use these methods in our career research.

- Similarly, we need more research to document exactly what kinds of learning occur in the context of developmental relationships. The Kram mentoring model provides an excellent list of the types of learning that could potentially occur. Also, the Hall and Kahn (2001) discussion of the types of learning associated with each type of relationship could provide some working hypotheses.

- Personality characteristics, rather than helping us predict career performance, are primarily useful in career development for selecting work environments that would best fit each individual. In general, I suggest that personality data are more useful for self-assessment than for organizational assessment for selection. In view of the massive amount of work that is done each day using various personality and other tools for self-assessment, it would be useful to measure empirically the effects of greater career self-awareness on career performance. Does better self-awareness, in fact, lead to better person-job fit and performance? To test this well, it would require rich measures of identity and longitudinal data. Again, one would expect that there are gold mines of data banks in the many career consulting firms that help people with career transitions.

- Regarding the two general types of predictive models described in the beginning of this chapter, it appears that both matching models and process models can be good predictors of career performance. How about some creative designs that combine the two approaches? One possible hypothesis is that good matches do not just happen but, rather, are the result of a long process of personal exploration and development. A competing hypothesis is that finding a good fit is the result of the person's self-awareness, such that some people are just better "fit finders" than others. Thus, we might study how a good fit comes to be seen by the person. In fact, both processes and fits exist within the person, so they should be related in some way. Research on such an interaction could help us develop stronger holistic person-based theory about the person-career synthesizing process.

Conclusion

In our discussion of factors related to career effectiveness, we examined the profession of management for illustrative purposes. Obviously, the ideas here apply to other types of work as well. In fact, it would be useful to compare the careers of people working inside an organization with those working independently or across a number of organizations. Perhaps factors in the individual, such as basic skills or personality, would be more important in the performance of independent workers than organization-based employees.

This completes our analysis of factors that facilitate task performances of managers in their careers: background factors, assessment data, personal characteristics, career process data, and person-organization fit. The following chapters examine the other three career outcomes: career attitudes, adaptability, and identity.

Note

1. This material is adapted from Briscoe and Hall (1999).

6 The Protean Career
Identity and Attitudes

See your life as a journey, pause at moments like this to see life's markers and the patterns that emerge, know yourself, be true to yourself, engage your whole self in everything you do ... trust your whole self and don't blink.

—Carly Fiorina, CEO of Hewlett-Packard (MIT commencement speech, June 2, 2000)

The notion of life and career as a journey is at once as new as the experiences of Ms. Fiorina at Hewlett-Packard and as old as the Greek philosophers and the derivation of the word "career." We have been talking about the career as being a protean, self-invented creation. We have viewed career development as finding one's "path with a heart" or one's "calling," which is a wonderful idea. The difficult question, however, is how do I pursue a protean career? What is the path with a heart for me? Do I have a calling, and if so, what is it? How do I move in that direction?

In Chapter 5, we discussed the many facets of career success, and we identified four dimensions of career development—performance, attitudes, adaptability, and identity. Because so much of the literature dealt with performance as a criterion, an entire chapter was devoted to that dimension. In this chapter, we discuss the two dimensions that relate to the subject of Ms. Fiorina's message: developing the whole person (as opposed to just task success).

The dimensions that help us round out the whole person are identity and attitudes. In this chapter, we examine career identity and attitudes, and in Chapter 7 we discuss adaptability. Because the literature on career identity, attitudes, and adaptability is not as extensive as that on performance, our discussion in these two chapters will not be organized in terms of the type of predictor data considered (background, career process, assessment, personality characteristics, and person-organization fit).

Career Identity

Personal Identity via Work Identity

From the point of view of the individual, identity is probably the most important of the four facets of career development. It is the person's sense of identity that, by definition, helps her evaluate herself. It tells her how she fits into her social environment. It also tells her about her uniqueness as a human being.

In Western society, the development of one's personal sense of identity is closely tied to the establishment of one's occupational identity. Often, a person "finds herself" through finding work that she loves; conversely, a person's work commitment may increase sharply after she resolves a personal identity problem. Therefore, we find that the age at which people generally work through their personal identity "crises" (late teens and early twenties) is also the age at which individuals in our society are expected to choose occupational identities. The question "What do you do?" is often a more acceptable way of asking, "Who are you?"

To give a strong sense of the self-discovery aspect of identity, Erik Erikson (1966) quotes William James:

> As a subjective sense of an invigorating *sameness* and *continuity,* what I would call a sense of identity seems to me best described by William James in a letter to his wife. "A man's character," he wrote, "is discernable in the mental or moral attitude in which, when it came upon him, he felt himself most

deeply and intensely active and alive. At such moments there is a voice inside which speaks and says, "*This* is the real me." (p. 149)

One way to think of career development from the individual's point of view is as a continuing quest for what one truly is and wants to do. As the person develops vocationally, there is a better fit in the integration of his sense of identity and the requirements of his work role. Erikson (1966) describes the growth and maturity of identity as follows: "For a mature psychosocial identity presupposes a community of people whose traditional values become significant to the growing person even as his growth and his gifts assume relevance for them" (p. 150). [We may speak, then, of a complementarity of an inner synthesis in the individual and of role integration in his group.] Finally, "And yet, just when a person, to all appearances, seems to 'find himself,' he can also be said to be 'losing himself' in new tasks and affiliations" (p. 151). This idea of career development as increasing the fit between occupational requirements and personal identity shows how career growth is a synthesizing process, integrating the person with his or her work environment.

Personal Identity and Social Identity

In the following sections, we examine two different facets of the person's overall sense of self: personal identity and social identity. *Personal identity* refers to those qualities in the person's self-perceptions that are unique to him or her. *Social identity* describes that portion of the overall identity that derives from the person's membership in a particular social group, such as a gender group or racial or ethnic group. Although both facets affect one's overall self-concept, the dynamics of each are so strong and so important that specialized areas of literature have developed around each one. Most of the early work on identity dealt with personal identity, whereas the area of social identity theory (SIT) became recognized as a distinct area of academic inquiry in the 1980s.

Obviously, the two facets are related. The way I see myself as a unique human being (my personal identity) has much to do with the way I deal with being a white American male. For example, consider my self-image in relation to issues such as educational attainment and financial well-being. My self-perception is that I have been able to achieve at a certain level, but that image is tempered by the knowledge of the educational and occupational advantages I have had by virtue of being a white male at this point in American history. Also, the way I feel about my social reference group is informed by my personal identity. That is, if my personal identity contains elements such as a value for fairness and equality, I might view my white maleness in terms of being concerned for issues of diversity and making connections with other social groups. For a more detailed discussion of these facets of identity, see Ashforth (2000). In our discussion of identity theory, we start by examining personal identity, the area in which the literature in our field started. Then we discuss SIT.

Personal Identity and Subidentities

A strong sense of identity is a prerequisite for pursuing a successful protean career. If the person is not clear on his or her needs and motivation, abilities, values, interests, and other important personal elements of self-definition, it would be very difficult to know where to head in life. As David Campbell suggests in the title to a book, *If You Don't Know Where You Want to Go, You'll Probably End Up Somewhere Else.*

As the main entity in the person's "self-system," the identity represents the person's image of himself or herself in relation to the environment (Hall, 1976, 1996b). Here, we use the term identity synonymously with related terms, such as self-concept, self-image, and sense of self. We will, however, use it as a distinct concept from self-esteem, which is an evaluation—the person's feelings or value he or she attaches to these personal qualities. Identity is descriptive (self-perceptions) rather than evaluative.

The identity has several components. For each social role that a person occupies, there is a *subidentity*, or a part of the identity, that is evoked by that role. Thus, I view myself in one way when I am with my children (through my subidentity as father). My self-perceptions are different when I am with a former college roommate (my subidentity as an old friend). For me, other subidentities include husband, professor (which can be further subdivided), neighbor and community member, brother- and son-in-law, hobbyist, and yard worker. The role represents a position in social space (Ashforth, 2000), with its concomitant expectations of behavior, whereas the subidentity represents self-perceptions as one responds to these role expectations (Hall, 1971, 1972, 1996b).

Career development and involvement occur as the person's career subidentity grows and becomes more differentiated. Thus, career development is, in fact, the creation of new aspects of the self that relate to the career. Therefore, career growth is a major way through which self-actualization occurs.

To illustrate these concepts, the sample career subidentities of two hypothetical people are shown in Figure 6.1. The top represents a person with low career involvement (i.e., a small portion of the identity engaged in the career role), and the bottom depicts a person with a higher level of involvement in the career.

Social Identity (Including Race, Ethnicity, and Gender)

Before discussing the impact of career processes on identity, we briefly discuss one other source of influence, background factors, which also have a bearing on identity development. Social identity theory describes the ways that gender, ethnicity, race, national background, and other aspects of social group membership can affect the type of identity a person develops and the way in which it develops. Minority group members in any setting are often discriminated against, with the result that they often must be "superpeople" to attain equal opportunities for good jobs and advancement. These extra obstacles can lead to identity perceptions that life's rewards are beyond the person's control, leading to feelings of helplessness, dependency, apathy, anger, and self-hate, which have sometimes been reported as part of the identity "baggage" of underrepresented members of any society.

Minority-group membership can also add to the difficulty of resolving identity issues. The article by Erikson (1966) is an eloquent statement of the interrelationship between the identity of a person and the communal identity of a people. Similarly, identity development has "two kinds of time: *a developmental stage* in the life of the individual and a *period* in history" (p. 160). Therefore, the member of a minority group must in a sense do double identity work, resolving what it means to be a mature human being and what it means to be a member of a particular group. Thomas and Alderfer (1989), in discussing how members of racial minority groups "often feel caught in a struggle between two distinct cultural worlds," quote Du Bois (1903, p. 45) and comment that his view of this tension "is perhaps even more apt today":

The Negro is a sort of seventh son, born with a veil, and gifted with second-sight in this American world—a world which yields him no true self-

Low Career-Involved Person

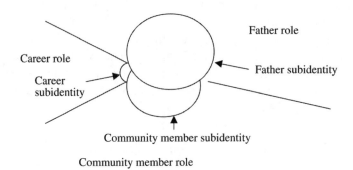

High Career-Involved Person

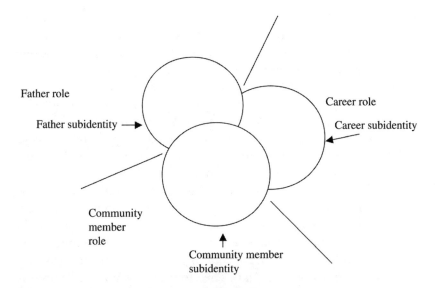

Figure 6.1. Roles and subidentities for two hypothetical people, one with high career involvement and one with low career involvement.

consciousness, but only lets him see himself through the revelation of the other world. It is a peculiar sensation, this double-consciousness, this sense of always looking at one's self through the eyes of a world that looks on in amused contempt and pity. One ever feels his twoness—an American, a Negro; two souls, two thoughts, two unreconciled strivings; two warring ideals in one dark body, whose dogged strength alone keeps it from being torn asunder. (p. 135)

Often, the minority person feels a strong sense of conflict between these two areas of identity. Examples are the career woman who believes she has to become less feminine to succeed or the black professional that feels more alienated from his former friends as his successes mount. They both may believe that they run the risk of "selling out" as the price for occupational attainments. In resolving their own personal identities, they also must resolve their group identity simultaneously. In actuality, this is an important aspect of the development of equality for the minority group as a whole, so in a real sense the person is performing double duty.

Ella Bell (1986, 1992) noted that because of this identity duality, black Americans are necessarily bicultural. She defines *biculturalism* as the "sociocultural repertoire of [racial minorities], as they move back and forth between the black community and dominant culture" (Bell, 1986, p. 21).

Bell (1986) explained this bicultural life structure as follows: The role expectations of the dominant American culture pull the person from one side and those of the black American culture pull from the other side. The dominant culture often influences individuals to suppress their racial identity, sometimes at the level of more surface symbols (e.g., hair, dress, and acquired tastes) and sometimes at deeper emotional levels (e.g., with whom one associates, where one lives, and one's political and social values). The strains between these two cultures are often aggravated by the fact that the white-oriented institutions in the dominant culture are often not conscious of these conflicting expectations. Also, conflicts can arise within the minority culture between, for example, members who are attempting to succeed within the dominant culture and those who identify primarily with the minority culture.

In her research on African American professional women, Bell identified three groups of women representing three types of bicultural life structure. One group was career-oriented women, whose lives were centered around professional activities. Their social relationships extended into both the black and the white cultures. Their stress derived from attempting to balance their work and personal lives and from the tensions of being boundary spanners between the two worlds.

The second group was black-community-oriented women. They were highly involved in the black community and had social and emotional distance from the white community. To the extent that they interacted with white people at work, they did not view these relationships as being as central to them as those with members of the black community. Their stresses came from inadequate resources available within the black community and from a lack of social support. They did not feel the conflict of marginality or double-identity strain that was experienced by the career-oriented women.

The third group was family-oriented women, for whom family was most central and work was less important. Their stresses came from a sense of not fully realizing their career aspirations. Their focus on the home meant that they focused less on race in forming relationships and focused more on common interests and personality.

This in-depth analysis of one social identity group illustrates the idea that it is not necessary to compare different groups to create learning about one group. Specifically, to learn more about the African American experience and identity, one does not necessarily need to have a comparison group of white Americans. Also, Bell's framework has applications to the study of other social identity groups. Of course, this study also offers important insight into an understudied topic, the black female career experience.

This comment notwithstanding, fascinating comparisons between African American and white women executives are made in a recent book by Ella Bell and Stella Nkomo titled *Our Separate Ways: Black and White Women and the Struggle for Professional Identity* (2001). This book discusses some of the authors' earlier work and provides rich qualitative and quantitative data. The former is provided by 14 in-depth interviews, 7 with black executive women and 7 with white executive women, and the latter by a national survey of 290 African American women and 535 white women managers. The data from both samples examine experiences at the intersection of race, gender, class, and history.

One theme that emerges from Bell and Nkomo's (2001) book is the biculturalism of the black women that was demonstrated in Bell's earlier work. The authors quote one of the black executives, Dawn Stanley, who described the black and white communities in her life as

two separate drawers, two separate faces, and two separate uniforms. I get up Monday through Friday and I think about acting, behaving, and interacting with one group of people where I am more formal and maintain an emotional distance. Then on Friday evenings, I close the door to my office. The weekend is back to me, back to family, back to being in safe territory. It's not that I don't do things with white folks from time to time, but my worlds are not very integrated, they are quite separate and distinct.... It's just two closets: They both work and I know what to expect in both of them. (pp. 11-24)

Another important finding from Bell and Nkomo's (2001) study is what the authors called "the racialized self." By this, they refer to "the ways in which race shapes a woman's identity, influences her overall sense of self, and informs her life. While race unleashes a black woman's voice, it silences a white woman's" (p. 11-1). In interviews, white women reported less awareness of race in their everyday interactions than did black executive women. Also, the survey data bore out these differences: Only 19% of the white women surveyed said they were conscious of their racial identity at work, whereas 81% of the black women respondents were conscious of their identity. One black woman, Brenda Boyd, described her identity as follows:

I experience myself as being exotic and mysterious to most white people. It is both the thing I enjoy the most and the most difficult part of my life. Being a black woman enables me—in spite of not having the right degrees, of not being the right color, of failing to be the right gender—to be what I am today. On the other hand, being a black woman is the thing that probably keeps me from moving ahead, because in a white world black women are simply unfathomable. That we have managed to get as far as we've gotten is unnerving to many whites.

Part of the majesty about being a black woman is that we have a great strength to draw from our grandmothers and our great-grandmothers all through our history. At some fundamental level, we always know our way home. Home is our anchor, our center. Our strength runs in our veins. As long as we keep dusting off, as long as we do not let the dust stay on us, then we realize that there is something quite extraordinary about being a black woman. (pp. 11-1, 11-2)

On the other hand, a white woman, Gloria Goldberg, described her identity experience differently:

I have never thought particularly about what it means to be a white woman. Instead I have focused on what it means to be a woman, because it was clearly in my way. So being female came into my awareness. (p. 11-2)

Bell and Nkomo (2001) make the following observation about the meaning of these differences:

> The racialized self-perceptions of black and white women are as different as night and day. Juxtaposing their perceptions illuminates one difference that keeps them apart. It also helps us comprehend how the infusion of race complicates or enhances the meaning of self for these women. (p. 11-10)

Identity Changes in the Career: What Affects Identity Growth?

Now that we have a sense of what the identity is, we can consider the following question: What facilitates the development of the growth of the person's identity? As previously discussed, race, culture, and history are part of the answer, but what else do we need to consider? This question can be examined in terms of two different time periods in the person's career. The first is when he or she is making an initial career choice, usually in high school or college. We examined this literature, which is extensive, in Chapter 3. The time period we consider here is the years following the initial choice—that is, the duration of the person's occupational or employment career. Unfortunately, we know far less about identity changes during the adult, working years than we know about adolescent changes as related to career choice.

Of the five types of information that predict career outcomes (background, assessment, personality, career processes, and person-organization fit), the one that seems to be the most useful in understanding the person's sense of identity is career process information. It appears that critical events and role transition may alter a person's identity or at least trigger personal explorations that later lead to identity alterations.

We now discuss the changes in identity that are stimulated by events in the process of the person's career. As discussed previously, the person's life history may be viewed as a series of passages from one role to another: high school student, college student, company trainee, engineer, manager, and so on.

Status Passage

The activities denoting these stages have been termed "rites of passage" (van Gennep, 1960). It is generally possible to identify three major phases: separation of the person from his customary environment, initiation from the old role into the new one, and incorporation or reintegration into the original or a new environment.

In a more contemporary setting, William Bridges (1994) discusses a similar view of change and transition. He describes change as a shift in one's external world. A transition, on the other hand, is the internal process, the identity change, that people go through as a result of that external shift. Like van Gennep (1960), Bridges sees this identity change happening in three stages. The first step is an ending, in which the person loses the old status. The next stage is a neutral zone, in which the person feels thrown into the chaos of change but does not yet see something else to replace the loss. Finally, there are beginnings, in which the person has achieved a sense of a new identity, with its new understandings, attitudes, and values.

The initiation phase is a highly visible component of institutionalized role transition. In it, personal changes are focused in a fairly short, intense time period. During the initiation the holders of the desired role test the newcomer to determine whether he will measure up to their standards. If he can, he is given public certification that he is now one of them. Because of this certification, he then begins to feel more like one of them—that is, his identity has changed so that he now sees himself as part of the new group. Perhaps the most clear and familiar example of this phase is the fraternity initiation, which we know can cause changes in a person's attitudes.

Although there are obviously few, if any, formal initiation rites in the work career, there are nevertheless many role transitions and turning points that serve the function of mini-initiations. For example, the recruitment and interviewing process is an important test of the candidate's abilities; the more difficult he thinks it is to obtain a job offer from a particular organization, the more he might identify with that organization if he is hired. Training programs and probationary periods, especially in firms with "up or out" policies, contain elements of initiation rites. Indeed, some initial job experiences, such as the audit function in accounting firms, are so routine and unsatisfying that they are often experienced as a form of hazing. A newcomer to a particular job may be tested by his boss, peers, or subordinates and may be very much aware of the particular point at which he won their confidence and became one of them. Of course, induction into career-related organizations such as management clubs or the Million-Dollar Roundtable in life insurance, which denote promotion to a particular level or a certain level of performance, is often treated quite ceremoniously and helps the person accept this advancement or achievement more readily into his sense of identity.

Role Transitions

Movement (transfer, job change, or promotion) into a new role can also induce considerable identity change, regardless of whether or not a form of initiation is present. Thus, another way to consider identity change is to examine the transition that occurs as one moves into a role—that is, not passages between roles but movement within a role. Nicholson and West (1988, 1989) identified a process of phases through which a person makes a transition into a role. First is a period of preparation, which happens before entering the role, in which the person develops initial expectations and the creation of an orientation to and attitudes toward the change. Next is the encounter with the new role— the initial entry process in which the person engages in exploration and sensemaking about the new role. Third is adjustment, in which the person changes in response to the role, shapes the role, and develops a network of relationships related to the role. In the final phase of the role transition, stabilization, the person achieves a level of personal and organizational effectiveness in the role.

There are certain predictable changes in identities that occur as the individual makes certain status or role changes during the course of the career. For example, when the recently graduated MBA becomes a manager, the expectations that she and other people associate with that role induce new self-perceptions and feelings of responsibility. Also, the more time she spends in the organization and the higher she moves in the hierarchy, the more investments she makes in the organization and, thus, the more strongly she will tend to identify with the organization (Hall, Schneider, & Nygren, 1970; Whetten & Godfrey, 1998).

In an early study of Roman Catholic diocesan priests making the role transition from assistant pastor to pastor (the manager or administrator of a parish), Hall and Schneider (1973) found that priests' identity perceptions became more favorable before the advancement. This reflects a process that sociologists call *anticipatory socialization* (wherein the person begins to adopt the attitudes, attributes, and self-perceptions associated with a particular role before entering it). During the 3 years immediately following the advancement, however, the new pastors' self-perceptions became less favorable. This was apparently due to the "reality shock" of the difficult work and responsibilities of the job, in contrast to the unrealistic expectations that had been developing during the many years of waiting for the promotion (22 years in this particular study). Research on members of other professions has shown similar decreases in self-perceptions following the initial work experience, which are often reported as disillusioning (Raelin, 1984, 1991).

On the other hand, studies of medical students (Becker, Geer, Hughes, & Strauss, 1961) and PhD candidates (Hall, 1968) indicate more favorable self-perceptions and increased identification with the professional role as the person moves closer to the aspired role during graduate training. Relating these studies to those of priests and teachers, the increases during graduate training may again represent anticipatory socialization, to be followed by a decrease in the favorableness of self-perceptions after the graduates assume their professional roles. There tend to be decreases in job satisfaction during the initial career years for employees in general, and this could be quite consistent with decreases in professional self-regard. That is, although the person may assume the role of manager as more a part of her identity, if she now values that role less or feels less competent in it because of the reality shock of the first job, her evaluations of herself could decrease (McCall, 1998).

Socialization

The process of influence that results in these identity changes over time is called *socialization*. For example, based on work by Fisher (1986) and Van Maanen (1976), Ashforth and Saks (1996, p. 149) describe socialization as a process that "focuses on how individuals learn the beliefs, values, orientations, behaviors, skills, and so forth necessary to fulfill their new roles and function effectively within an organization's milieu. ... Thus, socialization facilitates the adjustment of newcomers to organizations."

The model of socialization that has been most frequently applied to organizations was originally developed by Orville Brim (1966) and subsequently applied by Van Maanen and Schein (1979).[1] This model consists of six methods that organizations employ to modify the identities of new recruits. One dimension describes whether the socialization is individual or collective. That is, are new recruits processed by themselves or as part of a group? A second dimension describes whether the socialization is formal or informal—that is, whether the newcomer is explicitly defined as a new member and set apart in some way from more experienced members. A third aspect is sequential versus random, which describes whether there is a prescribed set of status passages in the process versus a more emergent process.

Of great relevance in contemporary organizations is the serial versus disjunctive dimension. Serial means that a current new member can learn from previous cohorts of new members, whereas disjunctive reflects a process of discontinuous change, such that current newcomers cannot learn from the experiences of previous generations. Finally, investiture versus divestiture describes whether the change process involves adding new elements to the person's identity versus stripping away elements of the "old" identity.

Gareth Jones (1986) developed these dimensions of socialization tactics to form a set of measurement scales, which have been supported by studies such as that by Ashforth, Saks, and Lee (1997). Jones, however, went beyond the original scales and argued that, in combination, they represent a continuum of two general approaches to socialization, an institutional approach and an individualized approach. The institutionalized style contains a combination of collective, formal, sequential, fixed, serial, and investiture tactics. The common element in these approaches is that the organization has a strong culture that is relatively stable, such that the person is influenced to change in response to the pressures from the organization.

Individualized socialization contains a combination of individual, informal, random, variable, disjunctive, and divestiture tactics. These focus more on the individual's unique experience and encourage him or her to create his or her own approach to the role, forming a more innovative role orientation.

Using this model, several studies, such as those by Jones (1986), Ashforth and Saks (1996), and Saks and Ashforth (1997), found that an organization's use of the socialization tactics was related to socialization outcomes, such as reduced role ambiguity, role conflict, and intentions to quit, as well as to increased job satisfaction and commitment to the organization. Furthermore, as one might expect, the use of institutionalized socialization tactics was found to be associated with a more custodial role orientation—that is, maintaining the status quo. On the other hand, the use of individualized tactics was found to be related to attempted and successful role innovation (Allen & Meyer, 1990; Ashforth & Saks, 1996; Jones, 1986).

Ashforth et al. (1997) concluded that although their data supported the existence of the six original scales, the tactics that were on the institutionalized end of the continuum did in fact seem to reflect a more structured approach to socialization. On the other hand, those tactics on the individualized end of the continuum seemed to be associated with a relative absence of structure.

Adult Development Processes

Another lens for viewing identity change during the course of the career is provided by the theories of adult development. These approaches were described in detail in Chapter 4, so we will not dwell on them here. The most important of the adult development models as they relate to identity change and career growth are those of Daniel Levinson (Levinson, 1996; Levinson, Darrow, Klein, Levinson, & McKee, 1978) and Robert Kegan (1982, 1994).

Levinson views the life course as a series of structure-building periods, called stages, separated by structure-changing periods (transitions). In the structure-building periods, the person's developmental task is to build a life structure that is appropriate for that era in the person's life. For example, the task in the 20s is to create an initial independent adult life structure after the person has left the parents and has entered the adult world for the first time. This task is quite different from that of the 40s, when an early structure has been created but one's roles are changing, requiring that a new structure be created to fit the roles and responsibilities of midlife. A life structure is an underlying pattern or design in one's life, and it is based primarily on one's total set of relationships. As these new structures are successively created, the developmental task includes not just engaging in new behaviors but also working through a new definition of self that is congruent with these behaviors. Also, if one is to be a whole person, one's attitudes and perspectives toward life must change and be brought into alignment as well.

A driving force in the person's life, according to Levinson, is the person's life dream, the ideal view of what kind of person he or she hopes to become. Movement in relation to the dream takes place in the transitional periods, during which much of the structure of the previous stage is undone, views of the self and of one's world are reexamined, and choices are made that will lead to a new life structure. (Some of this change is self-initiated, and some is forced on the person by the environment, by new roles such as work roles or the loss of same, by other people, by changes in one's body and health, etc.) Levinson reports that transitions generally last about 5 years, and he identifies specific ages at which people go through the various stages and transitions that he identified. He also notes that no one life stage is permanent, and he estimates that approximately half of our adult lives are spent in transitions (Levinson, 1986). Thus, in this view, life is a constant process of change and development. Each transition serves both as the ending of the previous stage and the beginning of the next.

Thus, we can see how the sociologists' and the social psychologists' theories of roles and role transitions and the developmental psychologists' models complement each other to help us fully understand role transitions. The role transition literature focuses on the old and new roles, their interface with the identity, and the dynamics of the change process as the person moves out of, into, and through each role. The adult development literature, on the other hand, adds the idea that most adults in a given culture tend to go through particular life roles in a predictable order and in predictable time periods in life. Although the developmental theorists also have an interactionist view (i.e., the interaction between the social environment and the individual), the primary focus moves inside to the identity of the person and how that develops in predictable ways.

Another developmental model, which is becoming increasingly important in organizational behavior, is that of Robert Kegan (1982, 1994). In his view, development occurs not so much in an age-driven manner but, rather, as a result of the person encountering new situations that contain increasingly greater complexity. As the person increases his or her capacity to deal with this complexity, the identity grows in its capacity to take in complexity and to integrate it in a way that permits committed action. Influenced by Piaget, the Kegan model proposes a series of levels of identity as the person moves from being very dependent and self-focused to being both autonomous and interdependent and able to comprehend a very complex system of relationships in which he or she operates.

A driving force in Kegan's model is the person's interactions with various "others" in the environment, where others include not just people but sources of influence, such as jobs, communities, and challenging tasks. A major source of developmental support is the *holding environment*, a setting containing relationships in which the person can be safe and vulnerable and can experiment with new behaviors. Kegan and Lahey (2000) provide a guidebook for good developmental conversations that people can hold and help them deal successfully with developmental tasks.

Longitudinal Occupational Studies of Identity Changes

Pioneering work on the analysis of identity changes during the course of careers in general (i.e., not any particular occupational group) was done by Strauss and Glaser. Classic works include Anselm Strauss, *Mirrors and Masks: The Search for Identity* (1970); Barney Glaser and Anselm Strauss, *Status Passage* (1971); and Howard Becker, Blanche Geer, Everett Hughes, and Anselm Strauss, *Boys in White* (1961). An overview of this work was reported by Barley (1989), and an excellent discussion of recent research on identity changes can be found in Ashforth (2000).

One of the most detailed studies of identity changes in the early career experiences of managers was conducted by Hill (1992), who followed 19 managers (14 men and 5 women) through their first year as sales and marketing managers. Before their promotion, all these people were individual contributors (called specialists, producers, or professionals).

Hill (1992) found that there were two key ways in which these managers' identities were transformed as they moved into their new roles. First, they moved from specialists and doers to generalists and agenda-setters. That is, rather than directly performing technical tasks themselves, they orchestrated diverse tasks and people. Psychologically, they had to switch their identification with their individual specialist tasks to identification with the business or with the role of manager.

A related identity transformation for these emerging managers was moving from viewing oneself as an individual actor to viewing oneself as a network builder. Psychologically, this meant changing from defining success through one's independent task accomplishment to valuing the accomplishments of others and to valuing interdependence. To make this transformation successfully, Hill (1992, p. 6) found that these managers had to master four key tasks:

- Learning what it means to be a manager
- Developing interpersonal judgment
- Gaining self-knowledge
- Coping with stress and emotion

Therefore, much of this learning is identity learning, or learning about oneself, and some is learning more about what the role requires. Interestingly, only one of these tasks relates to a specific competency area (interpersonal judgment). As Hill (1992) found, most of this learning did not happen intellectually; it happened experientially:

> The lessons were learned as the managers confronted the daily litany of interactions and problems in their new assignments. And they were learned incrementally, gradually. Sometimes the managers were aware that they were learning, but most often they were not. The learning consisted principally of "gradual and tacit change"; with the accumulation of evidence and experience came the erosion of one set of beliefs, attitudes, and values and buildup of another. (pp. 7-8)

Research by Schein (1996) developed the concept of *career anchors*, a central organizing force in a person's identity. Schein defines the career anchor as follows:

> A person's career anchor is his or her self-concept, consisting of (a) self-perceived talents and abilities, (b) basic values, and, most important, (c) the evolved sense of motives and needs as they pertain to the career. Career anchors evolve only as one gains occupational and life experience. However, once the self-concept has been formed, it functions as a stabilizing force, an anchor, and can be thought of as the values and motives that the person will not give up if forced to make a choice. Most of us are not aware of our career anchors until we are forced to make choices pertaining to self-development, family, or career. Yet it is important to become aware of them so that we can choose wisely when choices have to be made. (p. 80)

Schein's initial research in the mid-1970s identified five anchors: (a) autonomy or independence, (b) security or stability, (c) technical or functional competence, (d) general management competence, and (e) entrepreneurial creativity. Later studies in the 1980s found three additional categories: (a) service or dedication to a cause, (b) pure challenge, and (c) lifestyle.

For most of the 1970s and 1980s, Schein's research found fairly consistent percentages of managers in the different anchor categories, with approximate percentages as follows:

- General management: 25%
- Technical or functional competence: 25%
- Autonomy: 10%
- Security: 10%
- Remaining anchors: 30%

Surprisingly, Schein found a wide distribution of anchors in every occupation he studied, even though one might expect a particular specialized field to favor a certain anchor.

In speculating on the shifts in recent and future years, Schein (1996) offered the following descriptions of the career anchors:

Security or stability: People anchored in this category have had the most difficult time adjusting to the new, self-directed career environment— "It is not at all clear where the security anchored person of today can find his or her niche" (p. 82).

Autonomy or independence: This career anchor fits well with the self-reliance that is required in the current economy, and people in this category may become role models for the future.

Lifestyle: This is the category in which the most changes have been found since the early research in the 1960s and 1970s. Originally, geographic stability was part of the security anchor, but in research in the 1970s it became clear that geographical preferences were often related to two-career situations and larger life and family concerns. This anchor, like autonomy, also fits well with the new career contract because it reflects the perspective that the identity is primarily rooted outside of the employing organization.

Technical or functional competence: One problem with this anchor is that in many work settings people would prefer to climb the managerial ladder than build a career on a technical specialty. Still, however, a person needs to have a certain amount of technical proficiency to stand out in most places—to be viewed as a candidate for upward mobility. Another problem with this anchor is that obsolescence is occurring with greater speed so that continuous learning is imperative to permit this anchor to be effective. Who will take responsibility for this learning, the employee or the organization?

General managerial competence: This category is highly valued in most organizational cultures, even in today's delayered organizations. Increasingly, however, the managerially oriented person must also be strong functionally (i.e., in financial and analytic skills, marketing savvy, interpersonal and team skills, and emotional intelligence). Also, these managerial competencies have become important at increasingly lower levels in the organization; they are not clustered just at the top anymore.

Entrepreneurial creativity: With the explosion of electronic commerce and biotechnology and other technologies yet to arise, increasingly more of the economy will be based on entrepreneurial activity. For example, new business ventures, especially women-owned entrepreneurial ventures, represent the fastest growing sector of the U.S. economy. For the governments and societies of the world, a major challenge will be to resist the temptation to create excessive tax burdens on these new ventures, which might have a negative effect on the economic incentives for entrepreneurs.

Service and dedication to a cause: The number of people with this anchor is also increasing. It is often combined with the entrepreneurial anchor, creating new organizations dedicated to philanthropy, the environment, social justice, and similar causes. Also, increasingly, people going into more traditional roles within the private sector are searching for organizations with values and goals that promote social ends.

Pure challenge: This is a group that relishes competition, solving the unsolved problems, and overcoming impossible odds. Schein's impression is that there are increasingly more people in the workforce with this orientation, but it is not clear if this is because they have always had this predisposition or if it is an adaptation to a world that now presents more problems that require solution.

Schein's prediction about the career world of the future is as follows: "The only reliable prediction is that we will have to become perpetual learners, more self-reliant, and more capable than ever in dealing with surprises of all sorts. It should be a field day for those anchored in pure challenge" (p. 88).

Research Issues Regarding Identity

To conclude this part of the chapter, we consider some of the identity issues that could benefit from more empirical attention:

- There is (still) a need for more longitudinal research on the time-based process of identity change. There was significant research on identity changes during occupational role transitions in the heyday of the Chicago School of sociology in the 1950s and 1960s, but little of this type of work has been done in contemporary work organizations. The works of Hill (1992) and Ashforth (2000) are good models for future work.

- The measurement issues regarding identity are significant. It is inherently a clinical concept and has typically been studied with qualitative, clinical measurement methods. We need to develop more and better quantitative approaches to the study of identity issues.

- How does identity change as specific roles change over time? Most research on identity change has assumed that the role is stable while the person's identity is labile. Because speed is so prevalent in today's work environments, however, roles change as fast as people change. What are the mutually interactive processes by which roles and identities affect each other?

- How can we track changes in personal identity and social identity as well as their mutual interdependencies? In much the same way as roles are changing rapidly, so are social group roles and identifications. What does it mean to be a member of a particular minority group today versus 10 or 15 years ago? What does it mean to have been raised as part of a majority group and then have that group turn into a minority group? As in the case in certain parts of Eastern Europe or Africa, what does it mean to be socialized as part of a dominant group and then to have that group become a nondominant (and perhaps severely oppressed) group? How is the development of one's personal identity affected by these changes in social identity?

- Specifically, in the era of the protean career, how does the protean career identity act as a causal agent? That is, how does self-confidence affect career effort and subsequent success? Is there, in fact, a success spiral? When is the protean sense of self a causal agent, and when is it an outcome of some concrete experience?

- We need more research on short-cycle career processes. For example, research could be performed to identify changes resulting from role transitions, identity changes resulting from career learning cycles (negative and positive effects). There is also a need for more research on identity changes during daily role transitions (i.e., transitions from home to work and back, as described by Hall & Richter, 1988). A good example of such research on "microtransitions" is found in Ashforth, Kreiner, and Fugate (2000).

- How can we trace the mutual impacts of the objective career (e.g., role) and the subjective career (e.g., identity)? As objective careers become more boundaryless, how does the person "track" these changes onto his or her identity? If there is less sense of boundary or status passage in the career today, does that mean that there is less sense of career "progress" or growth?

- Regarding the previous point, in a larger sense, how do we define and measure growth in the career? In conversations with people whom I regard as having protean careers, it seems clear that a major issue for them is the lack of the traditional yardsticks by which to measure career success. They do not have the traditional progressions of jobs and titles by which to mark their progress. Although these are clear when they are learning and expanding their capacities, they worry that these are not visible to others. They certainly cannot be put on one's resume. Although there are skill-based or functional resumes, the growth of skills still does not have universal currency. We need fresh new ideas for framing, extracting, communicating, and valuing protean identity growth in the career.

Career Attitudes

As is the case with identity, career attitudes are strongly affected by career processes. Naturally, attitudes and values are also affected by personal characteristics because attitudes are important personal characteristics. Given the tendency toward consistency in the human personality, a person's attitudes are often related to his needs, wants, abilities, and other personal attributes. The general strength of these attitudes and values is related to personality characteristics, whereas changes in attitudes can be caused by events in the career process.

Following a decline in interest in attitudes in the 1960s and 1970s, in the past 20 years there has been a strong interest in attitudes, particularly cognitive approaches (Tenbrunsel, Galvin, Neale, & Bazerman, 1999). In particular, in the career field, much of the research on attitudes has centered on involvement and commitment to career, family, and the organization. Also, much work has been done on negative experiences related to involvement and commitment, such as burnout (Maslach, 1982; Maslach & Leiter, 1997). We will not attempt to discuss this area in detail but, rather, trace the origins of this research and give a sense of our current knowledge.

Role Transitions and Attitude Change

In addition to changes in identity as a career progresses, there are also concomitant attitude changes that occur in the first job and other early work experiences. These changes were first documented in a classic longitudinal study of graduate business students at Massachusetts Institute of Technology's Sloan School conducted by Edgar Schein (1967, 1978, 1996). Schein examined the attitudes of business students at three points in time—at the beginning of their 2-year graduate program, at the end of the 2 years of study, and after approximately 1 year of their first jobs. He also measured the attitudes of the management school faculty and those of a group of senior executives, representing the authorities in the educational and work systems, respectively. He measured attitudes in areas such as business in society, management theory and attitudes, attitudes toward people, and individual-organization relations.

As mentioned previously, Schein found that the attitudes of the senior executives and those of the business school faculty were quite different, indicating that their environments represent two quite different worlds. Critics of business schools view this gap as evidence that management education is hopelessly irrelevant to the training needs of business firms. Supporters view this discrepancy as a measure of the innovation the business schools create, introducing new attitudes and values into business through the newly hired MBAs. At the beginning of the master's degree program, the attitudes of the students were between those of the executives and professors.

Following the master's program, the students' attitudes moved closer to those of the faculty. Later, however, after some work experience, the students' attitudes moved the other way, closer to those of the senior executives. This indicates that the person's attitudes are affected by the climate and prevailing attitudes of the particular system in which he is working. This does not mean that every person changes or is socialized by his organization, but there is a clear tendency for people as a group to experience some attitude changes in a direction that is more congruent with the attitudes associated with the role.

Another important type of attitude is related to the person's satisfaction with his work and his organization. In the satisfaction literature, there is disagreement, but there seems to be a U-shaped relationship between satisfaction and age. Just after the person starts working, satisfaction is fairly high. Then, during the next few years, it tends to decrease, perhaps due to disillusionment with unchallenging initial jobs and promotion frustrations. Later, satisfaction begins to increase and continues to increase for the remainder of the career (Hall, 1976).

Research on young AT&T managers in the first 8 years of their careers noted a similar decrease in satisfaction over time (Campbell, 1968; Howard & Bray, 1988). There was an even greater decrease in career expectations, however, which may account for the decrease in satisfaction. On the other hand, there was an increase in occupational involvement.

This latter finding is consistent with several other studies, which have found increases in job involvement over time (Hall & Schneider, 1973; Lodahi & Kejner, 1965; Rabinowitz & Hall, 1977). The conclusions of Campbell's (1968) study seem to generalize well, based on the other research we have reviewed: The findings strongly suggest that the young manager goes through a process of adjustment and change during the early years of the career. The person's attitude toward the company becomes less favorable, and the high expectations are toned down considerably. Examination of case histories and the particular questionnaire items that show the most change indicate that the "negative" changes are realistic ones. For example, it is not uncommon in our samples to find a large percentage of the recently hired college graduates expressing sincerely and with conviction that they expect to become officers of the company. After a year or two of reality testing in the organization, expectations become more realistic. The same point can be made about attitudes toward the company. Some of the new recruits entering the first job of their managerial career have extremely positive views of the company. Their attitudes would be considered naive even granting that the company is very well managed.

Psychological Success and Job Attitudes

In the AT&T research, all four attitudes studied (company satisfaction, expectations, occupational satisfaction, and occupational involvement) were correlated with managerial success in both salary progress and management level attained. Expectations and occupational satisfaction were not related to success in Year 1, but they were correlated with success by the eighth year. The results are similar to those of Hall and Nougaim's (1968) success syndrome referred to earlier, in which increases in achievement satisfaction and work centrality were strongly related to success in the first 5 years of the managers' careers.

Based on the AT&T research and the early work of Porter and Lawler (1968), who found that good performance can lead to increases in work satisfaction, Hall (1971, 1976) developed a model of psychological success and career development. In this model, career development occurs as a self-reinforcing spiral of success experiences, starting with the person working on a challenging goal. If the person values the goal and has autonomy in determining the path to the goal, and if the goal is attained, then the person will experience psychological success as a result of that achievement. Psychological success is the feeling of pride and personal accomplishment that comes from knowing that one has done one's "personal best" (Hall & Mirvis, 1996).

The result of achieving psychological success on a career task is that one feels more competent so that one's self-perceptions (career sub-identity) become more positive. Because these are very positive, rewarding feelings, the person will be motivated to have more such experiences in the future. Therefore, the person is now more likely to choose another challenging goal for the future. Thus, the cycle is repeated, and success breeds success. Later studies at AT&T and elsewhere found additional support for the functioning of this sort of success spiral (Hall & Foster, 1977; Hall & Hall, 1976; Howard & Bray, 1988).

Although the rich get richer, it appears that the poor do not necessarily get poorer. In the AT&T studies, the work involvement of the less successful managers decreased only slightly (Bray, 1972; Hall & Nougaim, 1968). During a 20-month period of tight budgets and deteriorating job quality, the job involvement of research scientists and engineers remained unchanged (Hall & Mansfield, 1971).

Thus, the increased job involvement and motivation from task success results in the employee moving into a self-reinforcing success spiral, which directs his or her behavior toward greater task achievement. This idea fits well with the conclusions of perhaps one of the most prolific students of work attitudes during approximately the past 30 years—Edward E. Lawler, III. Consistent with his early work with Lyman Porter, which identified conditions under which positive work attitudes can result from strong job performance, Lawler's work throughout the years has documented the value of these attitudes for the effective functioning of a business. In the book, *From the Ground Up: Six Principles for Building the New Logic Corporation* (1997), Lawler goes beyond various fads and identifies core theoretical and empirical trends and patterns that represent the "new logic" for organizational functioning. One of the six principles in this new logic is that involvement is the most effective source of individual control. We can see in the psychological success model how this control (self-control) operates.

Self-Efficacy

This success spiral is also consistent with the prolific work of Albert Bandura and others on self-efficacy theory (Bandura, 1986; Hackett,

1995). Self-efficacy refers to the individual's beliefs about his or her ability to perform successfully a given task. According to Bandura, self-efficacy beliefs are powerful mediators of behavior and behavior change. If the person has low self-efficacy expectations related to a certain task, he or she will probably tend to avoid that task, whereas people with high self-efficacy beliefs will be more likely to approach those behaviors.

Bandura (1986) identified the following sources of information that can lead to changes in self-efficacy beliefs:

- Successful performance on the task
- Modeling or observing others performing the task (vicarious learning)
- Verbal persuasion (encouragement or support from others)
- Emotional self-management (e.g., reducing anxiety related to the behavior)

A rich empirical literature on self-efficacy has shown how interventions in these four areas can in fact increase a person's self-efficacy beliefs. In the career area, interventions aimed at increasing self-efficacy related to the tasks of given career fields have been shown to increase students' interests in and behaviors leading to pursuing those fields (Betz & Schifano, 2000).

For example, Betz and Schifano (2000) found that college women who received self-efficacy interventions aimed at what Holland called "realistic" career activities (e.g., using tools, assembling, building, and operating machinery) in fact later experienced greater confidence and interests in these activities compared to a control group. The interventions included building, repairing, and construction tasks. Professional craftspeople (equal numbers of men and women) demonstrated each task (modeling). Then, they helped the subjects complete their building and repair tasks (successful performance), encouraging and supporting them along the way (social persuasion). Also, hourly breaks were scheduled to affirm the participants' accomplishments with applause and verbal praise and to practice relaxation techniques with deep breathing and meditation (anxiety management). The full intervention took 7 hours. The results showed that women in the experimental condition versus those in the control group showed significantly increased self-confidence related to realistic activities (Betz & Schifano, 2000). The authors concluded,

In sum, the present study has demonstrated the effectiveness of an intervention to increase realistic self-efficacy in college women. The results suggest optimism concerning our ability to increase women's confidence with respect to activities traditionally viewed as "male domains." This in turn may eventually prove useful in facilitating women's pursuit of scientific and technical fields. More research related to both specific and more general effects of interventions based on Bandura's self-efficacy theory are needed. (p. 50)

Organizational Commitment

One of the most frequently studied career-related attitudes is the person's commitment to or identification with the organization. In contrast to satisfaction, which evaluates the person's affective response to the organization (positive or negative), identification and commitment tap the psychological involvement that the person feels with the organization and the extent to which his organizational membership is a significant aspect of his or her personal identity. In other words, the person feels a connection between the identity of the organization and his or her own personal sense of identity.

Organizational identity is a deeply held and stable sense of shared meaning for an organization and its members (Albert & Whetten, 1985). Organizations with a clear sense of identity are expected to reflect a high level of organizational commitment on the part of their members. A high level of member commitment indicates that the person personally accepts the goals and values of the organization, is willing to exert high levels of effort on behalf of the organization, and intends to remain in the organization (Mowday, Porter, & Steers, 1982). McCarthy (2000), in a review of the literature, reports the following:

> Firms which display clearer understanding of their organizational identity (collectively and consistently answering "who are we?" or, more telling, "who do we want to be?") may possess significant competitive advantage in harnessing the creative efforts of the diverse workforce in the face of complex market challenges (Barney, 1991; Eccles, Nohria, & Berkley, 1992; Fiol, 1991, 1994; Nkomo & Cox, 1996; Pratt & Foreman, 2000). (McCarthy, 2000, p. 10)

Two distinct orientations a professional person might take toward his career work have been identified (Gouldner, 1958/1959): loyalty toward the employing organization and loyalty toward the profession. People with mainly organizational loyalties are termed *locals,* and those with mainly professional loyalties are called *cosmopolitans.* At first, it was thought that these two orientations were opposite extremes (i.e., mutually exclusive), but subsequent research has shown that they are two separate dimensions. Thus, a person can be a cosmopolitan and still identify with a particular organization (a local cosmopolitan).

Three Types of Commitment

O'Reilly and Chatman (1996) proposed that there are three forms of commitment attitudes that an employee can develop toward an organization. *Compliance commitment* occurs when the person does not share values and beliefs associated with the organization but is conforming simply to receive certain rewards or to avoid certain costs. *Internalization commitment,* on the other hand, is the result of the member's sharing of important values with the organization. *Identification-based commitment* occurs when the person defines his or her identity in terms of membership in the organization and takes personal pride in being a member of that organization.

A related, but not entirely similar, typology was presented by Meyer and Allen (1997), who described the following components of commitment:

- Affective commitment: "the employee's emotional attachment to, identification with, and involvement with the organization"
- Continuance commitment: "an awareness of the costs associated with leaving the organization"
- Normative commitment: "a feeling of obligation to continue employment" (p. 11)

A variety of distal and proximal factors and processes have been found to be related to the development of the various forms of commitment. For example, a key factor influencing the person's affective commitment or identification with his organization is the extent to which he personally values the goals it is pursuing (Hall & Associates, 1996; Hall & Schneider, 1973; Hall et al., 1970; March & Simon, 1958). Organizational identification and commitment are not identical, although they are similar and are often used interchangeably, as they will be here.

For example, if I work for the U.S. Forest Service, an organization devoted to public service through effective land management, and if I strongly value public service, I will probably identify strongly with the organization. If I did not care less about public service, then other conditions would have to be present for me to be strongly committed to the organization.

One of these other factors is a challenging job (Buchanan, 1974; Gould, 1975; Hall & Schneider, 1973; Lee, 1971; Patchen, 1970). If I view the organization as a setting in which I can do stimulating, success-producing, satisfying work, that association may lead me to become committed to the organization. Two other conditions are position level and length of service in the organization. Generally, the higher one moves in the hierarchy and the longer one has worked for the organization, the more one identifies with it—indeed, the more in reality the person actually is a part of the organization (Gould, 1975; Hrebiniak & Alutto, 1973; Lee, 1971; Sheldon, 1971). Naturally, one's position level is a function of length of service, and in two organizations (the U.S. Forest Service and the Roman Catholic Church) the effects of position decreased markedly when length of service was held constant. When position was held constant, however, the effects of length of service were not greatly reduced (Hall & Schneider, 1973). In these two organizations, the effects of length of service were also independent of other variables that might help account for increased identification: job challenge, self-image, need importance, and satisfaction. Turnover and self-selection may have been factors, with the less committed people leaving early, but turnover was extremely low in both organizations. Hall and Schneider draw the following conclusions about the effects of length of service:

> With length of service a person probably accumulates a complex network of positive and rewarding experiences which become associated with membership in the organization: These eventually may generalize to the organization itself, so that organizational membership eventually becomes functionally autonomous as a motivating factor. Similarly, over time the priest's self-image becomes increasingly correlated with his organizational commitment. When one combines this increasing identity investment with (a) the declining number of outside opportunities as one gets older and (b) the dissonance-reducing process of assuring oneself that he has chosen his commitments wisely, it seems reasonable that time would lead to increasing identification. (p. 348)

Meyer and Allen (1997) make a similar observation about the effects of
tenure on commitment, but they offer a caution about how to view
time-based variables:

> Many potential antecedents of continuance commitment are of the sort that
> can accumulate over time. For this reason, some researchers have used time-
> based variables (e.g., age, tenure) as antecedent measures of continuance
> commitment. Findings obtained in these studies have been mixed and
> should be interpreted with caution. For some employees, the perceived costs
> associated with leaving an organization will increase as they get older and
> increase their organizational tenure. For other employees, however, the costs
> of leaving might actually decrease; as experience and skills increase, an
> employee's value to other employers might increase. For this reason, age and
> tenure are best thought of as proxy or surrogate variables of accumulated
> investments and perceived alternatives and not as direct predictors of con-
> tinuance commitment (cf. Cohen, 1993; Meyer & Allen, 1984). (p. 60)

As further evidence of the complexity of the links between time and
commitment, Beck and Wilson (2000) conducted a carefully designed
cross-sequential examination of changes in affective commitment with
tenure for a sample of Australian police officers. In contrast to what they
considered as a generally positive relationship between tenure and
commitment in previous research, Beck and Wilson found consistent
decreases in commitment over time in their sample. They also reported
that their findings were consistent with those reported in three other
studies of Australian police organizations. It is not clear to the authors
what factors might account for these results: the use of the cross-sequential
method, which controls for cohort effects and is thus stronger than the
more frequently used cross-sectional method, or the culture of the
organizations studied.

As part of the culture, the career patterns of employees, the promotion policies of the organization, and the external labor market seem to
affect the extent to which identification increases with length of service.
In an organization with a policy of promotion from within, where people
tend to spend their entire careers in that organization, identification
will probably be more strongly related to length of service than in organizations that hire managers and executives from outside the organization (i.e., where employees have multiorganization careers) (Hall &
Schneider, 1973). On the other hand, if the external job market for the

person becomes more positive with experience, as may be true for people in military and quasi-military careers (such as police professionals), this could weaken the person's attachment over time (Beck & Wilson, 2000; Meyer & Allen, 1997).

Another factor that seems to be related to identification in some organizations, but not all, is the personality of the individual. A study discussed in Chapter 5 indicated that people who are the "right type" undoubtedly identified the most with their organizations. In this study, the right type was nonconfronting and unaggressive. In research on two business organizations, the right type in the achievement-oriented firm had strong achievement needs, and the right type in the power-oriented firm had strong power needs. In the service-oriented Forest Service (a civil service system), high identifiers had strong needs for affiliation and security and viewed themselves as supportive and involved with people: Where the individual's personality is congruent with the climate of the organization, identification is more likely to occur.

Allen and Meyer's Model of Organizational Commitment

After reviewing an extensive literature on commitment, Allen and Meyer (1990, 1997) developed a model of antecedents and consequences of organizational commitment. The most distal factors that influence commitment are qualities of the organization, the person, socialization experiences, management practices, and environmental conditions. These impact on more proximal conditions, which include job and work experiences, role states, and the nature of the psychological contract.

These proximal influences in turn lead to certain processes. Affect-related processes, such as need satisfaction and attribution processes, might lead to high or low affective commitment. Norm-related processes, such as experiencing certain expectations and obligations, might lead to high or low normative commitment. Finally, cost-related processes, such as the extent to which the person has external alternatives or local investments, could affect the level of continuance commitment.

There are three major types of outcomes of commitment: retention (vs. withdrawal), productive behavior (attendance, strong performance, citizenship, and prosocial behavior), and employee well-being (psychological and physical health, career progress, etc.).

Meyer and Allen (1997) point out the value of considering the component of commitment that may be most influential when one is attempting to understand commitment-related behavior. For example, they note that research on affective commitment has shown the surprising finding that American workers are more committed than their Japanese counterparts, but Americans are more likely to switch jobs. Why? Quoting Near (1989), they suggest that Japanese workers stay in their jobs not because of strong affective attachments but, rather, out of a sense of obligation (normative commitment) and lack of available job opportunities (continuance commitment). Thus, to understand the complexities of commitment behavior, it is useful to have more fine-grained concepts for analyzing commitment attitudes.

If You Foster Psychological Success, Involvement, and Commitment, You Will Not Have a Burnout Problem

Although we have not discussed burnout explicitly, the good news is that if organizations take steps to provide employees with experiences that produce the kinds of attitudes that we just discussed—psychological success, involvement, commitment, and self-efficacy—there should not be a problem with burnout. Burnout happens when a person experiences frustration of his or her work goals over a prolonged period of time—in other words, when the conditions for psychological failure exist. As Maslach and Leiter (1997) have shown, burnout is not a problem rooted in the individual but, rather, it is a systemic problem whose roots lie in the organization.

Because the causes of burnout are in the organization, the solution does not lie in most of the current individually focused remedies, such as stress management programs, employee assistance programs, or better selection processes to find people who can handle stress. Rather, the key factors in combating burnout are those that we have already discussed as sources of success, self-efficacy, involvement, and commitment. We need to examine challenging job assignments and workload (so that work is challenging but not overwhelming), the amount of control and autonomy that the employee has over his or her work, and the rewards that are provided for a job well done. In the work context, it is important to have fairness in the administration of rewards, good supportive and development relationships and a sense of community, and a clear set of values with which the employee can identify.

One caveat should be raised, however: There can be hazards if growth is accelerated. The following is a case in point (Hall, 1999). Using the results of the previously cited research on the positive effects of early job challenge on success, Sears, Roebuck & Company implemented a system of constructing a careful progression of job assignments that would provide optimal "stretch." The result, they hoped, was that the company would be able to "grow" store managers faster than the 14 or 15 years that it had traditionally taken. As a result of using this pygmalion effect, Sears succeeded in promoting some people to the store manager role in 7 or 8 years. Thus ended a successful application of career research. The members of the team responsible for this new project wrote an article and declared victory (Wellbank, Hall, Morgan, & Hamner, 1978).

Harry Wellbank, who was Sears's head of training, took the logical next step and followed up on the later career experiences of these accelerated managers. What he found was troubling: Many had derailed, and many had left the company. At that time (in the 1980s), this was unheard of at Sears, a high-commitment company in which attaining a store manager role was a career-long ambition for most employees. As Wellbank dug deeper, he found the following causes of failure in the accelerated developers (Hall, 1999):

- They had not developed a personal network and a personal support system because they did not have time to do so during their rapid ascent.
- They had alienated people along the way, which further interfered with the development of a personal support system and network.
- They had not experienced any early, small failures or setbacks and had thus not developed resilience and hardiness.
- Because they had not had these setbacks, they had not had opportunities to build their skills related to identity (self-knowledge) and adaptability.

The lesson of this follow-up case is that we need to attend to the relational influences on career development. These relational influences include factors such as *interdependence* (the belief that people grow better in connection to others than independently), *mutuality* (approaching a relationship with the assumption that both parties will grow and benefit from it), and *reciprocity* (the expectation that both parties will have the skills and motivation to be both a teacher and a learner in the relationship). The role of these relational influences in the growth of career attitudes has been discussed by Fletcher (1996).

Research Issues Related to Career Attitudes

Here, we reflect on the material that we have just discussed and consider some of the issues that call for further research.

- There is more research on the antecedents of career attitudes than on their outcomes, beyond organizational outcomes such as retention. What about effects of career attitudes on personal outcomes such as life stress, work-home balance, and spouse and family happiness? How do the career attitudes of couples or of mixed-race or mixed-gender work groups interact and mutually affect the parties' personal outcomes?
- Can career attitudes feed back and affect career performance in some way? For example, what are the effects of career self-efficacy on career performance? Does self-efficacy lead to a more protean career or is causality in the opposite direction? Does self-efficacy contribute to being more protean or does it work in both directions in a spiral? We can theorize that there may be an upward spiral in which a certain base level of self-efficacy leads the person to take risks and then to achieve surprising results, which leads to greater feelings of self-efficacy—and the cycle continues. This idea has not been examined in terms of career behaviors over time, however.
- As the Sears study (Hall, 1999) suggests, we need more research on long-term effects of career experiences. How do career attitudes and experiences affect longer term personal outcomes (e.g., career identity, gender identity, ethnic identity, and the person's adaptability and ability to pursue a protean career)? One would think that satisfaction and pride in one's work and also feelings of meaning and purpose in work would have positive effects on a person's sense of identity and self-direction. In theory, this is how identity is formed and how it grows. What do the data indicate?
- Another critical issue is how people develop new or revised identities when they are going through an adaptation process. As Morrison and Hall (2001) found, one key issue in adaptation is whether or not the person has integrated the new behaviors into his or her conception of the self. If the person has changed but does not really value or accept that new behavior, viewing it instead as compliance with external demands ("it's not really me"), then that change may not last. What conditions increase the likelihood that new behaviors will also lead to new ways of perceiving and valuing the self so that the adaptation is internalized and stabilized?
- What more can be said about the cost-benefit issue? Is it worth addressing or are you lost before you start, if you focus on it? My view is that we need good work on both fronts. We need better measures of the costs involved in work-level interventions that affect career identity and attitudes as well as better measures of the benefits to the individual and to the employer. Also,

we need clearer theoretical and practical rationales, argued from a values perspective, in which central issue is, What is a life worth living? Thus, career identity and attitudes are important ends in themselves to be pursued for their own sake.

- How does leadership behavior affect career attitudes? Career attitudes could be an important micro-macro link here, connecting organizational leadership to individual motivation and performance. This link has always been an implicit part of leadership theories, which view leadership as the process of mobilizing others to want to strive for shared purposes (Kouzes & Posner, 1995). The question, then, is what do "mobilizing" and "striving" look like? How might we track the process by which some people dedicate their lives to a lofty purpose?

Conclusion

In the information economy, the rapid rate of change puts positive attitudes, identity growth, and adaptability at a premium. The good news is that all these personal qualities are developable—that is, they can be influenced by the individual and by the organization. Also, they tend to go together and to reinforce one another. As Staw and Barsade's (1993) research has shown, people with positive attitudes tend to make jobs into satisfying, developmental experiences; that is, they adapt effectively to frustrations in the work environment. Knowing oneself enables the person to choose wisely whether it is in line with their interests and values to make such adaptations or whether it is better to move on and select a new place to work. In turn, effective adaptation creates new skills and relationships, which in turn leads to a change in the person's self-identity. There's an old saying to the effect that all good things tend to go together (e.g., intelligence, achievement, health, status, and appearance). This is especially true with these metacompetencies for the protean career.

Note

1. This model is usually inaccurately attributed to Van Maanen and Schein rather than to the original source, Brim (1966), which is cited in Van Maanen and Schein (1979).

7   Career Adaptability

ROBERT F. MORRISON
AND DOUGLAS T. HALL

Like identity, adaptability is a long-term component of career effectiveness. Also like identity, adaptability is a high-order quality that we call a *metacompetency* (Hall, 1996b)—if you can master a metacompetency, it will give you the capacity to master many more specific skills. In contrast to identity, which deals primarily with the person, adaptability has more to do with the (changing) task. This is not a totally clear distinction, however, because people learn about themselves through task success, and people stretch their task capacities in part through changing themselves and the way in which they approach new tasks.

In this chapter, we distinguish between adaptability (which is the capacity to adapt or change) and adaptation (the action process involved in responding to a new situation). We define adaptability and adaptation as follows:

Adaptability is the predisposition and readiness to consciously and continuously

> scan and read external signals and develop or update a diverse set of role behaviors so that they maintain an effective response to constantly changing environmental requirements and influence the environment (response learning);
>
> strive for a more complete and accurate fund of knowledge about the self to develop the potential to modify or maintain one's identity (identity exploration);
>
> maintain congruence between one's personal identity and those behaviors that are timely and appropriate responses to the ever-changing demands of the environment (integrative potential); and
>
> be willing to develop adaptive competence and apply it to a given situation (adaptive motivation).

Adaptation is the process of (a) using insight and learning to maintain equilibrium between the personal identity (self) and an ever-changing being, (b) developing modified role behaviors so that they provide an effective response to constantly changing task and role demands, and (c) negotiating and maintaining an effective integration or balance between the persona and personal goals and the environment.

We realize that these are complicated definitions with multiple elements. We "build" these definitions as we review the theory and research on adaptability and adaptation.

Why Adaptability Is Critical to Contemporary Career Development

The Importance of Environmental Influences on Careers

In view of the current turbulent environmental change, there are serious questions about whether individuals are capable of continuously responding in a competent manner over a complete life span. In the employment setting, the global "New Economy" has resulted in restructuring, downsizing, rapid growth, new technologies, and worldwide operations that have left millions of workers lacking the skills necessary to support themselves. A traditional, stable career that is primarily within and controlled by the same organization is becoming increasingly less common, leading to the need to adapt to constant change in a career. The "new protean career" requires that employees function in an autonomous, proactive, and self-directed manner, recognizing where and when to develop the required new skills (Hall & Mirvis, 1996; Hall & Moss, 1998). Mission and role[1] changes require military officers to be very adaptive to changing tasks, technologies, and the world (Edwards & Morrison, 1994). So-called "boundaryless" organizations require concomitant permeability in the internal career systems of those organizations (Gunz, Evans, & Jalland, 2000).

In personal and private life, the complexity and rate of change in family and other social systems demand a level of adaptive skills that is "over the heads" of the majority of people (Kegan, 1994). The life span impact on individuals has been magnified because they are living so much longer that they need to learn to modify their lifestyles as they age to accommodate their declining physical and mental states (Baltes & Baltes, 1990). With an aging population, maintaining the employability and skills of older workers is a critical human resource issue not just for employers but also for the larger economy (Hall & Mirvis, 1996, 1998). Adaptability is a construct that aids us in moving from static models of behavior to dynamic ones.

Adding Adaptability to Career Choice and Decision Making

Chapter 3 presented several models of career choice and decision making. Now, we complicate the picture by adding the notion of adaptability and its correlates to the list of influences on a person's career choices once the career is under way. Specifically, we argue that when we examine career changes (such as changes in the person's duties, skills, field, occupation, or job function) (Latack, 1984), in addition to the predictive factors described in Chapter 4, we also need to examine environmental change and personal adaptability to help explain these changes (Grezda, 1999). This does not mean that the person-environment fit models or the decision process models described in Chapter 3 are less important when we are studying career change. In fact, when a person is making a major change, we argue that the change is usually in the direction of an improved fit. The question, however, is what enables the person to extract herself from one work situation and go through the difficulties of a major career transition for the sake of arriving at a better fit? We argue that adaptability is a key enabling factor (a metacompetency) in making such changes.

As noted previously, the other major metacompetency that enables major career decisions is identity, which was discussed in Chapter 6. If the person did not have the identity skills to enable a good, honest self-assessment of the quality of the current fit, he or she would be less likely to recognize the need to make a change. Thus, both identity skills and adaptability are instrumental to making major career changes.

The purpose of this chapter, then, is to explore the concept of adaptability. We examine primarily the level of the individual, not the group, organization, or society (although we recognize that these more macrolevels are where the forces for change usually originate). First, we argue that adaptability is not just a matter of ability or competence but that it also has a motivational component. That is, the person must be motivated to adapt and also be capable of adapting. Thus, adaptability is a function of adaptive competence and adaptive motivation.

Furthermore, we view adaptive competence as having three components—personal identity changes, behavioral responses, and integrative. We discuss the importance of all three aspects of this adaptive competence for an effective change process. This will complete our discussion of our general model of the nature of adaptability. Next, we discuss the factors that lead to adaptability and those influences that inhibit the adaptation process. Finally, we examine the consequences of adaptability.

To identify these facets of adaptability and its related concepts, we review both the empirical and the theoretical literature covering the entire life span and multiple societal roles because work and nonwork roles are closely and inextricably intertwined (Blustein, 1997). Our focus is on the individual in the work environment, however. In an attempt to further our overall understanding of this complex phenomenon, we present a comprehensive model of adaptability and some propositions for future testing.

Observing the Experience of Adaptability

The root of the word "adaptable" is "apt," meaning to learn or understand (Savickas, 1997). We are faced with the need to learn or understand when we are faced with a novel situation—one that requires us to change in some way. Adaptability helps a person deal with change.[2]

To help us understand adaptability, we consider a person at equilibrium. Our person, Chris, is successfully employed as a middle manager in a health care delivery organization (an HMO). Chris is also near the end of an educational program, an executive MBA (EMBA) program. Changes are happening here at many levels. At the macrolevel, the health care industry is in flux, with national health care still being debated, with expensive new technology and rising costs, and with an aging (i.e., expensive) client population to serve. At the organizational level, hospitals and HMOs are experiencing severe financial problems, with some going bankrupt. At the individual level, Chris, as part of the EMBA program, has gone through a process of intensive self-assessment and career review and is approaching a career decision point at the end of the graduate program: stay in the current organization or do something different.

In other words, Chris is in an *adaptation episode*, a period when the environment is shifting and a personal response is called for. What is required for Chris to make a good response? The following is the first issue to address: How do we define "a good response"? We argue that a good response is one that (a) involves an appropriate, reality-based reaction to the environmental changes and (b) serves Chris's long-term interests, values, and goals (i.e., fits with Chris's identity).

What does Chris do to arrive at a good decision? First, she becomes aware of the need for a personal decision and the need for change. Even if she stays in her current organization, she will have to change: With her new MBA degree, she will view herself and be viewed by others as a different person. She may be moved to a new assignment soon, her organization may be restructured or merged, she might get a new boss, and so on.

Second, she takes a long, hard look at herself with the aid of psychological instruments, 360-degree peer feedback, self-reflection, observations of her behavior, and other self-assessment activities. Not only does she get a clearer picture of who she is but also she learns the skills of learning about herself: asking for feedback, enlisting the support of others, reflection skills, behavioral observation skills, use of self-assessment tools, and so on.

Third, Chris examines her environment and obtains information on the demands and opportunities that are confronting her. What needs are emerging, what skills are in demand, where are the rewards, who and where are her sources of support, and so on?

Therefore, what does Chris do next? She combines the results of her identity learning and her assessment of the environment, and she develops a course of action that integrates the two. In her case, she realizes that she values achievement, action, teamwork with people she likes and respects, and entrepreneurship, and she sees many opportunities in the emerging world of electronic commerce. In her final step, she joins a "dot.com" health care delivery business that was started recently by four good friends of hers. A year later, she is happily ensconced in her new role with the startup firm and is performing at a high level. She has demonstrated her good adaptability via successful adaptation.

A General Model of Adaptability

Our general model will posit the following:

Adaptability = (adaptive competence) X (adaptive motivation)

That is, to adapt to a change in the environment, the person must be able and willing to change.[3] The person's competency for change could be extremely high, but if the motivation equals zero, then his or her adaptability is also zero. The same is true regarding competence: The person's motivation to change could be sky high, but if his or her competence for change is zero, then the adaptability is also zero. In discussing this model, we focus first on competence, and then we discuss motivation.

Three Components of Adaptive Competence

There are three general ways that adaptive competence has been defined in the literature. First, some writers define adaptive abilities in terms of dealing with external demands (Baltes & Baltes, 1990), especially those that are unique or stressful. A very general definition such as this needs more specification before it can be used in theory building, research, or application. Specifically, in this view, adaptability is seen as the behavioral effectiveness of the transactions between self and environment with "positive" adaptations maximizing gains over losses in functioning (Featherman, Smith, & Peterson, 1990). This perspective refers to the external manifestations of adaptability in the form of appropriate behavioral responses.

At the opposite pole, adaptability has been defined as an internal phenomenon, in which there is resilience, positivity, and flexibility in personal changes (Phillips, 1997). In this view, the stress is on the individual's clarity of personal direction and ability to stay on his or her own "path with a heart" (Shepard, 1984).

A third definition includes abilities in both the internal and external domains. In this perspective, adaptability entails "a generalized capacity to respond with resilience to challenges arising from one's body, mind, and environment" (Featherman et al., 1990, p. 53). Thus, the term adaptability should encompass both internal and external states and processes, not just one or the other. We consider each of these approaches to adaptive competence in turn.

Identity Exploration[4]

Piaget (Super & Knasel, 1981) introduced an early model of adaptation as a process by which the self develops through interchanges with the environment. His model was based on two processes, assimilation and accommodation. During assimilation, the individual impacts on the environment by assimilating some aspects of his or her environment into his or her already existing schemata. During accommodation, the individual is influenced by the environment and modifies his or her schemata to accommodate certain other aspects of his or her environment. In Piaget's model, the individual is a responsible agent acting within a dynamic environmental setting.

In the context of a protean career, Hall and colleagues postulate that a key to the constant adaptation required by such a career is "one's ability to reinvent oneself and one's career, to change one's personal identity, and to learn continuously throughout the career" (Hall, Briscoe, & Kram, 1997, p. 322). In this vein, adaptability is a "meta-skill" that enables people to incorporate new roles and responsibilities into their personal identities (Mirvis & Hall, 1994). These recent articles have built on Hall's early formulation (Hall, 1971) in which adaptation occurs at two levels, internal and external. At the internal level, individual adaptation takes place by the growth or modification of personal identity.

Because personal identity is composed of subidentities and each subidentity is linked to a specific social role (e.g., professional, parent, or spouse), the subidentity needs to change with each role transition or modification. The process of changing the subidentity may start before entering a new role if people begin to modify their personal identities by adopting attitudes, attributes, and self-perceptions consistent with those represented by the new role (Hall, 1976).

Block and Kremen (1996) propose a third approach to adaptability that centers on the internal level. They characterize human adaptability using a theoretical approach based in psychological abstractions. Their characterizations include ego strength, emotional stability, coping, competence, self-efficacy, hardiness, and self-regulation, with ego resiliency an analog for adaptability: "The linkages of the ego structures that keep the personality system within tenable bounds or permit the finding again of psychologically tenable adaptational modes are what is meant by the construct of ego resiliency" (pp. 350-351). Consistent with this approach is the idea that change may not be the culprit that produces problems. It may be the individual's ability to adapt to change (i.e., to cope). The key to minimizing the harmful effects of change appears to be resiliency—that is, the ability to bounce back and effectively deal with (adapt to) the effects of change. Too rapid change produces stress—that is, the inability to adjust and to bounce back at a commensurate pace (Buffington, 1992). Although ego resiliency is an interesting construct and adaptation to internal capacity constraints is imperfect but important (Cohen, 1993), ego resiliency alone is incomplete because it considers only internal events, omitting external events that are also included in adaptation (Goodman, 1994).

Featherman and colleagues (1990) developed a three-dimensional model of adaptability. Two of these dimensions are internal and are composed of strategies and skills used in (a) emotional coping in response to stressors and (b) problem solving (cognition manifesting itself in problem-solving heuristics). In their paradigm, adaptability is an expert knowledge system about one's functioning in the world and about the nature of tasks that must be performed effectively. Adaptive persons change between rational problem-solving and reflective planning cognitive styles in response to the situation, using the latter as their primary approach.

Vaillant (1977, 1993, 2002) presents a narrow depiction of adaptability but emphasizes an important factor. Vaillant's research has its cornerstone in the Grant study, a longitudinal project that was started at Harvard University in 1939 and continues today. The funding (and hence the name) came from 5-and-10-cent store founder W. T. Grant, and the sample started with 268 members of the Harvard classes of 1941 through 1944, who signed up for a lifelong study of "normal" adult development. Vaillant's 1977 book, *Adaptation to Life*, was based on his interviews with the participants at their 25th class reunion.

Vaillant's latest book, *Aging Well* (2002), represents a "final report" on the Grant Study. It also adds data from two other longitudinal studies, one of inner-city men in Boston and the other of California women selected for unusually high intelligence. (Presumably, this would give the overall trends greater generalizability, with more diversity in the sample.) In this work, he assessed their overall mental and physical health and sorted his sample into four groups: "happy and well," "happy and sick," "sad and well," and "sad and sick." Vaillant found that six factors assessed by age 50 were "excellent predictors of those who would be in the 'happy-well' group ... at age 80: a stable marriage, a mature adaptive style, no smoking, little use of alcohol, regular exercise, and maintenance of normal weight" (Lambert, 2001, p. 46).

The following is Vaillant's (1977) view of adaptation:

Health is adaptation. ... If you have not the strength to accept the terms life offers you, you must, in self-defense, force your own terms on it. If either you or your environment is distorted too much in the process, your effort at adaptation may be labeled mental illness. (p. 13)

In his later work (Vaillant, 2002), he relates this positive coping approach to emotional intelligence (Goleman, 1995, 1998). Lambert (2001) noted,

"Being old, healthy, and without friends is not fun," writes Vaillant. Socially isolated men died at younger ages. A mature coping style strengthens relationships because being able to handle the emotional issues gracefully removes barriers between people. Advancing age impairs some motor skills, but maturation can make people sharper at *emotional* tasks. "What test could you have given these men at age 30 that would predict significantly improved life outcomes in their later years?" asks Vaillant. Borrowing a phrase from author Daniel Goleman, he answers his own question: "It would be a test of emotional intelligence." (p. 47)

"Adaptation" and "defense" are used interchangeably. Lives change, and the course of life is filled with discontinuities. The key ingredient that Vaillant adds to our understanding of adaptability is its dynamic nature over time because he believes that what is adaptive at one time may be mental illness later. Vaillant observes that human development continues throughout life, and truth can be discovered only longitudinally. Vaillant (1977, 1993) studies adaptive mechanisms to make sense of psychopathology.

What do we know about individuals who display high levels of identity exploration? A summary of relevant research shows the following behavioral manifestations of this component of adaptive competence:

- Self-assessment: self-initiating, self-correcting, and self-evaluating; seeking, hearing, and acting on personal feedback; open to criticism
- Stabilized values, ego resiliency, and moods; broadly ranging interests; exploring, communicating, and acting on personal values
- Sense of mastery within a wide range of life domains; autonomous functioning
- Accepting and integrating varied perspectives
- Perceptive and insightful
- Symbolizing personal experience and environments
- Positive and energetic approach to life
- High quality of one's memory and cognition and of one's ability to cope with stressful events

Response Learning

In the second perspective, adaptability has been seen in terms of facile behavior, the predisposition to learn and change performance in a manner consistent with significant changes in environmental requirements related to one's multiple roles (Morrison, 1977). Such a definition is consistent with Hall's (1976) second level of adaptation, in which adaptive behavior is demonstrated via performance. Although such definitions include effective performance and social competence (Featherman et al., 1990) and also role flexibility (Murphy & Jackson, 1999), they are incomplete.

A complete definition needs to consider changes in the total environment (Mumford, Baughman, Threfall, Uhlman, & Costanza, 1993), a complete constellation of occupational and nonoccupational roles (life space), and how the emphasis among different roles in the set changes over a lifetime (life span) (Morrison, 1974; Phillips, 1997). In this context, individuals constantly move among diverse sets of roles and related role expectations, modifying responses to the demands of each with varying degrees of ease. Response learning is expressed by the effectiveness of the transactions between the self and a dynamic environmental setting, with the person acting as a responsible agent who maximizes gains over losses in functioning (Featherman et al., 1990; Super & Knasel, 1981). Response learning becomes most apparent when unpredictable social or technological change occurs in both work and nonwork roles. The dynamic nature of adaptability is reflected in the tendencies within our species to create novel experience and to be proactive, not just reactive.

In most theoretical approaches to adaptability, the assumption is made that only the environment influences the individual, who must respond by changing. Adaptability should not imply that change is only a one-way proposition, however. As Piaget proposed, individuals influence and change their environments (assimilation) as well as change themselves (accommodation) (Goodman, 1994; Super & Knasel, 1981). Some common examples of individuals changing their environments include employee turnover, divorce, and early retirement.

Others approach the learning component of adaptive competence differently by including cognition as a core element—that is, learning is not just behavioral but also cognitive. Featherman and colleagues (1990) posit that an expert knowledge system (expertise) about one's functioning in the world and about the nature of tasks that must be performed effectively in a role is a major part of adaptability. Smith, Ford, and Kozlowski (1997) also focus on expertise so that the adaptive individual is capable of modifying previously learned methods and using existing knowledge to generate new approaches. Hesketh and Neal (1999) combine cognition and affect in specifying learning, self-confidence, and coping ability as keys to approaching new tasks.

Cognition is a primary component of Super and Knasel's (1979) model of "career adaptability" in which both analytical skills and knowledge are emphasized. The analytical skills are brought into their model via the inclusion of three factors. One factor requiring analytical ability is planfulness, the ability to identify tasks that need to be accomplished in the near or more distant future and the tendency to cope with them. Analytical skill is essential to their second factor, exploration and establishment, involving the consideration of a range of possibilities, examination of some of them in-depth, and the desire and effort to become established in one of these. Analytical skill is also needed in their third factor, reflection on experience, consisting of an awareness of and tendency to analyze one's experiences. Knowledge is brought out by two factors. One knowledge factor is information, which includes knowledge of the world of work in general and of the relevant field(s) in particular. The other knowledge factor is decision making, requiring knowledge of the principles of career decision making and the ability to apply them. Knasel (1982) proposes that decision readiness is an indication of adaptive competence in individuals allowing them to interact proactively and effectively with the environment via assimilation and accommodation.

In summary, the literature provides the following behavioral profile of individuals who show adaptive competence in the area of response learning:

- Flexibility; openness to new and diverse ideas and people; responding differentially to a varying environment—for example, modifying a personal leadership style so that it remains consistent with the requirements of the varying cultures of different work groups or communicating differently in concert with each different work group's capability
- Engaging in and acting out the results of personal development activity
- Planning activities
- Maintaining overall and effective task performance in both well- and ill-defined situations and during turbulent change
- Seeking new challenges in unexplored territory; exploration; seeking learning opportunities
- The absence of disciplinary problems
- Congruent developmental and chronological ages
- Interpersonal skills and social poise
- Using a variety of strategies during problem solving—for example, adaptive decision making involving the use of intuitive, consultative (imitative), and emotionally expressive as well as rational strategies; another possible way of describing this is "responding effectively to changing environmental demands; for example, using a simplistic decision style or making quick decisions under time constraints and taking more time or using a more complex decision style when more time is available"
- Performing effectively during an extended period of time in a variety of roles representing contrasting aptitudes, values, interests, and behaviors—for example, (a) a special forces officer at work versus at home as a family member (spouse, parent, sibling, or child) or performing well on both traditionally masculine and feminine tasks or (b) changing performance consistent with changes in performance requirements in more than one of six managerial roles (technical or professional, interpersonal, formal organization, political, boundary, and personal)
- Revising norms and expectations as a response to the environment rather than ignoring pressure from the environment to change them and appearing to accept and enforce current rules of behavior; learning from mistakes

Integrative Potential

The personal and behavioral elements of adaptive competence are not complete in themselves. They are separate entities without any cohesion. Identity exploration without action is simply "navel-gazing." Also, response learning that is not linked to one's values and path with a heart is blind reaction. Savickas (1997) postulates that to engage in the process of adaptation, people must be willing and able to develop and maintain congruence between the self and its fit among many life roles when the environment requires constant change in those roles. For adaptation to be a meaningful way of promoting the development of the individual, there is also a third necessary process, one that integrates personal identity and new learned behavior and produces action. It is this integration component with its increased congruence that is necessary to enable the adapter to develop the self toward greater wholeness and engagement in the world.

Block and Kremen (1996) introduce the notion of integration by stating that "individuals vary widely in their effectiveness of adaptation, in their ability to equilibrate and reequilibrate in response to their ever-changing being and their ever-changing world" (p. 349). Savickas (1997) takes it a step further by proposing that people adapt to better implement their self-concepts in situations. By increasing the congruence between themselves and the roles in which they are engaged, they develop toward greater wholeness and engagement in the world and, concurrently, becoming the people they want to be.

A foundation for balancing identity exploration and response learning is provided in Super and Knasel's (1979) model of what they call "career adaptability." Their anchor consists of work salience and work values, representing the importance ascribed to having a working career and the values sought in it. This basis can be applied more broadly by substituting "role" for "work" and renaming their anchor role salience and role values, representing the importance ascribed to performing a role and the values sought in it. Their factor of autonomy, comprising the sense of agency, individuality, and control over one's own life and career, provides the mechanism for balancing the persona and the external demands. Without integrative potential, the person could be very self-aware and very attuned to the shifts in the signals from the environment—and stagnant if all the previously described factors do not produce action.

Even with both identity exploration and response learning combined via integrative potential, this could result in an individual who is capable of adapting but has not actually adapted. Integration must lead to action and change for the person to be truly adaptable. As a result, it is more accurate to apply the term adaptive competence rather than adaptability to the aggregate of the three factors described previously.

Synthesis: The Three Components of Adaptive Competence

Rather than debate which of these three perspectives is most valid as a way of understanding adaptive competence, if we consider our earlier discussion of Chris's changes, we can argue that, in fact, all three are necessary components in a general capability for a self-directed adaptive change process. One part of adaptive competence is internal to the individual—one's self-knowledge and the ability to learn about one's self, to increase one's self-awareness. We define this internal component of adaptive competence, identity exploration, as follows:

Identity exploration is the continual striving for a more complete and accurate fund of knowledge about the self to develop the potential to modify or maintain one's identity.

Thus, identity exploration is the first step in a process of psychological development in which the person's awareness of the self becomes more varied and more complex, and the person's ability to learn about the self (e.g., through feedback seeking, greater openness to feedback, reflective observation, and learning from experience) increases. This evolution of identity takes place through a progressive series of stages, which are driven by successive interchanges between the self and the external environment (Kegan, 1982, 1994; Levinson, 1986).

The second component of adaptive competence is the ability to reflect accurately on one's own behavior, to scan and read the environment, to sense when behavioral changes are needed, to learn new behaviors, and to be able to apply those behaviors appropriately in a timely fashion. We define this second component of adaptive competence as follows:

Response learning is the conscious predisposition to continuously scan and read external signals and to develop or update a diverse set of role behaviors so that they maintain an effective response to constantly changing environmental requirements and influence the environment.

The third important quality is the ability to integrate the first two—that is, to react to one's changing environment in a way that fits with one's identity. Thus, the actual personal changes must be true to one's self and true to the realities of the environment. This is what produces the whole person who is competent to adapt.

Thus, putting it all together, we define integrative potential as follows:

Integrative potential is the ability to continuously maintain congruence between one's personal identity and those behaviors that are timely and appropriate responses to the ever-changing demands of the environment.

In summary, we have the following "formula" for adaptive competence:

Adaptive competence = identity exploration + response learning + integrative potential

Adaptive Motivation

As mentioned previously, the adaptable individual must add adaptive motivation to adaptive competence to be considered high in adaptability. The need or motivation to adapt has many causes. Hall (Goodman, 1994) summarized these issues very well when he proposed that triggers in the organization or society, roles, and person lead, with the right support and circumstances, to an awareness of choices, renewed exploration, subidentity transition, a new establishment, increased adaptability, and a heightened sense of self. We define adaptive motivation as follows:

Adaptive motivation is the willingness to develop and apply adaptive competence to a given situation.

Examples of environmentally driven (society, organization, role, etc.) causes are the incidence of novel and ill-defined problems (Pulakos, Arad, Donovan, & Plamondon, 1999), new people and teams (Murphy & Jackson, 1999; Pulakos et al., 2000), different cultures (McCall,

1998; Pulakos et al., 2000), challenging physical conditions (Pulakos et al., 2000), contingent work (Murphy & Jackson, 1999), use of technology (Murphy & Jackson, 1999; Pulakos et al., 2000), life role changes (Morrison, 1974), and individual mental or physiological change (Wilson, 1991). In one example of transition from one culture to another (Haddad & Lam, 1988), the majority of immigrant husbands who had both working spouses and preschool children continued to perform their traditional, old-country roles and shared part of their wives' roles. The one third who did a limited amount of domestic chores reported limited choice due to "situational constraints," whereas the remaining 12% did not adapt.

Although we usually anticipate that adaptation will take place in response to an external stimulus, the need to adapt can be internally motivated. Adaptability (Featherman et al., 1990) represents tendencies within our species to actively seek stimulation, to create novel experience, and to be proactive, not just reactive. Adaptability involves a lifelong capacity for motivated self-expansion and expression grounded in collective cultural experience but also seeks uniqueness within it, the "competent self." In other instances, the fear of change or lack of self-esteem reduce the individual's adaptability. In both cases, we expect the individual's adaptability to influence his or her motivation to adapt.

From the opposite viewpoint, individuals who lack adaptability also show a certain profile of behaviors (McCall, 1998). First, there is a failure to learn and develop as the surrounding context changes. Prior strengths become weaknesses. Second, the person shows arrogance because she does not know what she does not know. Third, preexisting flaws develop into full-scale weaknesses as the person is exposed to novel environmental demands and is found wanting.

Now that we have described the ingredients in the person's capacity to change (adaptability), the important question is how does this ability translate into actual adaptive behavior? This takes us from the realm of adaptability to adaptation.

Adaptation: The Process of Adapting

If adaptability is the potential and preparedness for dealing with a variety of demands, then we need a separate construct for putting it into action because adaptability is not always perfectly translated into action. Adaptation is the attempt to actively resolve apparent contradictions from one's experience into a more encompássing, adequate structure or synthesis (Kramer, 1986) and is a process term, not a trait or state like adaptability. In one view (Featherman et al., 1990), revisionist psychologists have redirected the study of human intelligence to include adaptational processes in broadly encompassing terms. Examples are accommodating reactions to limiting conditions, active manipulation of constraints and opportunities within a setting, and purposive exits from unfavorable environments for more optimal ones. Another viewpoint (Cohen, 1993) focuses on adaptation to the application of knowledge, to dynamic and rich task environments, and to the performance of a decision strategy across the spectrum of tasks in a domain. Both concentrate on behavioral responses to the need for change.

As with adaptability, this is an incomplete picture of the adaptation process because adaptation must take place intrinsically and extrinsically. Internally, personal adaptation is the process by which individuals improve or maintain acceptable implementations of their self-concepts in situations (Savickas, 1997). That is, effective long-term adaptation requires that change occur not only in the person's behavior but also in the individual's sense of self or identity. Thus, for complete adaptation, individuals need to develop congruence in the fit between their identities and their roles while simultaneously moving toward becoming the persons they want to be.

Early propositions stated that the process of adaptation occurred in fixed stages that were chronologically keyed (Hall, 1971, 1976). It has become apparent, however, that the process must occur continuously (Hall et al., 1997; Morrison, 1974).

The Identity Adaptation Process

A traditional definition of adaptation is for the individual to make the self or identity more suitable (congruent) by changing—flexibility in responding to the environment (Savickas, 1997). This interpretation gives purpose to change because it emphasizes congruence. This conceptualization is incomplete, however, because the influence goes only one way—that is, the environment affects the individual. A previously introduced, more appropriate model that is applicable to internal adaptation is Piaget's, with its basis in the two processes of assimilation and accommodation (Super & Knasel, 1981). In accommodation, the individual modifies his or her schemata to reconcile it with certain aspects of his or her environment; thus, the environment impacts on him or her.

Vaillant (1977) amplifies Piaget's ideas by taking them one step further. As stated previously, if you cannot accept what life offers you, you must, in self-defense, force your terms on it. Any extremes in such adaptation may be labeled mental illness (Vaillant, 1977). Vaillant emphasizes the dynamism of life by noting that what is adaptive at one time may be mental illness later.

Defining Identity Adaptation

Using the preceding models of personal adaptation, we propose the first of three elements in a definition of adaptation. Identity adaptation involves consciously and continually using insight and learning to achieve equilibrium between the personal identity (self) at any point in time and an ever-changing being throughout life.

Indicators of Adaptation Within the Individual (i.e., Identity Development)

Based on the relevant literature, the following behaviors represent a profile of an individual who has demonstrated adaptation in the area of identity growth:

- Purposeful and accurate self-assessment accompanied by self-correcting activity; obtaining and performing in accordance with personal feedback
- Increased stabilization of values, ego resiliency, and moods; an increased range of interests; sense of mastery within a wide range of life domains
- Autonomous, competent functioning; engaging in and acting out the results of personal development activity
- Accepting and integrating varied perspectives
- Perceptive and insightful
- Symbolizing personal experience and environments
- Positive and energetic approach to life
- Assimilating appropriate aspects of the changing task and environment into the already existing schema while concurrently modifying the schemata to accommodate other, appropriate aspects of the environment
- Dialectic reasoning, which represents a high degree of adaptation to the social world
- High quality of one's memory and cognition and ability to cope with stressful events

The Behavioral Adaptation Process

Behavioral adaptation is the process by which individuals learn, negotiate, enact, and maintain the behaviors appropriate to a given environment. Ashford and Taylor (1990) noted that "'appropriate' indicates some degree of fit between the behaviors demanded by the environment and those produced by the individual such that the individual is able to achieve valued goals" (p. 4). Adaptation is expressed by behaviors demonstrating flexibility, openness to new and diverse people and ideas, exploration, dialogue skills, eagerness to accept new challenges in unexplored territory, and comfort with turbulent change (Briscoe & Hall, 1999). In many situations, behaviors will reflect adaptation to the current dynamic situation during its changes. A common example involves systems in which people work in teams that have short lives. Moving frequently from one team to another places a premium on the individual's ability to be rapidly and effectively assimilated into different teams (Hollenbeck, LePine, & Ilgen, 1996). The diversity and breadth of behaviors that are required during adaptation have been demonstrated in several studies. For example, individuals need to perform well on both masculine and feminine tasks to adapt effectively (Orlofsky & Windle, 1978).

One description of adaptation is provided by Schneider (1999), who states, "by adaptation, I mean the acts of coping and adjusting" (p. 350). His definition, however, does not fully articulate the complexity of adaptation. The complexity of the phenomenon is introduced by Kramer (1986) when he posits that "dialectic reasoning would represent a high degree of adaptation to the social world, providing a more coherent and integrated structure by which multiple perspectives and changing cultural/historical contexts can be coordinated into an encompassing framework" (p. 286). The diverse skills required in adaptation are demonstrated in decision making that involves using many decisional strategies (Phillips, 1997). During adaptation, decision making should include intuitive, consultative (imitator), and emotionally expressive strategies as well as rational strategies.

A key ingredient in the adaptation process is learning (Savickas, 1997), especially learning from experience (McCall, 1998; Morrison, 1996). Experience-based learning emphasizes seeking opportunities to learn, learning from mistakes, being open to criticism, seeking and using feedback, and seeking broad knowledge of the environment. Such behaviors allow the individual to adapt to cultural differences and a wide variety of role changes. Failure to learn and develop as the surrounding context changes results in nonadaptation so that prior strengths become weaknesses and preexisting flaws become important under changing conditions.

Defining the Behavioral Adaptation Process

Using the preceding models of behavioral adaptation, we propose the next contribution to the definition of adaptation. This second element consists of consciously and continually developing and performing a diverse set of role behaviors and modifying the environment so that an effective response to constantly changing task and role demands is provided.

Behavioral Indicants of Adaptation by the Individual

The following profile of the individual who has shown behavioral adaptation emerges from the literature:

- Planning activities
- Performing effectively over an extended period of time in a variety of roles representing contrasting aptitudes, values, interests, and behaviors
- Responding differentially to a varying environment; openness to new and diverse ideas and people
- Revising norms and expectations as a response to the environment; learning from mistakes
- Maintaining overall and effective task performance in both well- and ill-defined situations; coping with stress
- Using a variety of strategies during problem solving
- Exploration; seeking new challenges in unexplored territory; seeking learning opportunities
- Congruent developmental and chronological ages
- Interpersonal skills and social poise
- The absence of disciplinary problems

The Integrative Adaptation Process

Integrative adaptation has been described by Block and Kremen (1996), who state that "individuals vary widely in their effectiveness of adaptation, in their ability to equilibrate and reequilibrate in response to their ever-changing being and their ever-changing world" (p. 349). Savickas (1997) proposes that change is given purpose when the adaptation process includes developing congruence between the self and the environment. Adaptation allows the individual to better implement his or her self-concepts in situations, with increased congruence developing the self toward greater wholeness and engagement in the world. Causation (Hall, 1976) is represented by a sequence in which behavioral adaptation results in the psychological success that leads to personal adaptation. This causal sequence indicates that both levels of adaptation must be congruent with each other to be effective.

Defining the Integrative Adaptation Process

Using the preceding models that describe the need for integrating the individual and the environment, we propose the final contribution to the definition of adaptation. Integrative adaptation is consciously and continually negotiating and maintaining an effective balance between the persona and personal goals and the environment.

Adaptation Defined

In summary, we define adaptation as follows:

Adaptation is the process of (a) using insight and learning to maintain equilibrium between the personal identity (self) and an ever-changing being, (b) developing modified role behaviors so that they provide an effective response to constantly changing task and role demands, and (c) negotiating and maintaining an effective integration or balance between the persona and personal goals and the environment.

Summary of Adaptability and Adaptation

Here, we recap the distinction between adaptability and adaptation.

The Definition of Adaptability

Adaptability consists of three facets—identity exploration, response learning, and integrative potential. In the aggregate, adaptability is the predisposition or propensity to consciously and continually (a) maintain identity equilibrium between the self and an ever-changing being throughout life (b) update and perform a diverse set of role behaviors and influence the environment so that an effective behavioral response to constantly changing environmental requirements is achievable and compatible with personally desired role behaviors, and (c) maintain an effective integration or balance between the ever-changing being that the individual desires to be and environmental demands.

The Definition of Adaptation

Adaptation consists of the same three facets comprising adaptability—that is, identity, behavioral, and integrative. In the aggregate, adaptation is the process of consciously and continually (a) using insight and learning to achieve equilibrium between the personal identity (self) at any point in time and an ever-changing being throughout life, (b) developing and performing a diverse set of new role behaviors and modifying the environment so that an effective response to constantly changing task and role demands is provided, and (c) negotiating and maintaining an effective balance between the persona and personal goals and the environment.

An Integrated Model of Adaptability

Based on this research, our proposed model includes an array of cognitive and noncognitive individual differences that influence the individual's actual and perceived adaptive competence. Different sets of individual differences affect identity exploration and response learning. There is a reciprocal relationship between adaptive competence and adaptive motivation. Both adaptive competence and adaptive motivation comprise the construct of adaptability, whereas demographics moderate their impact on adaptability. Adaptive motivation is directly affected by environmental factors. Adaptability directly influences adaptation, with that relationship moderated by a set of contextual factors.

Adaptation affects future adaptability and produces outcomes that vary in concert with the level of adaptation achieved. The relationship between these concepts is illustrated in Figure 7.1.

Applying These Ideas: Maintaining Adaptability

What are some of the action implications of these ideas about adaptability? Faced with areas of strength and threat, the individual (or the organization) has two courses of action available to maintain adaptability.

Correcting Weaknesses Versus Using Strengths

One approach is to correct the person's weakness and help her become updated technically through continuing education seminars, job rotation into work that demands technical learning, independent study, and so forth. A second alternative is to play to her strengths by further improving relational and strategic, integrative skills (Fletcher, 1999). We assume here that she is, in fact, relatively skillful interpersonally; this seems reasonable because with experience, the person acquires what Levinson (1996) calls "wisdom" and certain political skills, which are largely social and essential to survival in most complex organizations.

Colearning

There is another way to use the relational strategy to accomplish multiple objectives: developing subordinates and bridging the "generation gap" in the organization. This involves working with new, young employees in a coaching capacity. In this way, the older employee can impart to the newcomer her wisdom, political skills, and the ability to "sell" her ideas while learning the latest technical concepts and methods from the new member, who is relatively current technically. By working as a team, the older person combines the complementary strengths of both people and helps them both overcome their weaknesses. Each person can feel confirmed and successful. A win-lose situation has been converted to win-win. This strategy is what Kram and Hall (1996a) termed "colearning."

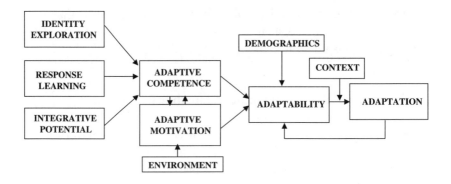

Figure 7.1. The Components of Adaptability and Adaptation

Selection and Placement

Another way of tapping the benefits of age is to place the older person into a job that places a premium on the overall perspective and wisdom he has acquired. Middle age is not a period of hot creativity and insight but of cool reflection and integration, making the person skillful in activities such as long-range planning and adaptation.

At this point in time, the middle-aged manager ideally should be exercising a different kind of leadership and dealing with different organization problems. In middle age, the stage Erik Erikson called "the period of generativity," Harry Levinson (1969) advocates a switch in role and self-identity from "player" to "coach":

> If he opts for wisdom, he becomes an organizational resource for the development of others. His wisdom and judgment gives body to the creative efforts to younger [people]. . . . He shifts from quarterback to coach, from day-to-day operations to long-range planning. He becomes more consciously concerned with what he is going to leave behind. (pp. 59-60)

Because personal qualities such as intrinsic motivation seem to distinguish adapters from nonadapters, an effective way for organizations to combat obsolescence is through effective techniques of selection and placement. Good selection ordinarily consists of a job analysis and identification of the personal attributes necessary for success. In using selection methods for adaptability, the organization would take the additional step of a strategic job analysis (Schneider & Konz, 1989). Here, the focus would be on the future job requirements, especially those that are likely to change the most, and on the personal attributes that will be needed for today's employee to be successful tomorrow. In contrast, most organizations select people for today's jobs and then wonder why their employees are not suited for tomorrow's jobs (Briscoe & Hall, 1999; Seibert, Hall, & Kram, 1995).

Other personnel practices that are helpful in dealing with obsolescence are midcareer assessment centers, career counseling, and more flexible retirement policies (early or late, depending on the person's ability). For example, in an early experience of downsizing, Alcan was forced to terminate (i.e., fire) many of its managers to help meet a budget crisis (Cuddihy, 1974). After the people who were to be fired were notified of the decision, the company put them through a program of assessment, counseling, and coaching in the skills of job hunting. The reason these managers had to be fired in the first place was that they were not essential in their current jobs and were not adaptive enough to be used in other, necessary jobs. The company obviously was partially responsible for this situation and intended to continue using these selection and development methods for all employees following the firings. In this way, maintaining employee adaptability can become a standard personnel function that should eliminate the need for future "prunings" if done well. This Alcan program was a precursor of a much more widespread use of self-assessment and career development as part of a well-managed corporate downsizing process, which became more widely practiced in the 1980s and 1990s (Hall & Associates, 1996; Latack, 1990).

Factors in the job and organization climate help maintain adaptability (Kaufman, 1974; McCall, 1998; Pelz & Andrews, 1966). Specifically, early in-depth exposure during a 3- or 4-year period to all areas of one project (i.e., early job challenge) is important. An experienced, older colleague acting as a coach or mentor is also helpful. It is also critical to reward the person for good performance (with recognition, pay raises, and good assignments) in the first 10 years. Then, in her thirties the person should be pushed into a new project in a new area so that she cannot "rest on her laurels." Also, she should be given increased independence from her supervisor or coach.

Selection is a strategy that can also be employed by the individual and the organization. Selection along with optimization and compensation, as three strategies available to older workers to adapt to the work content and context, were studied by Abraham and Hansson (1995). In their research with 224 working adults, they defined these strategies as follows:

> *Selection* is a set of strategies that persons might use to narrow the focus of their jobs—do only important tasks, delegate to others, etc.
>
> *Optimization* consists of a set of strategies that persons might use to maximize their performance in their more critical areas of job responsibility—polish and update their critical skills and knowledge.
>
> *Compensation* strategies use the knowledge-based pragmatics (the culturally based knowledge systems developed over the life span) and technology (eyeglasses, hearing aids, etc.) to minimize the impact of functional losses.

The study found that males (who tended to hold higher-status positions) used selection more than females, whereas females (who tended to hold lower-status positions) used optimization and compensation more. Only optimization contributed to the maintenance of ability and performance, whereas selection and optimization contributed to goal attainment. We do not know what specifically activates these strategies. The relationships were low, possibly because most individuals' job requirements were not sufficiently taxing to have them reach the limits of their reserve capacity (Abraham & Hansson, 1995).

Questions for Future Research

As we consider the vast literature on career adaptability, there are several critical questions that future research might usefully investigate:

- How and when do people learn to adapt to change in a career marked by several learning cycles? Earlier chapters presented the idea that in addition to longer adult development stages in the career, there are shorter (on the order of 5 years) learning cycles that characterize career growth. What triggers the initiation of exploration activity that gets a person moving from one realm of career activity to another? Are certain people more prone to change than others? How much impact do changes in technology and markets have?

  As Grezda (1999) pointed out, although many investigators (DeFillippi & Arthur, 1993; Latack, 1990; Weick & Berlinger, 1989) noted the dramatic environmental changes that were taking place in the 1990s, there was very little empirical research on their effects and on how people adapted. These changes are ongoing, and they represent great opportunities for study as natural field experiments. Time series designs would be useful for tracking longitudinal effects. In-depth case studies could help test change models such as the one presented here. Cross-lagged correlational designs would be useful for testing specific causal hypotheses about the predictors and consequences of adaptability. Examples of good qualitative data on the experience of making significant career changes as a result of environmental changes can be found in Noer's (1993) study of the broken psychological contract; Hall and Moss's (1998) study of companies whose career contracts changed; and Arthur, Inkson, and Pringle's (1999) study of career changers in New Zealand.

- To what extent is adaptability a function of personality or age and state versus a skill and outlook that can be developed? From the literature, it appears that the answer is that it is both. There is a need for careful research that would measure a combination of key person variables and key situational variables, however, so that we might quantify the relative contributions of each set of variables to the variance in adaptability motivation and behavior. Although this question always seems to be "lurking" in the literature, it has not been addressed directly.

- What can organizations (and society) do to help people adapt? What specific kinds of training and developmental assignments work best to generate adaptive motivation and adaptive competence? It could be illuminating to search for differences in the developability of these two components of adaptability. Is it easier to change adaptive motivation through activities such as self-efficacy training? Is it easier to put people into assignments that demand change, where adaptive behavior in a sense is forced? We need to develop a typology of strategies for adaptability, and we need systematic research on the effectiveness of these strategies.

- What kind of firm should emphasize and develop adaptability in its people and what kind should acquire talent outside? Mirvis and Hall (1994) raised this question as an alternative to the old familiar "buy versus make" debate (i.e., should you grow your own talent or hire it from the outside?). Again, this may be more of a both-and issue rather than an either-or. A given organization might do both. Some organizations might be better suited to leaning more in the grow-your-own direction, whereas others might do better with more external hiring. We need more research that would help an organization decide which approach is best for them at that point in time, however.

- How do people acquire complex, adaptive, and stable behaviors? Developmental change must be studied using a dynamic, longitudinal tracking procedure because acquiring behavior is an interaction among learning opportunity and physiological readiness (Thelen, 1992). Although much has been written about the fact that careers are now protean and boundaryless for many people, there has been very little empirical work on exactly how people change from traditional careerists to being protean. Careful documentation of this change process would be extremely valuable.

- How can our knowledge about adaptation be applied specifically to the careers of older workers? The issue of the older worker has been with us for ages, but it seems that we periodically have to "rediscover" it. Vaillant's data from the Grant Study show that positive and relational adaptation strategies are positively related to health and longevity and, by implication, to career longevity as well. More research on the separate components of adaptability and adaptation in older workers (e.g., adaptive competence, adaptive motivation, and integrative competence) would be helpful so that we can determine which facets of the adaptive process are most critical. Also, to what extent can the components of the adaptive process be learned later in life? Vaillant states that positive adaptive skills lead to good later-life outcomes, but are these adaptive qualities pretty well "set" in the older person or can they be developed with education, training, coaching, and social support? My hunch, based on our work on self-confidence (Hollenbeck & Hall, 2001), is that there is more potential for development here than the age stereotypes would have us believe.

- In turn, we should examine in depth the career experiences of older workers to shed more light on our basic theoretical understanding of the adaptive process. Older workers, in contrast to the stereotype, are hitting obstacles and novel situations (internal and external) all the time, and they are often forced to become "experts" on adaptation. As the saying goes, old age is not for sissies. Thus, as Vaillant's research suggests, healthy and happy older workers can provide new understandings about successful adaptation.

- A particular type of older worker adaptation that we need to understand better is the experience and success of senior leaders. In particular, technologies need to be developed (and studied) to identify potential senior leaders who are adaptable. We need to develop methods for forecasting changes in future leaders' roles (Edwards & Morrison, 1994). Although there is no validated measure that can be used to assess adaptability directly (Rothstein, 1999), promising tools to measure qualities such as "learning agility" have been created. Examples include such instruments as Lominger's Choices and the Center for Creative Leadership's Learning Tactics Inventory (Hoehn, 2000). These tools are being applied in many organizations, and there are plenty of organizational data available to document our experiences with these tools.

Conclusion

As noted previously, we view adaptability as a metacompetency because it enables the person to develop other competencies. In much the same way that reading is a metacompetency (once you have learned to read, you then have access to a world of knowledge in print), adaptability lets the person be more open to feedback from the environment, to get help from other people, to experiment with new behaviors, and to learn from his or her own experience.

It is useful to break out the separate components of adaptation so that we can understand the process better. Some people fail to adapt because the motivation is lacking, in which case we need to understand the person's construction of his or her world and self. In other cases, it is a lack of competence. In these cases, it is necessary to consider three components: the person's behavioral responsiveness and flexibility, the person's ability to explore his or her own identity to learn about necessary personal changes, and the ability to integrate new behaviors into a revised sense of personal identity.

In the contemporary career environment, with protean careers characterized by cycles of continuous learning, adaptation is the "coin of the realm." There is no topic more critical to the study of successful careers than the issue of how people reinvent and redefine themselves, in ways that bring them psychological success, over the span of their work lives.

Notes

1. *Role* is defined as "a set of norms and expectations applied to the incumbent of a particular position" (Reidy & White, 1977, p. 228). The common usage of the term has only considered the interpersonal or social aspects of the position, but we need to be careful to include an awareness of the physical environment and task technology as well (Cairo, Kritis, & Myers, 1996; Pulakos, Arad, Donovan, & Plamondon, 1999).

2. In fact, many different terms are used along with adaptability to characterize what occurs prior to and during the time that individuals change. Some of these terms concentrate on the predisposition to or involvement in change that occurs within the individual. Ego resiliency, ego strength, emotional stability, coping, competence, hardiness, self-regulation (Block & Kremen, 1996), resiliency (Buffington, 1992; Phillips, 1997), maturity, coping (Dix & Savickas, 1995; Knasel, 1980), self-efficacy (Block & Kremen, 1996; Gist & Mitchell, 1992), adaptive expertise (Smith, Ford, & Kozlowski, 1997), category flexibility (Mumford, 1991), and positivity (Phillips, 1997) are associated by the various authors with the individual's internal state or process during change. Adaptivity (Baltes & Baltes, 1990; Morrison, 1977), behavioral plasticity (Baltes & Baltes, 1990), avoiding obsolescence (Hall, 1976), ability and willingness to change (Kegan, 1994), adjustment to demands (Nelson, 1975), flexibility (Phillips, 1997), adaptive performance (Hesketh & Neal, 1999; Pulakos et al., 1999), role flexibility (Murphy & Jackson, 1999), and the individual's proficiency in self-managing new learning experiences (London & Mone, 1999) are used by authors to describe the individual's external state or process during change.

3. We thank friend and colleague Michael Arthur for pointing out the multiplicative nature of this relationship.

4. The terms "identity" and "self" are used synonymously in this discussion, along with related terms, such as "sense of self" and "self concept."

8 Managing Protean Career and Life Roles

In recent years, a huge literature has evolved on work/life issues. From the organizational perspective, the issues center on how to maintain organizational flexibility, how to create programs to recruit and retain good workers, and how to best design work. From the employee's viewpoint, the issues center on how to maintain personal flexibility, how to have a life worth living, and how to have fulfilling and rewarding work. In fact, flexibility in work has been found to be a major correlate of both work satisfaction and family well-being (Clark, 2001). In addition, a growing issue here is work/life equity, the extent to which all employees (e.g., single, child-free, and married and parenting) enjoy equal access to the same work/life benefits.

To analyze this issue, we review some earlier work to provide a context. Then, we "fast-forward" to what is known today and what the organizational and career implications are of this current knowledge.

Early Work: Interrole Analysis
and Dual-Career Couples

Role Conflict

In the early 1970s, as women's participation in the U.S. workforce was starting to increase, there was a concomitant growth of interest in home and work roles as a method of understanding the conflicts between the demands of these two domains. In an early study, Hall and Gordon (1973) analyzed the different roles that represented the major life choices of college-educated married women: full-time at home, full-time employment, and part-time employment. They made the obvious prediction that satisfaction would be related to the extent to which women actually engaged in the kinds of activities that they would ideally prefer to do. This prediction was supported for women who were doing full-time home-based activities but not for those employed either part-time or full-time. In other words, this straightforward prediction was supported in reference to the traditional activities but not in the case of employment activities. The results were interpreted as suggesting that

> The career choices of the work-oriented married women are more difficult to implement successfully than are the choices of home-oriented women. Home-related tasks and volunteer activities are part of the traditionally accepted roles of wife and mother. The woman who by her own choice prefers to do these activities will find external role support, acceptance, admiration, and intrinsic satisfaction for doing them. Since employment is outside the traditional home roles, the woman preferring to work may encounter increased role conflicts, time pressure, prejudice, and discrimination when she seeks employment. These problems may offset the satisfaction which a work-oriented woman would otherwise receive by doing what she prefers to do. (p. 47)

Using data from that same study, Hall (1972) examined the relationships between coping strategies and the degree of satisfaction experienced by women in the different role groups. Using Levinson's (1959) concept of the role enactment process, which views the role senders' expectations of the role incumbent, the incumbent's perceptions of the received role, and the incumbent's actual role behavior as three separate facets of the role-enactment process, Hall found that women developed coping strategies linked to each facet. For example, Type I coping was an attempt to redefine role expectations at their source by negotiating revised role demands with role senders (e.g., hiring child care help so that the mother was not expected to be at home during the day). Type II was personally redefining the role (e.g., changing one's own attitudes about the role, such as adopting the perspective that a spotless house had lower priority than other home and work tasks). Type III coping was trying to change one's own behavior (e.g., through better planning, organizing, and time management) to permit one to meet all the role senders' expectations. (An instrument to assess these three types of coping is reported in Hall and Hall (1979). The results showed that the strongest correlation with satisfaction occurred with Type III; people who used this reactive style of coping tended to be less satisfied than others. Additional analysis of the data suggested that what mattered more than the specific type of coping was whether any conscious coping was used at all. People who used some form of coping tended to be more satisfied than people who did not consciously use a form of coping with role stress.

Other early study by Evans and Bartolome (1981, 1984) and Korman and Korman (1980) provided rich interview data documenting the conflicts that couples experienced between work and home. Also, as subsequent research has confirmed, they found that when work roles and home roles come into conflict, work usually wins. Thus, success in the career often comes at a high price.

Later research used this typology of roles and coping to analyze additional aspects of work and family roles (Greenhaus & Beutell, 1985; Greenhaus & Parasuraman, 1999). This research found that a wide range of pressures from work roles and family roles can interact to generate role conflict. Even "good" experiences, such as job involvement and job satisfaction, can take time away from family involvement and be in conflict with family role activities. Greenhaus and Beutell identified three types of work-family conflict: time-based conflict, strain-based conflict, and behavior-based conflict. Various studies, cited in Greenhaus and Parasuraman, have found that the direction or causes of the conflict can vary. Sometimes, work demands can interfere with family life (WF conflict), and at other times family can interfere with work (FW conflict). Not surprisingly, the results from many studies have been consistent: WF conflict is more common that FW conflict (Greenhaus & Parasuraman, 1999).

What about gender differences in role conflict? Given the traditional view of men as providers and women as caregivers, one might expect that because women would experience more pressures from family roles, they would also feel more conflict between work and family roles. The results are surprising, however. Most of the studies did not find significant differences in role conflict between men and women (Blanchard-Fields, Chen, & Hebert, 1997; Voyandoff, 1988), but (here the results may not be so surprising) when a study did find a gender difference, it found that women felt more conflict than men (Hammer, Allen, & Grigsby, 1997).

Dual-Career Couples

Roles and Conflicts

Some of the earliest research on dual-career couples was conducted by Robert and Rhona Rapoport (1969, 1975). The Rapoports' research established this topic as a field of study and lay the groundwork for analyzing the issues by separating out the component parts: her career, his career, her family roles, and his family roles. They also identified basic styles in couple members' orientations toward their careers and their relationships. For example, accommodators, where one member subordinated his or her career to that of the other, often found career and family decision making to be less stressful than that in families in which the two careers were both primary and thus in conflict.

The Rapoports also studied the characteristics of happy versus less happy two-career couples. They found that there were four qualities that differentiated these two groups. First, the happier couples tended to have a strategy for coping with work/family conflicts (consistent with the Hall [1972] study reported earlier). Second, the happy couples had more flexibility than the less happy group. This flexibility could be in many places: in their work, in their relationship, and in their individual personal styles. Third, they had a high level of mutual commitment. This included strong commitment to each other's careers and their own as well as commitment to the relationship. Fourth, they simply had high levels of energy. As one couple in our research reported in an interview, "You just learn how to get by on less sleep!"

Hall and Hall (1979) expanded this notion of couple styles based on the four possible combinations of career and family involvement (Table 8.1). Accommodators are couples in which one partner is high in career involvement and low in home involvement. The second partner is just the opposite—high in home involvement and low in career involvement. Thus, each accommodates the other. One assumes primary responsibility for home and family roles, whereas the second partner assumes primary responsibility for career and breadwinning. If both partners are truly involved in their respective roles and value both work and family, then conflicts are minimized.

If both partners are highly involved in their careers and only minimally involved in home or family roles (but both value a well-ordered and rich home life), they may be described as adversaries. The identity of each is defined primarily by career, and the home roles are important to them but remain undone by either of them. This is probably the most stressful structure for couples because they are competing over priorities. Major changes, such as relocation or having children, can be threatening because they represent a difficult change in an uneasy status quo. Each wants to delegate home responsibilities (which could include the responsibility to hire and manage help—it is still a big job!) to an unwilling mate.

Many couples are highly involved in either career or home, with little identity tied up in the other: These are the allies. As with the accommodators, their priorities are clearly defined and compatible. If they are both career involved and not home involved (Table 8.1, Type IIIb), they are not overly concerned with preparing gourmet dinners or entertaining at home frequently; hosting people at a restaurant can work fine for them. The major stress for them is finding enough time to devote to their relationship. For couples who are both primarily home involved (Table 8.1, Type IIIa), the two incomes provide enough resources for a comfortable life, but they make career choices that minimize spillover from work into the home. One source of stress for family-involved allies might be an occasional pang of doubt about "what if" they had chosen to pursue their careers more aggressively, especially when they compare their careers to those of peers (e.g., at college reunions). Overall, however, allies represent low stress and conflict.

Table 8.1   Dual-Career Couple Types

Type	Work Involvement	Home Involvement
I. Accommodators	Spouse A high Spouse B low (or vice versa)	Spouse B low Spouse A high (or vice versa)
II. Adversaries	Both high	Both low (but both value a well-ordered home)
III. Allies	IIIa. Both low; or IIIb. Both high	IIIa. Both high; or IIIb. Both low (with low value for a well-ordered home)
IV. Acrobats	Both high	Both high

SOURCE: Hall and Hall (1980).

The final type is the one that is such a popular subject of articles on "the" two-career couple, those folks who want high-involvement careers and high involvement in a wonderful, full family life—the 2.4 kids, the house in the suburbs or the town house on Beacon Hill, the Volvo wagon, and live-in help. They are the couples who want it all—they want to have their cake and eat it too. Their identities are not restricted to one particular role; they are ego involved and seek fulfillment in all of them. This group is hypothesized to have the highest degree of stress and conflict.

In fact, there can be two kinds of conflict for the acrobats. One type is interpersonal conflict between the two partners as they attempt to juggle the overload of role demands on them. The other type is intrapersonal, the internal conflict of trying to do well in all role areas—being successful at work, being a loving, supportive spouse, being a caring, involved parent, providing a comfortable home, and so on.

This typology is not static. Couples often move from one type to another as their career and life stages develop. For example, a young couple might begin as allies, where both are going flat-out on their careers while they live in a modest, low-maintenance apartment and have no children. Their social life may consist primarily of evenings out or at home for dinner with other ally couples. Then, as they start a family, and as a well-ordered home becomes more important, they may move to one of the other types. They could become adversaries if no one assumes responsibility for the home, with constant bickering about who is going to call the baby-sitter or who is going to take care of the sink full of dishes from last night's party. If one partner switches to a more flexible work option, they could become accommodators. If they want it all, they could become acrobats. In my observation, the most frequent switch for young couples is from allies to accommodators, perhaps with a stop at acrobats along the way. This is often caused by financial necessity, and as soon as they can afford it, one partner cuts back on work hours. I leave it to the reader to guess which gender is more likely to make this accommodation.

There are three common forms of stress among two-career couples, and it is important to consider each one separately. The first and most common source is role overload. This is caused by the sheer number and intensity of demands on the couples' time. Overload pressure is especially high for young couples (at a career stage in which financial resources are tight) with children. The sheer number of demands on the partners exceeds the time and energy to do them.

Individuals vary in the extent to which they can handle different degrees of role demands, however. When does "load" become "overload"? Although the common belief might be that the more role demands a person has, the more stress and the less satisfaction the person will have, the opposite may be true. Hall and Gordon (1973), in a study of married women, found that the more roles a part-time worker had, the more satisfied she tended to be, and the opposite was true for full-time workers. Furthermore, the difference between these two correlations was significant. That is, part-time workers derived significantly more satisfaction from having many life roles than did full-time workers. Thoits (1992) found that the more roles a person had (both men and women), the better the person's mental health. Similarly, Barnett and Baruch (1985) and Gore and Mangione (1983) found that people who hold multiple roles experience good mental and physical health.

There could be problems in the context in which multiple role demands are occurring. Sekaran and Hall (1989) argued that role overload pressures are more problematic when there is asynchronicity in the work and family roles of each party. That is, each role has a life of its own, with cycles of peak and low demand. For the parent role, September is a high-demand time, when children have to be outfitted for school, they are making a difficult transition to a new school or a higher grade, and new activities are getting started. For the work role, this is a time when many people are starting back to work after a summer vacation. In the church and community, many organizations are also getting started, needing volunteer assistance and expecting participation. Thus, many roles are peaking simultaneously, and the effects of the overload are intensified. On the other hand, if one partner could find a way to reduce the workload in September (e.g., by taking vacation then, by doing more work at home, or by taking on more work during the summer months), this could make the couple's roles more in sync. (More detail on the specific ways that synchronicity can work is found in Sekaran & Hall, 1989.)

The second type of stress for dual-career couples comes from conflict, the incompatibility of different role expectations. One type of conflict is interrole conflict, in which one partner's different roles make mutually conflicting demands—for example, when a person, as an employee, is expected to be out of town next Friday for a client meeting and is also expected, as a parent, to be at his child's school for the fifth-grade play. It is not possible to be in both places at the same time (although people may be tempted to do so electronically). There is also intersender conflict within a role. An example is when a father is home alone taking care of his daughter and she wants him to let her stay up past her bedtime to watch a special TV show, but the mother had left strict instructions that the daughter should be in bed on time.

A third type of conflict is intrapersonal conflict (within the person), in which a person feels torn between two valued activities (e.g., attending the son's band concert or the daughter's all-star softball game). It could also be a conflict of unmet expectations, in which the person believes he or she is simply not measuring up to the standards set by other people he or she respects ("I could never be the father that he is" or "I'll never be as successful as she is").

The third source of stress is change. This is certainly not unique to dual-career couples, but with the two careers they may be more likely to experience relocations more often than one-career families, and a relocation can trigger all sorts of other changes—new jobs, new home, new friends, new schools, new community, new culture, often a more expensive house and the concomitant financial stress, and so on. Again, synchronicity is an issue: The more roles that are changing simultaneously, the more the stress is compounded.

Jobs and Interdependent Systems

Examining one role in depth (as opposed to across roles), if the person experiences the demands of one role as being "too much," that could contribute to a feeling of overload. Barnett and Brennan (1995, 1997) documented the interdependent relationships between one partner's career experiences and the quality of the partners' relationship. Specifically, they found that stressors in one partner's job affected the distress that the other partner experienced. Barnett and Brennan (1997) studied the effects of high levels of what they called "job demands," which they operationalized with three items: "Having too much to do," "Having to juggle conflicting tasks or duties," and "The job's taking too much out of you." In a carefully designed longitudinal study in which they controlled for many potentially related variables, such as gender, job control, and other job characteristics, Barnett and Brennan found that as these feelings of excessive job demands increased over time, a person's psychological distress (i.e., perceived anxiety and depression) increased correspondingly. Similar cross-role effects have been reported by Williams and Etzion (1995).

Another kind of interdependence—between job design, work/life balance, and job performance—was identified by Bailyn (1993) and colleagues. In research with teams of engineers, they found members of engineering project teams who were encouraged to design their work process in a way that would make their lives more livable. The result of the job design changes was that the engineers' lives seemed more in balance, which was the desired and expected result. There was another, entirely unexpected result, however: The quality and productivity of the teams' work also showed dramatic increases. New product development teams were setting records for completion of new products, product quality, and budget performance. Thus, not only is designing work in a way that enhances work/life balance or integration beneficial for the employee but also it leads to higher business productivity.

Protean Careers and Dual-Career Relationships

It has become clear from recent research such as that of Bailyn, Barnett, and colleagues that we need to be more mindful of the design of work and of the systemic interdependencies among various work and life role experiences if we are to understand and ameliorate work/life issues more fully. When we talk about the design of work over a period of time, we are talking about the design of careers.

Therefore, we return to the career issues we have been examining throughout this book (e.g., protean careers and shorter career cycle times) and consider the implications of shorter career cycles for dual-career couples and their families and other committed relationships.[1] We highlight the key aspects of the protean career and of current organizational forms, and then we consider what this all means for work and family relationships.

As discussed in Chapter 4, traditional theories of career stages posit a life cycle approach to development, in which the work career unfolds over a regular series of stages during the course of the person's work life: exploration, trial, establishment, maintenance, and disengagement (Hall, 1976; Super, 1957). It is becoming increasingly clear, however, that these stages represent the "old career contract" notions of the "one-life, one-career imperative."

The Protean Career and 4 F Organization

As mentioned in Chapter 2, the protean career has replaced the organizational career. The implication of the protean career is that increasingly the individual will have to reinvent himself or herself in the work setting to meet the demands of a changing economy. The protean career has the following characteristics (Hall & Associates, 1996):

- The career is managed by the person, not the organization.
- The career is a lifelong series of experiences, skills, learnings, transitions, and identity changes.
- "Career age" is important, not chronological age.
- Development is
    continuous learning;
    self-directed;
    relational; and
    primarily driven by work challenges, not formal programs.

As work settings have become "3 D" (decentralized, delegated, and diverse), they have come to require "4 F" qualities in organizations and people (fast, flexible, facile, and fun). We know from early work in organization design (Duncan, 1971; Lawrence & Lorsch, 1967; Scott, 1992) that the more an environment possesses the qualities of complexity and change, the more nimble an organization must be to be effective. It is also becoming clear that to obtain the high commitment from employees that organizations need for innovative, independent decision making and problem solving, work has to be designed in a way that makes it intrinsically rewarding (i.e., fun) to work for the organizations. (A company such as Southwest Airlines is a good example.) These 4 F qualities enable an organization to adapt successfully.

Individuals and organizations in an environment of complexity and turbulence need to exhibit 4 F qualities. One specific implication of this flexibility for individuals is that we need to modify our models of career stage development. I argued in Chapter 3 that the life stage model of career stages (Super, 1957) has been replaced by a model of much shorter (e.g., approximately 5 years) learning stages. In the learning stage model, the critical issue is career age (time in that career field) rather than chronological age.

For example, my son works in the Internet software industry. He started as a public relations specialist, remaining in this position for a couple of years. Then he wanted to work on the company side, so he took a position as head of marketing for a start-up firm and remained in this position for approximately 1½ years. Then, seeing the need for Internet start-ups to develop more strategic business savvy, he moved into a strategic business development role with an Internet consulting and service firm and remained in this position for less than 2 years. Then, with some friends he started a new company, an Internet incubator, and he has been involved with this company for approximately 3 years. Thus, in less than 10 years, he has had what he experiences as four careers. In each, he had an exploratory stage, in which he gathered information to help him decide whether to make the switch or not. Next, he had a trial stage, in which he did some work on his own time in the role to which he was considering entering. For example, he did some marketing work for the start-up, which had no marketing function at that time, on weekends while he was still with the public relations firm). Then, in the new role, he had an establishment stage, in which he ascended a steep learning curve. Finally, he entered a performance or mastery stage, in which he was able to deliver value. Thus, at the ripe old age of 30, his career has already been a series of many learning cycles, containing "ministages" of exploration, trial, establishment, mastery, and transition.

Protean Careers and Dual-Career Couples

What does this new learning cycle model imply for two-career couples and their relationships? How do individuals and couples manage the boundaries between their work and family roles? Previously, we discussed using roles as a lens for viewing work/life relationships. Now, we go a step further and examine time and role boundaries. We also distinguish between psychological boundaries and physical boundaries (Hall & Richter, 1988). Our lens for viewing this boundary management is the various transitions that the two individuals make—for example, between work and home domains, between one work domain and another over time, and between one home domain and another over time. A central question is how individuals and couples are managing these transitions in a context in which role structures are becoming increasingly complex and cycle times are increasingly compressed. As the work of Barnett and others demonstrates, the number of roles a person holds or the number of hours worked alone do not necessarily lead to greater stress. The problems appear to lie in the ways in which the person copes with interrole conflict (Hall, 1972) and the extent to which he or she attempts to adapt work schedules to meet the needs of oneself and the family (Barnett, Gareis, & Brennan, 1999).

Boundaries and Transitions

A boundary serves two functions in relation to a person's life roles. First, it serves to define or indicate the extent or domain of a role. Second, it separates that role from other roles. Thus, it both defines a role and separates that role from other roles.

Although there are many ways to study the relationships between roles, one way to make the relationships between roles stand out in bold relief is to examine the process by which a person moves across the boundary between two roles. Because the boundary separates the roles, the differences between the roles are heightened at the point of boundary crossing (Hall & Richter, 1988).

Boundary demarcation may be either physical, in which the markers are time and location, or psychological, in which the individual's "life space" and "subidentities" (where a subidentity is the portion of one's identity that is engaged in a particular role) are separated into role-linked regions. Thus, transitions can be either physical (e.g., when the person commutes between work and home) or psychological (in which the person's attention or involvement shifts between roles).

There are three basic styles of crossing physical and psychological boundaries during daily transitions between work and home: anticipatory, discrete, and lagged. In an anticipatory transition, the person becomes psychologically engaged with the role that he or she is moving into before the physical departure. An example is a person who takes a shower at home in the morning and rehearses a presentation to be given at work later in the morning. A discrete transition is one in which the psychological and physical engagement with a role coincide. Continuing the presentation example, in a discrete transition, the person would not begin thinking about it until entering the work space. A lagged transition is one in which the person continues to be psychologically engaged with the departed role after entering the new one. An example is when a person continues to think about a home issue after entering the work space.

I hypothesize that the effects of protean careers on work/life conflict are complex. The autonomy and flexibility and self-control that one has in a protean career give one more "slack" for attending to family and personal activities. Thus, one hypothesis is that couples in which one or both partners have a protean career will experience less work/family role conflict than couples in which both partners have traditional organizational careers.

I also hypothesize that as organizations become more flexible and responsive to employees' work/life issues, psychological role transitions will become more problematic than physical role transitions. In other words, the physical issues caused by time conflicts, which make it difficult for a person to be present for both home and work roles, will decrease as the employee gains more options and flexibility regarding the use of his or her time. Thus, for example, a parent may be free to leave the office early to attend a child's softball game. That parent, however, may still be thinking about the work issue he or she was attending to upon leaving the office (a lagged transition). In fact, Hall and Richter (1988) found that much of the stress caused by work and family roles occurs at the boundary—that is, at the transition point when the person is moving from one role to the other. Therefore, as the person's work role becomes more flexible, with more permeable boundaries, this gives the person more degrees of freedom to juggle and integrate roles, but it may create more frequent psychological (if not physical) transitions back and forth between the different roles.

To provide a concrete example, I offer my own experience. As a college professor, I have wonderful autonomy and flexibility about where and when I do my work. Except for meeting with classes and attending various meetings, much of the work I do involves research, writing, designing courses and class sessions, reading student work, and the like. This work can be done anytime, anywhere. Thus, as a father in a two-career family with a school-age child, I often work at home, often on short notice because of unforeseen events (such as snow days at school, child's illness, and housework being done). Also, whether I am physically at home or at my university office, I am constantly available to role senders from the other role through the telephone, e-mail, and fax. (Somehow, this boundary permeability seems especially pronounced at home.) Because of the uncertainty about what crisis a telephone call might bring and because I now more often receive expectations from both roles simultaneously, there seems to be more work/family conflict and stress now than there was when my work was less flexible (i.e., when I was primarily at the office, dealing primarily with work responsibilities). Thus, for me, greater role flexibility and boundary permeability seem to create greater role conflict and stress.

Another kind of flexibility that is often touted for dual-career parents is reduced-hours work as a way of giving parents more flexibility and more time at home with family. This has become especially important in view of an increase over time in the average length of the workweek for professional employees (Jacobs & Gerson, 1997). Many professional workers would like to reduce their work hours (Bond, Galinsky, & Swanberg, 1998; Jacobs & Gerson, 1997), but there is a perception that reduced hours carries a risk to one's prospects for career advancement (Carr et al., 1998). Despite the view that reduced-hours employment would contribute positively to the quality of life of working couples, the research on the topic has not supported these positive effects (Ozer, Barnett, Brennan, & Sperling, 1998). What seems to be resulting from the research is a more complex view of the situation. "Remedies" such as reduced hours involve making difficult choices and trade-offs. We are not talking about reduced hours as the choice of a "good" option (home and family) over a "bad" option (work) but, rather, as a trade-off between two valued options. Therefore, this is not an easy choice. In fact, the more difficult the trade-off is for a person, the more likely the person is to suffer a reduced quality of life (e.g., anxiety and depression, lower job role quality, and increased thoughts of quitting) (Barnett & Gareis, 2000). What seems to be most important is not the actual number of hours worked but, rather, the personal fit between the work schedule and the person's needs (Barnett et al., 1999).

Thus, as work/life programs have progressed, we have made progress in helping employees deal with physical role transitions, but the emotional transitions are still largely unexplored territory (and they are much more difficult to cope with than issues of physical presence). Not only is it necessary to create flexibility in the work environment but also it is critical to find ways to help individual employees go through the difficult soul-searching about what is the best arrangement for their particular personal and family situations.

Research Issues for Protean Careers and Dual-Career Couples

What implications do the new short-cycle careers have for dual-career couples and their relationships? Here, a few are suggested:

- We need to learn more about everyday psychological role transitions. Preliminary research has found gender differences in transitional styles for daily role transitions. How are transition styles developed? Can they be altered? What are the psychological and relational correlates of different styles? How do they affect outcomes at home and at work? An excellent start in this direction was made by Ashforth, Kreiner, and Fugate (2000), who provide a goldmine of theory and ideas for further research.
- We need to go beyond examining relationships between roles to study relationships between changes in roles. It is not enough to know in a static sense how one partner's work role affects the other partner's work or home role or their relationship because that work role changes very rapidly. In time, if the roles did not change, both partners could most likely adapt successfully to each other's work demands. In earlier research, the dynamic elements considered were the longer period adult life stage transitions and life cycle career stage transitions. Although these transitions could be difficult, they tended to occur only a handful of times, and then a relatively stable new life/career stage configuration would be reached that might last 10 or 15 years. In the New Economy, these career transitions often happen annually.

(We know from the work of Barnett and Brennan [1997] that increases in job demands lead to increases in psychological distress. Can positive changes in other job or life characteristics lead to changes in positive outcomes?) What effect does the continuous learning caused by the New Economy (and its attendant chronic stress) have on a relationship?

- Career metacompetencies are also relational metacompetencies. We need to study metacompetencies as they relate to the two-career experience. Elsewhere (Hall & Associates, 1996), I have discussed the futility of trying to predict which career competencies will be critical in the future and have proposed that organizations instead focus on developing in their workforce two "career metacompetencies," which would enable employees to learn how to learn in a much more protean, self-directed way. These career metacompetencies are identity change and adaptability. Adaptability is key to enable the person to sense weak signals in the environment that call for personal change. Identity change is the ability to learn about oneself, to be self-aware, to have a clear sense of personal direction, and to pursue one's calling, or what Herb Shepard called the "path with a heart." Adaptability without identity is simply mindless reaction; the person could be changing with the environment, but it may not necessarily be a change that is in the person's best interests. Also, identity change without adaptability means awareness without effectiveness.

I argue that we could consider these metacompetencies in the context of a dual-career relationship as well as in one person. First, career turbulence requires that both parties possess both metacompetencies. If only one partner has them, then that person will change and the other will not. Under this condition, the first partner could be making successful career adaptations, but these changes could be slowly undermining the relationship. For example, one partner might decide to quit a company and spend full-time on his own business (an activity that had been a second source of income previously), but if his wife's identity was rooted in having a stable, constant income and in being married to a large-company executive, and if her identity did not change, the relationship would be headed for trouble.

Second, the relationship must possess adaptability and identity change. The expectations and contributions of each party must change with new roles, and the partners must be aware of and in control of these changes. Although both parties might be quite protean in their career and home identities, if the relationship cannot change, there could be problems. For example, if a relationship were based on one party's being the primary homemaker, but the work roles of both parties changed so that both had to do a great deal of traveling, and if they were unwilling to hire help for the home roles, their relationships and both of them as individuals would come under increased stress.

- A secure base supports transitions. We need to study how secure personal relationships can facilitate successful career adaptation. Research on individual development has identified the importance of a "secure base" (Kahn, 1996). This term derives from attachment theory and describes the "felt security of children who engage in unworried explorations, trusting their parents/attachment figures to come to their aid should difficulties arise" (Kahn, 1996, p. 162). Caregiving behaviors that create secure base conditions include communicating empathy, warmth, and respect and giving encouragement, comfort, and information. Kahn argues that a work environment that has these qualities of a secure base can help employees cope with the anxieties and ambiguities of the uncharted waters of the New Economy, which in turn lets them engage in exploratory and other learning behavior required for a successful protean career. As Kahn points out, there is a paradox here: "Individuals are only capable of being fully self-reliant when they experience themselves as supported by and attached to trusted others" (p. 161).

  We can extend this notion of secure base beyond the work setting to the dual-career relationship. The more the relationship possesses the qualities of a secure base, the more both parties are psychologically free to explore changes in their lives.

  We can also apply the causal reasoning in the other direction: The more the career provides the qualities of a secure base, the more psychological freedom and flexibility the relationship will have. What would be a "secure base" in the career role? It could mean a sense of mastery and self-confidence with one's work role, receiving rewards and intrinsic reinforcement from work, feelings of pride and success at work, and a feeling of acceptance by and respect from coworkers. The more psychological success one feels in the work role, the more capable one is of risking one's accomplishments in the home role.

- We need to move beyond the conflict paradigm in our research on work/life issues. Experience is the best teacher for metacompetencies. We need more research on ways that work and life experiences build metacompetencies. The bad news about careers and relationships being buffeted by more frequent transitions is that transitions can be stressful. The good news is that the metacompetencies for weathering these transitions can be developed. In fact, the stressful transitions can build the metacompetencies. Although there may be some personality characteristics, such as hardiness and flexibility, that may be linked to the metacompetencies, it is clear that we have identity change and adaptability "muscles" that strengthen with use (Briscoe & Hall, 1999; Hall, 1986). In fact, identity change is at the core of the process of adult development, and most people are capable of "growing" their identity with the appropriate challenges and with a certain amount of psychological safety (Hall & Associates, 1996; Kegan, 1982).

The problem is that under the old career contract, people would embark on a career and, after becoming established, would settle into a midlife plateau, during which little change was demanded. Then, when the employing firm encountered the New Economy and had to restructure, employees were hit with the sudden demand for massive adaptation and identity change. Some were able to meet the challenge, and some were not.

If, on the other hand, the person experiences ongoing changes from the beginning of the career, he or she learns how to learn much more easily and less stressfully. Thus, it appears that workers in their 20s would have a much easier time developing their adaptability and identity change abilities than did those who were older. Also, among older workers, those with more transitions in their career history probably had an easier time adjusting to the protean career than did those with more stable careers.

Experiences related to work and family can be powerful triggers for developing one's identity and adaptability. In fact, work/family issues and conflicts may have more impact on a person's development than work experiences alone. In all the research on work/family conflicts, to my knowledge, there has been no recognition of the developmental potential of these issues. As discussed previously, work/family issues have been framed almost entirely around their conflicts. The literature on adult development (Kegan, 1982, 1994; Levinson et al., 1978, 1996), however, makes it abundantly clear that personal and family experiences are a major "engine" of growth, moving the person from one life stage to the next. We need to add a developmental frame to the way we view work and family issues, and we need research on the ways that dealing with these issues can contribute to personal and career growth.

Conclusion

It appears that the shorter life cycle of a career will necessarily make for more frequent transitions in dual-career relationships (but, I hope, not for shorter life cycles of relationships). Whether the relationship's life cycle is also shortened may depend on the "metacompetency muscle" that gets built into it. Being able to manage the paradox of creating secure bases while facing incredible risk and turbulence will be the key to success. Part of the answer is to learn more about managing the psychological role transitions that occur in everyday life. Creating good boundaries in one's life, to separate the secure base from the areas of risk, and then learning to transit those boundaries can be a way to resolve the paradox. Also, expanding the domain of work/life research to include these positive developmental outcomes that can arise from dealing with work/life experiences can contribute in important ways to our understanding of personal and career development.

Appendix

Additional Work/Family References

The following references were provided by the Sloan Work and Family Network at the Boston College Center for Work & Family. Some, as noted, can be accessed directly on the Web. Look for current references (and join the network, if you are interested) at www.bc.edu/wfnetwork.

Bowen, G. L. (1999). Workplace programs and policies that address work-family and gender equity issues in the United States. In L. L. Haas, P. Hwang, & G. Russell (Eds.), *Organizational change & gender equity: International perspectives on fathers and mothers at the workplace.* Thousand Oaks, CA: Sage.

Burke, B., Cropper, A., & Harrison, P. (2000). Real or imagined—Black women's experiences in the Academy. *Community, Work & Family 3*(3), 297-310.

Domsch, M. E., & Ladwig, D. H. (Eds.). (2000). *Reconciliation of family and work in Eastern European countries.* New York: Lang. (ISBN 3-631-36713-9)

Drago, R., & Kashian, R. (2001). Mapping the terrain of work/family journals. *Journal of Family Issues.* (The journal has kindly given permission for the authors to post the article: http://lsir.la.psu.edu/workfam/journalevaluation.pdf)

Galinsky, E., Kim, S., & Bond, J. T. (2001). *Feeling overworked: When work becomes too much.* New York: Families and Work Institute. (To view and download the executive summary: http://www.familiesandwork.org. To request a copy, please contact Erin Brownfield: ebrownfield@familiesandwork.org; phone, 212-465-2044, extension 210)

Hertz, R., & Marshall, N. L. (Eds.). (2001). *Working families: The transformation of the American home.* Berkeley: University of California Press. (For more information on the collection: http://www.ucpress.edu/books/pages/9187.html)

Lewis, S. (2001). Restructuring workplace culture: The ultimate work-family challenge? *Women in Management Review, 16*(1), 85-92.

MacDermid, S., Galinsky, E., & Bond, J. T. (Eds.). (2001, Summer). [Special issue]. *Journal of Family and Economic Issues, 22*(2). (Free online sample copy: http://www.wkap. nl/journalhome.htm/1058-0476)

Moen, P., Kim, J. E., & Hofmeister, H. (2001). Couples' work/retirement transitions, gender, and marital quality. *Social Psychology Quarterly, 64*(1), 55-71.

Peters, J. K. (2001). *Not your mother's life: Changing the rules of work, love, and family.* New York: Perseus.

Rayman, P. (2001). *Beyond the bottom line: The search for dignity at work.* New York: St. Martin's.

Reynolds, A. J., Temple, J. A., Robertson, D. L., & Mann, E. A. (2001, May). Long-term effects of an early childhood intervention on educational achievement and juvenile intervention: A 15 year follow-up of low-income children in public schools. *Journal of the American Medical Association, 285*(18), 2339-2346. (For more information, see the University of Wisconsin summary of the study: http://www.waisman.wisc.edu/cls/index.html. Study author Arthur Reynolds can be contacted at 608-263-1847 or 608-263-3837.)

Scanzoni, J. H. (Ed.). (2001). The household in its neighborhood and community [Special issue]. *Journal of Family Issues, 22*(2).

Note

1. The term family is used in this discussion to refer to a person's loved ones, with whom he or she is in a committed relationship, the relational network that represents the person's private life.

III

Implementing Career Concepts

9 Reflection

SELF-DEVELOPMENT
FOR THE GROWTH OF
IDENTITY AND ADAPTABILITY

One morning, as I was going through the daily routine of checking the mail, I saw something that instantly perked me up—a letter from one of my favorite students from last semester, Ralph Davis. Ralph, a pharmaceutical company research manager, was a student in the executive MBA program and had been unusually active in relating the content of the organizational behavior course to his own work and life, which is very rewarding for a faculty member in an area that is often viewed as less than relevant to pressing business issues. I read Ralph's letter first:

AUTHOR'S NOTE: I gratefully acknowledge the helpful comments of Kent Seibert on an earlier draft of this chapter.

Dear Tim:

I thought you'd be interested to hear about an experience I had that grew out of the career planning activity that we did in your class.

Although it was difficult for me at first to "slow down" as you requested and reflect back on the peaks and valleys of my life and career to date, I was amazed at the ideas that seemed to whiz into my head. After I wrote down my key insights from the career life line that I constructed, it became very clear to me what I wanted to do. Although my background is in science, as you know, I am currently in this new role of manager of my department. I had always thought of this as a sort of rotational assignment (you know, serving my turn for the group). But as I reflected on the incredible amount of learning I am doing in this role, especially about my relationships with and impact on people, I realized just how much satisfaction I am getting out of it. (It is fashionable in the lab here to "dump" on administrators and administrative work, and I realize that I had fallen into that mind-set, without thinking much about it.)

Anyway, I came to the conclusion that I really wanted to test myself as a leader, to give this management career path a real shot. So my action plan in the career reflection exercise was to make an appointment with the CEO, tell him of my interest in learning more about leadership, and ask him if there was some way I might be assigned to work that would bring me in contact with some of the most senior people in the firm. That way I could learn by observing and relating to our top leaders, and in turn I could see how I stacked up compared to them. So I made an appointment.

I'll get to the bottom line quickly: The outcome of this conversation with the CEO was that he asked me to be his special assistant. Since he's new to the company and I've been around awhile, he sees this as a way to help him settle in, and learn about the people and the issues, in addition to my helping him on various projects. And, after talking it over with my family, I've decided to do it. And I'm tremendously excited about it!

But I just wanted to let you know that if I hadn't been forced to reflect on these recent career experiences, I would have continued viewing my department manager job as temporary and would have moved back to my very comfortable technical work in a year or two.

Many thanks for the experience.

Sincerely,

Ralph

Earlier in this book, we discussed the importance of two meta-competencies that are critical to providing the sense of direction and the creative energy for the protean career: identity growth and adaptability. A critical question, however, is the following: How can we help people cultivate these two metacompetencies? I argue that along with the traditional trilogy of developmental experiences (challenging assignments, developmental relationships, and formal training), there is a potent and drastically underused self-development process that anyone can use: reflection.

The U.S. Army has adopted these two metacompetencies and the process of self-development as part of their new training and development principles (Army Training and Leader Development Panel, 2001). The Army views the relationships among the metacompetencies and self-development as intrinsic to two key development principles: Know yourself and lifelong learning:

> **Know yourself.** Self-aware and adaptive leaders are the basis for successful spectrum operations. The relationship between self-awareness and adaptability is symbiotic. The greater self-awareness gained by assessment against measurable standards, the more adaptive the leader. Through a commitment to lifelong learning enabled by self-development, leaders can narrow the knowledge gaps not provided through educational and operational experiences.
>
> **Lifelong learning.** Part of the Army's culture should be the commitment by its leaders to lifelong learning. Learning organizations support self-awareness and adaptability. Lifelong learning requires standards, tools for assessment, feedback, and self-development. (p. OS-21)

In this chapter, we examine the nature of reflection as a self-development activity and the ways that it can be used to promote continuous career learning.

What Is Reflection?

Here, we do some reflecting of our own—on the opening letter from Ralph Davis. What was striking to me as I read that letter was how little time the class had spent in this career reflection exercise (approximately

1½ hours) but how significant the resulting changes were for Ralph. Ralph's claim that he probably would not have otherwise realized how interested he was in seriously exploring leadership opportunities seemed reasonable because he was in a very fast-moving, high-stress environment that provided no time for reflection. All that counted was meeting the project deadline. Then it was on to the next project. Thus, the personal reflection experience, simple though it was, seemed to have a powerful effect.

What is it about reflection that has this impact on a person's career and life? Kent Seibert and Marilyn Daudelin (1999) have done path-breaking research on how reflection works and how to facilitate it. One of the surprises in Kent Seibert's (1999) work is that, in contrast to the popular stereotype, managers do engage in reflection on their everyday experiences. Perhaps this may not sound like such a revelation after you hear it, but before Kent began his dissertation research, many friends, faculty, and executives were telling him, "You're crazy to waste your time studying managerial reflection. That term is an oxymoron!" Kent was told that managers are simply too busy to reflect. In their Henry Mintzberg world, in which life is a series of 5-minute interactions (Mintzberg, 1990), and which Tom Peters once called the "nanosecond nineties," reflection is a luxury only academics can imagine, or so went the thinking.

Seibert, however, found that the managers in his study did a lot of personal reflection. In fact, he found that precisely because things are so turbulent and are moving so fast, it is essential for a successful manager or executive to be able to learn from experience—and to learn quickly. This means that she or he does not necessarily have time to attend a training program or a university executive program to learn about what is happening in today's business world. Instead, it is necessary to engage in continuous learning and to learn on the fly, as the changes she needs to learn about are actually occurring. The way this happens is through what Seibert and Daudelin (1999) called "active reflection," often aided by help from one's friends and colleagues, to help make sense of it all.

Reflection is an intentional cognitive process in which the person attempts to increase his or her awareness of personal experiences and, therefore, his or her ability to learn from them (Hullfish & Smith, 1961). In terms of our metacompetencies, increasing one's awareness of personal experiences represents identity growth. Also, increasing one's ability to learn from experience means enhanced adaptability (Boyd & Fales, 1983).

Seibert and Daudelin (1999) define reflection formally as "a cognitive activity managers engage in to make sense of an experience" (p. xvii). Mezirow (1991) described several different types of reflection:

- Introspection: Becoming more aware of one's experiences
- Content reflection: Thinking about what we perceive
- Process reflection: Thinking about how we perceive
- Premise reflection: Thinking about why we perceive as we do; exploring whether "good" or "bad" are relevant

Reflection: Stereotype Versus Reality

Qualities of Reflection

Seibert (1996a) learned that the nature of the reflection that managers actually do is quite different from the stereotype most of us have of reflection. Specifically, he found that reflection did not have the following qualities:

Qualities	... *that would lead development professionals to think*
Passive	"There must be something we can do to get people to sit still long enough to do some thinking."
Contrived	"Let's design a reflection workshop."
After the fact	"We'll schedule people to attend the month after their assignment is ended."
Time-consuming	"It'll take at least 2 hours."
Narrow	"We'll have people list the new job tasks they can perform."
Context-independent	"We'll make sure there are no interruptions by doing this off-site."

In contrast to this conventional view of reflection, Seibert (1996a) found that effective managers engage in real-time reflection. Thus, reflection and learning are connected to the context in which action occurs; they are not just something the person does in an "ivory tower" setting after the fact. As the experiences of these managers showed, reflection was a highly active process, which was a natural part of doing one's work in a planned, thoughtful way. This means that reflection is necessarily often quite brief, with an "in-the-moment" quality. Also, the questions raised during reflection were often quite broad and general— that is, they often led to insights about long-term career goals and strategies.

What do these real-time reflection qualities imply for the continuous-learning manager? The following questions, from Seibert (1996b, p. 253) could be usefully asked by the developing person to capture the most meaning from personal experience:

> Reflection characteristic questions for the developing person
>> Active: "This experience is mentally stimulating. What's the most productive way to do that thinking?"
>> Natural: "I can't help but ask, what's going on here? What does this all mean?"
>> Brief: "What 'windows of opportunity' are there in my workday to reflect? While I'm waiting for a meeting to begin?"
>> Broad: "What am I learning about this job, this organization, my coworkers, myself? How do I feel about all this? How does this affect my thinking and my career?"
>> Context-connected: "What regular work activities promote reflecting? Writing progress reports? Preparing presentations?"

To illustrate, Seibert (1996b) gives the example of Steve, a manager in a consumer products company:

> Steve found that his best reflecting was done in the context of meetings. Having to present and then defend his ideas to others forced him to think issues through thoroughly before going into a meeting. Being prepared to write trip reports also provided a natural opportunity to reflect on critical issues identified in the field. These reports were usually written on the flight home. Since he traveled so much, his days in the office were often filled with back-to-back meetings. This left little free time to mentally process the results of meetings. Steve found that the brief time he spent walking from one meeting to the next could be used productively to identify and catalogue key issues. (pp. 252-253)

How a CEO Reflects

In a study of how CEOs learn, my colleague David O'Connell and I found many examples of ways in which the individual learning of a person at the top of an organization can have profound effects on the strategy and direction of an organization. Consider, for example, the work of Stanley Goldstein, former CEO of CVS, a highly successful chain of retail pharmaceutical stores. Stan was one of the founders of CVS in the 1960s. When the founders sold CVS to the Melville Corporation 5 years after CVS's founding, Stan expected to stay for approximately 1 year and then move on because he had never worked for a large New York Stock Exchange firm. He found he was learning so much by observing and working with Frank Rooney, Melville's CEO, that he stayed, and he eventually succeeded Rooney as CEO.

In conversation with Stan, one hears him talk much about other people he has observed, reflected on, and learned from during the course of his career. He reports that he spent much time reflecting on Rooney's performance to draw lessons for himself. He can describe in great detail what he learned by observing a delivery truck driver he worked with when he was a kid:

> When I was a kid my dad had a small wholesale business and in the summertime I worked on a truck as a delivery guy, a 10-ton truck, delivering stuff to grocery stores. And the driver was a French-Canadian who hadn't gone to the sixth grade, and the lesson I learned in those several summers was how smart this guy was.... He had very strong opinions about world politics and issues that were social and otherwise, and [I saw] how damn smart he was.... It was really a lesson learned that you can learn from a lot of people.... The consumer group we're trying to go after, you can be fooled—they are smart as hell. And you have got to treat them with respect, and treat them the way you want to be treated.
>
> So all the phrases about continuous improvement—we didn't know those phrases. But it's, again, common sense and logic. And we are not the ones to be able to do it, because we don't know what the hell is going on. They are the ones that do it. So you can learn from everyone.

He also describes himself as the firm's "designated golfer," and he also loves to spend time sailing, enjoying the opportunities to reflect in solitude or with trusted friends.

At its peak, Melville owned approximately 10 well-known retailers, such as Marshalls, Bob's Stores, Linens 'n' Things, and Thom McAn shoes. CVS was about half of the volume and profit of the total corporation, however, and by the 1990s it became clear to Stan that a change had to be made because the business had become flat. He described his thinking as follows:

> So we started to really rethink what we wanted to do, and it didn't look as though anything materially was really going to change. The capacity wasn't going to come out of the retail business. There was more space being put on every year, and in fact, it was going to get even worse.
>
> I kind of handled it in the conventional way, in a lot of discussion with the board of directors, saying, "I think we have to do something." And they felt the same way.

He also talked to consultants and bankers, and their ideas confirmed his. After much more individual reflection and discussions of these ideas with his board and other industry leaders, Stan and the Melville board reached a decision: They would spin off and sell the various businesses and would end up eventually with CVS on its own. Concerning Stan's future career, he would stay with CVS and work to groom his successor, as he planned for eventual retirement. The entire process took about 2½ years.

Mr. Goldstein also consciously uses his board as a source of learning, as this restructuring indicated. For this reason, he wants a strong, smart board:

> Many people are cynical about boards. I always thought you get the strongest, smartest board you can possibly get because it's a lot easier dealing with smart people than not so smart people. They have been very, very supportive and helpful. I'm very open with the board.
>
> They are the kind of people that want it that way. I encourage feedback and unvarnished feedback, and we have a good process.

When asked his advice to someone just moving into a CEO role about how he or she can best learn, he argues for mutual reflecting with one's management team:

> I have a good friend who has an expression, "No one knows what all of us know." No one knows what all of us know. And that's true. I've always phrased it in a different way. I know about 75% of the answer, but you put three other people in the room, and they will end up with 92% of the answer.... Always something comes out of an interplay amongst people who are bright and have a lot of common sense, and you can come to a better conclusion.

On February 10, 1998, the front page of the *Boston Globe* carried the headline, "CVS to Buy Detroit Drugstores for $1.48b." With the acquisition of Arbor Drugs in Michigan, CVS became the largest drugstore chain in the United States (moving past Rite Aid, Eckerd, and Walgreens). Also, Stan continued to run CVS, bringing along his successor, and he is now very happily retired.

Reflection in the Heat of Battle

You may be thinking at this point,

Sure, it's fine to go off and reflect when you have spare time to do so, whether you're commuting to the office or out on your boat. But what about those moments of crisis? You know how the saying goes: When you're up to your rear end in alligators, you forget that your original objective was to drain the swamp! What do you do when the events of the day leave you no time to reflect? The urgent always drives out the important!

You know what? There is always time to reflect. Stan Goldstein, CEO of the United States' largest drugstore chain, had time for it. Also, Hal Moore had time for it.

If Hal Moore could do it, you can do it. As Gordon Sullivan and Michael Harper (1997)described the scene in their book, *Hope Is Not a Method*, Lt. Col. Hal Moore was leading the 1st Battalion, 7th Cavalry, in the Ia Drang Valley of the central highlands in Vietnam in 1965. In the first major clash between U.S. forces and the North Vietnamese army, Col. Moore led his troops into a longtime Communist stronghold, where they were quickly surrounded and outnumbered four or five to one. They engaged the North Vietnamese in a fierce, bloody battle that lasted 4 days. At the end, half of Moore's battalion had died, along with hundreds of North Vietnamese. As Sullivan and Harper described the scene,

Moore's command had distinguished itself against an enemy that was far superior in numbers and that had held the initiative throughout much of the battle. Ultimately, both sides would claim victory, but the tenacity of the 7th Cavalry and its indomitable spirit are a monument to effective leadership.

There was a mystery in Moore's command behavior, however:

> During the fight, Moore established his command post in the center of the
> primary landing zone, partially protected by a large termite hill. With his
> radio operators, forward observers, and others he worked the artillery, air
> support, and resupply while he led the battalion in fight. From time to time
> he was observed to withdraw, appearing to those around him to be shutting
> down and blocking them out for brief periods of time.

What was Moore doing during those periods of withdrawal? After the
battle, Moore and his men were debriefed in detail to draw lessons
about how the North Vietnamese had fought. What was learned,
though, about Moore's leadership behavior?

> When asked about his periods of seeming withdrawal, Moore said that he
> had been reflecting, asking himself three questions: "What is happening?"
> "What is not happening?" "How can I influence the action?"
>
> > The leader's reconnaissance
> >   What is happening?
> >   What is not happening?
> >   What can I do to influence the action?
>
> Moore's behavior captured the essence of strategic leadership. Moore
> was scanning his environment, thinking about his situation, then determin-
> ing his best course. The future was winning the battle, not simply parrying
> each thrust. The genius to Moore's approach lies in his second question. *By
> reflecting on what was not happening, he was able to open his mind to broader
> opportunities, to see the full range of his options.* He was better able to antici-
> pate what might or might not happen next and to plan his moves to best ad-
> vantage. (Sullivan & Harper, 1997, pp. 46-47)

What strikes us about leadership behaviors such as Stanley Goldstein's
and Steve's and even Hal Moore's is that they sound so ordinary—they
are just good, simple observation, logic, and reasoning. There is nothing esoteric or "New Age" about this sort of reflection. This is simply a
matter of using (or taking) brief moments of free time to examine one's
experiences, to ponder over them, to reflect with others, and to draw
conclusions and action ideas from them.

Identity Growth Through Self-Reflection

Another quality of managerial reflection-in-use, according to Seibert's study, is that it is natural for managers to think about themselves as well as about business problems or other task-focused matters. Indeed, as previously noted, one of the most important metacompetencies that a manager can possess is identity development. This is the ability to learn about oneself, to solicit and hear personal feedback, to ask questions about the self (questions directed at oneself and to others), and to change one's sense of identity to fit with changes in one's skills, competencies, and experiences (Briscoe & Hall, 1999; Hall, 1986). One of the ways of developing this metacompetency of identity awareness is through engaging in reflecting about the self.

Reflecting about the self involves a relatively deep level of inquiry. One can think of reflection in terms of different levels of questions that a person might address. These questions form a ladder of inference, shown in Figure 9.1. As Figure 9.1 shows, inquiries into basic information and factual data and into how things work represent the most basic form of reflection, whereas questions asking about purpose and about how the experience relates to one's self represent the deepest level. These deeper questions have the greatest potential to lead to personal transformations for the individual.

Self-reflection for identity development is aided through processes such as 360-degree feedback, which provided developmental feedback from the observations of oneself, superiors, customers, subordinates, peers, and sometimes family and friends. Indeed, my belief is that the more a 360-degree feedback process is preceded by an initial self-reflection so that the feedback from others can be viewed as a way of confirming or adding to one's own self-perceptions, the more the person feels like the active agent of the personal change process—and thus the more effective the external feedback.

Indeed, unless the person is capable of examining and revising one's sense of self when going through a change process, one runs the risk of being "chameleon-like," simply reacting to each environmental demand without having a core or anchor to keep headed in the direction of one's own "path with a heart." Indeed, it is not until one has incorporated changed behavior into one's sense of identity that one has fully completed the adaptation process.

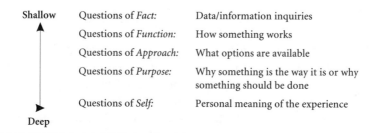

Shallow	Questions of *Fact:*	Data/information inquiries
	Questions of *Function:*	How something works
	Questions of *Approach:*	What options are available
	Questions of *Purpose:*	Why something is the way it is or why something should be done
	Questions of *Self:*	Personal meaning of the experience
Deep		

Figure 9.1. Ladder of Inference for Questions Formed in Inquiry (reproduced with permission from Seibert & Daudelin, 1999, p. 79)

Conditions That Promote Good Reflection

Based on his research, Seibert (1999) identified conditions in a person's job environment that can promote good reflection. They are summarized in Table 9.1.

A certain amount of autonomy in a job provides the person with the discretion and stimulus to engage in reflective activities, whereas feedback provides "grist for the mill," data on the outcomes of one's job actions on which one can reflect. Interactions with others provide the opportunities to get new raw material for reflection as well as the support for reflection and ideas for new perspectives to inform one's reflections. Job pressures can have the positive effect of stimulating reflective thinking, as can moments of solitude.

It is also possible to use these contextual conditions to help identify specific tools and activities that will promote reflection. Table 9.2 contains a list of such activities that Seibert (1999) identified in his research.

In addition to reflection that happens naturally in the person's everyday experience (or "in action" reflecting, as Seibert [1999] calls it), it is also possible to create reflection through an intentional process of coaching. In her research, Daudelin (1995) used mentors to help people reflect on a learning experience in addition to teams. She also gave people the assignment of reflecting by themselves. She found that the processes of reflecting with a coach and individually were both linked to effective learning. (Team-assisted reflecting appeared to be less effective, perhaps because of the distracting effects of group dynamics because the groups were in their early stages of formation.)

Table 9.1 Conditions That Promote Good Reflection

Reflection Condition	*Definition*
An Immediate Work Environment That Offers	
Autonomy	Ample freedom and discretion to structure one's work as one sees fit
Feedback	Information on the results of one's actions Information as the raw material of reflection
Interactions with other people	
• Access to others	Encounters with skilled and knowledgeable people
• Connection to others	At least one caring interpersonal relationship
• Stimulation by others	Encounters with people who provide new ideas and perspectives
Pressure	
• Promotive pressure	Significant performance demands resulting from time limitations and/or large amounts of new information
• Directive pressure	Significant performance demands resulting from the visibility and importance of the work
Momentary solitude	Periodic, brief occasions at or away from work to process new information alone

SOURCE: Seibert, K.W. (1999). Reflection-in-action: Tools for cultivating on-the-job learning conditions. *Organizational Dynamics, 27*(3), 58. Reprinted with permission.

Thus, we know from Daudelin's (1995) research that coached reflection can be effective, and we also know from Seibert's (1999) work that in-action reflecting can enhance learning. Table 9.3 summarizes in more detail the distinctions between coached reflection and in-action reflection.

Working with a peer coach can be a powerful aid to reflection in a self-assessment process. Also, other types of naturally occurring relationships (such as project teams, professional associations, interactions with customers, family, community, and support groups) can be used consciously to facilitate an individual's reflections (Hall & Kahn, 2001).

Steps for Leveraging Learning Through Reflection and Questions for Research

What are our lessons from the ideas in this discussion? On the basis of work by Kent Seibert and other research in our Executive Development

Table 9.2 Cultivation Tools for Reflection

Reflection Condition	Cultivation Tools
Autonomy	Clearly define the scope of the learner's authority in the assignment and define it broadly. Clarify expectations between learner and boss. Genuinely empower the learner.
Feedback	Establish formal and informal mechanisms for obtaining feedback from superiors, peers, and customers. Look for feedback in the work itself (financial data, status reports, etc.).
Interactions with other people	
• Access to others	Connect with customers, functional experts, suppliers, etc. Pursue breadth in variety of personal contacts. Make it OK to ask naive questions.
• Connection to others	Develop one or two deep relationships at work. Find a superior, peer, mentor, or friend who can help support the learner emotionally. Try to build a relationship involving mutual support.
• Stimulation by others	Connect with people who think differently. Embrace diversity in others. Interact with others who will challenge the learner's perspectives and assumptions.
Pressure	
• Promotive pressure	Establish stretching deadlines. Immerse the learner in large quantities of new information. Approach decisions decisively.
• Directive pressure	Establish the importance of the assignment to the learner and to the organization. Publicly announce goals and timetables. Seek opportunities to share the status of the work with people who matter (executives, customers, etc.).
Momentary solitude	Note brief moments alone as chances to reflect. Reflect while engaged in activities that do not require conscious thought, such as sitting through unproductive meetings, eating lunch alone, and traveling.

SOURCE: Seibert, K.W. (1999). Reflection-in-action: Tools for cultivating on-the-job learning conditions. *Organizational Dynamics, 27*(3), 58. Reprinted with permission.

Roundtable, the following are lessons of reflection (Seibert, 1996b, pp. 261-263). Along with each lesson, there is an important research issue— usually, how can we maximize the likelihood that this will happen in a work setting.

Table 9.3 Two Types of Reflection

Coached	In-Action
An intervention designed to promote review of an experience	A spontaneous mental process intended to make sense of an experience
Facilitated by someone other than the learner	Conducted by the learner himself or herself
Occurs at discrete points in time	Is ongoing
Is planned using formal, structured tools	Is unplanned and informal
Occurs by physically removing the learner from the experience	Occurs in the midst of the experience while it is happening
Is contemplative	Is active

SOURCE: Seibert, K.W. (1999). Reflection-in-action: Tools for cultivating on-the-job learning conditions. *Organizational Dynamics, 27*(3), 58. Reprinted with permission.

1. Embrace intentional inquiry. Be curious and get into the habit of asking questions. Remember that the "old competency" was the ability to say "I know …" and the "new competency" is the ability to say "Let's ask …." Ask many "why" questions to try to get to the root causes of experiences.

The following is the research question here: Why does this reflection not generally happen in everyday work practice? What steps could an organization or a leader take to make this inquiry happen more frequently?

2. Recognize and harness natural thinking abilities. Stop and notice what conditions or experiences stimulate you to reflect naturally. It may be when you encounter a surprise, something totally unexpected. Take advantage of those occasions to push yourself to think deeper. Try to build reflection into your everyday life.

Again, we need research on the most effective ways to help people build reflection into their everyday lives. We could start by comparing people who do reflect on a regular basis with a matched sample of people who do not. What is the profile of the regular reflector?

3. Inbrief. Do not wait until after an experience to "debrief" it to yourself. Instead, do what Seibert calls "inbriefing"—reflecting on experiences in the moment as you are having them. If Col. Moore can do inbriefing during the heat of the Ia Dang battle, you can do it in the midst of your annual budget planning.

Research here would have to be more subtle than that addressing the previous issues. We need to find unobtrusive ways of identifying and measuring inbriefing. Although it could be studied retrospectively, if it is not done in real time, we are not doing justice to the concept. The technology of wireless communication devices may provide creative new ways of doing this during the next few years.

4. Identify brief windows of opportunity for reflection. When you think about it, there are countless times during the day when you have pauses or "down time." It may be while you are commuting or traveling—we find one of our best times for reflecting is when we are 30,000 feet above the world in a plane. There is something about the physical perspective that this altitude provides that has a profound effect on our attitude as well. Other great opportunities are when you are on hold on the telephone, when waiting for an appointment or for the kids after school, or perhaps when mowing the lawn. Remember Stanley Goldstein's time on his boat and on the golf course. You do not even have to force yourself to think about work issues—just free your mind, and the thoughts will come.

All the time management books tell you to capture these spare moments, and I say use them for reflection, not just for more task accomplishment. (Indeed, task efforts should be more productive if they are undertaken mindfully vs. mindlessly.)

On the research front, some people are naturally better at seizing everyday moments than others. Therefore, one kind of research could be simply comparing people who do this with those who do not. Then, we could study interventions aimed at creating more daily reflection for people who do not do it naturally.

5. Build developmental relationships with "reflectors." As Marilyn Daudelin's (1995) exercises suggest, other people can be a great source of assistance in learning through reflection. Seek out other people who share your interest in learning. Try some of these exercises together. Form a support group. Contract with a colleague to serve as peer coaches for each other. Form a reading and discussion group. Form an investment club. Build peer-coached reflection into your regular meeting activities. Remember everything Stanley Goldstein learned from the truck driver and from his predecessor, Frank Rooney.

Here, it would be interesting to do research on people who have reflectors in their social network compared to people who do not. Does this behavior "rub off" naturally, or does the nonreflector have to consciously attend to this learning?

6. Reject the myth that we "learn from experience," and accept the reality that we "learn by reflecting on experience." Just realizing that you have to

exert conscious effort to capitalize on your experience will take you a long way in capturing the learnings.

We have seen from Daudelin's (1995) research that adding the process of conscious reflection heightens the person's learning from an experience. To help an individual appreciate fully the value of this reflection, it might be interesting to study people as they do their own personal experiments in which they do reflection after some experiences and not after others. Then, measure the learnings from both sets of experiences after a period of time. Determine if the person has captured more learning, as assessed by himself or herself, after doing the reflections.

7. Develop a language for talking about reflection that fits the organization's culture. It is easy to slip into a lot of jargon when discussing the ideas about reflection. Perhaps we have done that here. In making reflection part of your everyday life, find ways of discussing it that fit with the everyday language of your work environment. Perhaps words such as thinking or analyzing sound more familiar to your friends and coworkers than terms such as reflection or inbriefing. Use your own words when you enlist others in this kind of learning.

For research, it would be very simple to compare organizational cultures in which reflection was part of the talk and the culture versus those in which it is not. For example, in the U.S. Army, in which activities such as the after action review (AAR) capture lessons learned are very familiar to the average member, it is very easy and natural for a person to say, "Let's do a quick AAR as a team." One would expect reflection and learning to be higher where there is a language of reflection.

8. Use questions to aid your reflection. One of the best tools for reflection is the use of questions to help you focus your thinking. Remember Col. Moore's three questions: What is happening? What is not happening? and What can I do to influence the action? Other questions may work better for you. Experiment and find what works best for you.

For research, a simple experiment, similar to Daudelin's (1995), could be devised. One group could be asked to do reflection on an important experience in their own way, with no questions specified. The other group could be given focusing questions. Then, learning would be measured following the reflections to determine if the group with the questions had learned more than the other group.

9. Encourage bosses to promote career reflection conversations. Managers and executives need to be educated about the value of reflection. Executive

development activities should incorporate reflection tools. Developmental activities, such as performance appraisal discussions and career discussions, should be designed with time for individual and peer reflection. In fact, in my experience, the most productive kind of performance appraisal is one that is conducted as a career reflection conversation. In this process, the boss asks the employee to reflect back over the most rewarding times in his or her career. Then, after the employee discusses some of these satisfying times, the boss asks, "Now, what kind of future work assignments could give you more of those good experiences?" Then comes the current performance question: "Now, what do you have to do in this assignment to prepare and position yourself for this career move?"

Research on this issue could be similar to studies of mentoring processes. In the same way that we assess the extent to which a mentor engages in the various mentoring task behaviors or does not, we could examine the extent to which a leader enables and encourages reflection and career dialogue. We could also study whether the leader models this behavior in his or her own daily work.

10. Build reflection into regular work activities. Make capturing the learnings a regular part of doing business. Make it an explicit part of strategic planning sessions, problem-solving meetings, status update meetings, and discussions with customers. Create the norm that you never finish a major piece of work without asking, "What did we learn from this? What can we do differently next time, based on this learning?"

This process could be studied the way we study job design because this action would essentially make reflection part of a person's formal job. Then we could compare jobs that have been "enriched" by reflection with jobs that have not been changed. We could also use survey research to simply assess current practice and identify the various ways that organizations are now doing reflective activities.

Remember, "Experience is the best teacher—if you can learn from it!"

Appendix

Tools to Promote Reflection

Here, we consider some specific "tools" that help people do this reflection and capture the lessons of their own experiences. First, some tools are presented for you to do this capturing of lessons learned by yourself. Then, we consider ways of doing this personal reflection with the aid and support of other people.

Learning Logs

A very simple way of promoting reflection is to get into the habit of making regular entries in your personal "learning log." This is a journal that can take various forms. To make it most accessible, I recommend a simple, small, lined notebook in a size that fits easily into your purse, pocket, or briefcase. The key is to always have it available so that you can pull it out and enter your thoughts on the spur of the moment—while you are waiting for a bus, plane, appointment, or a meal in a restaurant. Some people prefer to use a computer for a learning log. If you carry a computer around with you, this can be effective as well. In my experience, using a desktop computer does not work as well because the machine is less available to you on the spur of the moment. One way a desktop computer learning log can work well, however, is if you sit down and use the computer on a regular basis. For example, some people I know do their journal every night on their home computer before they turn in for the night.

I suggest that you think of four key questions in relation to each entry in your learning log:

1. What happened? What was the experience? Write down the details of what happened: Where were you? What did other people do? What did you do? What was the result? and so on.

2. Why did it happen? What are the lessons of the experience? What did you learn from it? What generalizations can you draw from the experience?

3. What can I do about it? What action can or should you take as a result of this learning? What would you do differently next time in a similar situation? How can you get help from other people to support you in this behavior?

4. With whom can I share it? One of the best ways to learn something is to teach it. Whom do you know that would benefit from learning what you have just learned? When and how can you best share it with them?

To help prompt you, you might make up your own learning log with the following questions written on each page in a format such as that shown in Exhibit 9.1.

EXHIBIT 9.1

A Learning Log

Date: _____

1. What happened?

2. Why did it happen?

3. What can I do about it?

Peer-Coached Reflection

Marilyn Daudelin (1995) found that the learning from reflection can be multiplied if you do it with another person, with each of you acting as a coach for the other. This is just one of the many ways that a relationship can enhance learning.

Daudelin (1995) recommends the following procedure for peer-coached reflection:

Step 1: Individual reflection (20 minutes)
  Write about a recent experience, using the questions in your learning log (see Exhibit 9.1).
Step 2: Paired reflection (20 minutes—10 minutes per person)
  Read the one or two sentences that capture the essence of the experience.
  Briefly describe what happened.
  Report on insights and their implications for future action.
  Collect feedback from partner.
  Record any new insights in your learning log.

Step 3: Learning reports (30 minutes) (in small groups, four or five people maximum)
    Read the one or two sentences that capture the essence of the experience.
    Report a couple of the most significant insights and their implications (no discussion at this point, please!).
    Progress in order around the circle until all have reported insights.
    Discuss insights and learning themes.
    Record any new insights in learning log.

Step 4: Closure exercise (10 minutes)
    Form a large circle.
    Each person reports one insight surfaced during the exercise.
    Record any new insights in learning log.

This peer-coached reflection exercise can be done in the context of a team meeting, a retreat or workshop, a department meeting, a support group, or any other gathering of people interested in new ways of learning together. Although the design looks very simple and straightforward, it can yield powerful insights, especially if the people in the group have shared similar kinds of experiences so that their individual insights can potentially be generalized to other members.

Getting the Most Learning From a Meeting or Seminar

One of the most troublesome aspects of many meetings or seminars designed to promote learning is that they cover a lot of material, but often in a didactic way, and there is little opportunity to reflect on how the material relates to one's own life or work. It could also be a rich, experiential activity, full of insights and excitement, but then it may end without a real linkage being made to everyone's everyday life. Often, such meetings or programs end abruptly because the time is up, and everyone has to dash out of the room.

The following is a design that Marilyn Daudelin (1995) created for rescuing a meeting or seminar from these frustrations:

Step 1: Individual reflection (10 minutes)
    Use the questions in your learning log to jot down specific insights that occur to you.
    Be sure to answer the question about implications for future action.

Step 2: Discussions with a partner
    Pair up with another person.
    Discuss a few of the more significant insights that you recorded.

Write down (in your learning log) any new insights that occur as a result of this discussion.

Step 3: Group discussion (20 minutes)

One person begins by reporting two significant insights—one about the content of what was presented during the meeting or program and one about his or her personal learning.

Proceed around the circle, with each person sharing two insights, keeping the report to simple statements of learning.

Record any new insights in your learning log.

I have used this design to capture learnings from all kinds of learning experiences, and it is remarkable how useful it is for people to hear what others have learned. It creates reactions such as, "Oh, yeah, I noticed that, too! That *is* a good lesson!" It helps move ideas from a vague, intuitive sensing to a very concrete conclusion.

10 Toward More Strategic and Self-Directed Careers

To: Rachel Thompson, CEO
         SystemsWork Corporation

From: Andrew Morton
         Chair, Board of Directors
         Chair, Board Executive Committee

Subject: Enhanced Career Development

Rachel,

Now that we have merged, acquired, downsized, outsourced, outplaced, and transformed the business, how are we going to strengthen the organization, by retaining and growing the leadership talent that remains? How will you avoid what some have called the "cesspool syndrome," the stark possibility that, as a result of all of the corporate trauma that you have been through (and perhaps also because of the imperfect way that you have managed your people during these changes), the good people have left for greener pastures and only the dregs remain?

According to McKinsey & Co., we are now at a point where there is a "war for talent." With new technologies and information systems becoming cheaper and more available to all, with more competitors getting very smart about strategy, the playing field is being leveled. The critical factor now is execu-

AUTHOR'S NOTE: I am grateful to Kathy Kram and Lisa Cheraskin for their helpful comments on earlier drafts of this chapter.

tion. Those firms that can attract and provide career growth for the most talented professionals and leaders will be the ones that thrive and survive.

What is the plan for identifying and developing the leadership and workforce that SystemsWork will need to take us to the next level? How can we link the strategic growth of our business with opportunities for our employees to develop and fulfill themselves in their careers? As we have discussed in the executive committee and in full board meetings, you have the full support of the board of directors in making the investments necessary, including board time, to accomplish this career development. Right now this lack of leadership bench strength is the #1 barrier to our future growth.

We would welcome a discussion of your plans for leadership/career development at a meeting of the executive committee in the near future.

How would you, as a senior human resource professional, respond if the CEO burst into your office Monday morning and asked for your ideas on an integrated, business-driven plan for career development in your organization? Oh, and by the way, she needs it in 2 weeks for the next executive committee meeting. What would your recommendation be?

Although this particular vignette is not real, the situation is real in many companies. This is a composite based on real companies' experiences. In many contemporary business organizations, a major limiting factor in corporate growth is the bench strength and quality of their leadership resources. I hear increasingly from senior executives responsible for corporate management and executive development programs, including our business partners in the Boston University Executive Development Roundtable, that a major problem is the attraction, development, and retention of leaders and professionals in critical skill areas. How would you respond to the CEO's request for a comprehensive leadership development plan?

Over the years, I have had the opportunity to study or consult with or both many organizations as they designed programs for executive succession, leadership development, and career development. This chapter represents an effort to pull together some lessons from this work—in the form of basic ingredients and a plan for an integrated leadership development process. It is presented here in the form of a design for a hypothetical organization, the SystemsWork Corporation.

SystemsWork is a technology-based firm, relatively new in the grand scheme of things but definitely not a start-up. It was created in the mid-1970s by an engineer-entrepreneur, and the business has been very successful. After many years of rapid growth, it has slowed recently, with sales hovering at approximately $800 million. It has been difficult to reach the billion-dollar level. The market is there, and the products are acknowledged to be industry leaders in performance and quality, but the organization has not been able to move to the next stage of operating more independently of the founder and CEO. Also, the CEO feels besieged because she lacks critical skills, such as marketing strategy, in her top management team; therefore, she believes that "I have to do it all myself."

The Business Need for a Career Development Plan

Perceived Future Business Challenges

When I have asked senior executives in several firms similar to SystemsWork (i.e., well-managed, growing, technology-based and financial services companies) what critical business challenges their firms will face during the next 5 to 10 years, the responses generally have come down to a basic issue: sustaining strong corporate growth. As they grow, companies often reach a certain size barrier, like SystemsWork, at which the company seems to have hit a temporary plateau (e.g., the $1 billion or $10 billion barrier).

The major factor that is now causing this limit to corporate growth in many companies is the quality (and the bench strength) of their leadership resources—the talent is not being grown inside. This fact has been well documented by McKinsey's (1999) influential study of the "war for talent." Thus, in this competition for strong leaders, the executive search firms are enjoying a booming business as increasingly more companies look to the outside market for senior talent. As we hear from our business partners in the Boston University Executive Development Roundtable (and these firms are viewed as the leaders in executive development), a major problem is the attraction, development, and retention of leaders in critical skill areas ("We can't pay them enough or offer enough stock options to hold on to the stars"). Also, to complicate matters further, true development of leaders involves not only changes in skills and competencies but also transformations of their basic identities (how they view themselves and the world), and this is hard work (Heifetz, 1994).

We often hear that a company would have to have managers and executives with a different set of skills over the next 5 years (e.g., better communication and interpersonal skills, better team skills, more identification with the whole company rather than one's own "stovepipe," better strategic thinking, and increased ability to understand and manage complexity). As one executive in a technology-based firm stated, "The set of skills necessary to take us to where we are now is different from what we need to take us to the next level."

How do these leadership competencies relate to firm performance? In the McKinsey (1999) study's top quintile companies, 65% of their top executives rated their company's talent pool as "much stronger" or "somewhat stronger" than the competition (vs. only 35% in the mid-quintile firms. Also, in these top quintile firms, the average annual shareholder return between 1986 and 1995 was 22% (vs. 12% for mid-quintile companies).

Not only do they want better talent but also executives often would prefer to see these new skills developed internally. In firm after firm, one hears examples of very visible outside hires at senior levels that were viewed as not successful, supporting the idea that a corporation must "grow its own" talent. The "stick rate" for external hires is often in the range of 30% to 40%.

My personal view is that although hiring from the outside at senior levels can be risky, there is a need for a mix of internal and external hiring in certain circumstances: (a) when the critical competencies are not available internally and (b) when there is a need for more bench strength overall. Certainly, it would be ideal to have a sufficient range of competencies and depth of talent so that the company could rely primarily on internal development; to reach that point, however, a certain amount of external recruiting will probably be necessary.

Perceptions of Needed Management Skills

In informal surveys, I have asked executives if they would be interested in participating in a formal management education and development process or program. The consensus is clear and positive. When I ask what kinds of development work they personally would like to do, they often mention skill areas such as the following:

- Communications and interpersonal relationships skills (especially when working across organizational levels). These include the following:
  Active listening
  Giving and receiving constructive feedback
  Negotiation and confrontation skills
- Leading and working in teams (Several executives described themselves as "lone wolves"—very effective in individual activities but feeling challenged by the growing need for teamwork.)
- Developing a true team at the top (the senior executive group)
- Knowing when to seek participation and consensus and when to be decisive
- Knowing how to manage change and how to deal with resistance to change
- Integrative thinking (managing for the good of the whole [SystemsWork Corporation] and getting out of the "stovepipe mentality")
- Developing long-term planning and strategic skills; aligning short-term activities better with long-term goals
- Keeping up with the technical side of the business and its products

Many of these skill areas can be viewed as people skills, or what Daniel Goleman (1995, 1998) calls emotional intelligence. My sense, however, is that these go beyond simply people skills and also cover business skills, leadership, technical and product understanding, and change management skills.

This is a long list of skills, but it is not exhaustive. How can we ever expect one person to master such a diverse set of skills and also be able to acquire new ones that become important in the future? To get to my own "bottom line," there are two things we need to do: We need to have a clear strategy for developing managers, and we need to focus not just on skills but also on the process of learning (i.e., metacompetencies, or how people learn competencies).

A Strategic Framework for Career Development

In today's customer-focused, cost-conscious corporations, it is critical that functions such as career and leadership development be done in a way that moves forward the business strategy while developing the individuals involved. Thus, it is important to capitalize on the natural resources for development that are already present in the organization.

Rather than having large, complex, long-term career development systems, increasingly more organizations are searching for career development activities, especially for managers and executives (Seibert, Hall, & Kram, 1995), that have the following benefits:

1. Help promote the business purpose and strategy
2. Promote learning and career growth through real work (action learning)
3. Can be done quickly
4. Are low cost
5. Use available resources (e.g., other people in the organization)
6. Can be recognized and retained in memory as career development experiences

The basic purpose of developing stronger managers is to support the strategic objectives of the company (Hall, 1995). Creating a management development process involves creating the strategic linkages shown in Figure 10.1. From the business strategy and the direction of the future needs of the business, it is possible to identify the competencies that will be needed in the company's leaders, its executives and managers. Next, there must be a method of identifying and assessing those competencies in managers and executives. There must also be a process or program for developing those competencies.

The company's staffing process needs to include moving people who already have the needed competencies into the right positions as well as placing people into challenging assignments that will stretch them and strengthen or grow additional competencies that they need. Finally, the company's reward system (e.g., compensation and formal and informal recognition) must reinforce the development and demonstration of these new managerial skills.

Furthermore, in addition to having all the management development elements shown in Figure 10.1, it is critical that these activities be managed and integrated (McCall, 1998). Some very large corporations with excellent human resource functions are very strong in the separate aspects of this framework, but these firms lose competitiveness because these activities are too highly specialized and poorly integrated.

Ultimately, as the human resource capabilities of an organization grow, all elements of Figure 10.1 will be developed and integrated. At this time, it is important to start with what is already present in the organization and then to build from that. Therefore, the focus in this chapter is mainly on needed competencies and methods of developing

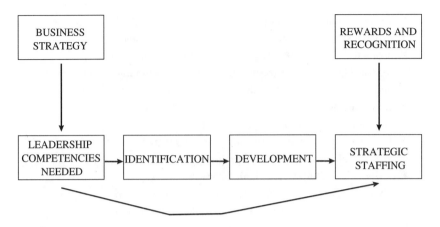

Figure 10.1. Model of Strategic Career Development

them. We discuss staffing primarily as a means of development (through challenging assignments).

Naturally Occurring Resources for Development

Increasingly, organizations are realizing that several naturally occurring resources offer these qualities by using the everyday work environment as a development tool (Hall & Associates, 1996; McCall, 1998). Thus, in our work on contemporary careers, we need to understand more about these natural processes as a way of meeting management development needs in a more constrained corporate environment.

Elements in the natural work environment that can be used to aid career development include the following:

- Challenging assignments (e.g., jobs, teams, task forces, and committees)
- Rapid change (in technology, products, and industry)
- Feedback (e.g., 360-degree or multirater, performance review)
- Developmental relationships (e.g., mentoring)
- Coaching (e.g., skill building, not just remedial)

The following qualities in the organization are critical (Hall & Moss, 1998):

- Corporate purpose (e.g., human meaning)

- Corporate values (e.g., for personal identification)
- Strong respect for the individual and individual potential
- Strong leadership climate (e.g., inspirational and empowering)
- Formal skip-level employee-manager/executive communication processes
- Support for employee career development (e.g., development culture)
- Commitment to diversity (e.g., valuing individual employees)
- Human resource leadership and support
- Formal management education and training programs
- Formal individual development programs
- Business-linked succession planning process
- Job rotation (e.g., cross-functional and cross-business moves)
- Easy access to career information (e.g., online information)
- Value for balance, the whole person (e.g., for sustainability)
- Corporate entry-level recruiting of technically trained people with management education and potential

Again, not only do these organizational qualities need to be present but also they need to be integrated and managed.

At the individual level, the following activities are becoming essential:

- Participating in leadership development education programs
- Using self-assessment resources (e.g., 360-degree and PC-based instruments)
- Reflection on own behavior (e.g., learning logs and peer methods)
- Individual networking and benchmarking (internal and external)
- Ability to ask for help (e.g., from peers, boss, and friends)
- Ability to adapt (e.g., go for novelty and learn new skills)
- Career and life planning (e.g., with family and partner)
- Development action plans (e.g., linked to performance review)
- Developmental action (e.g., willingness to risk, move, and take nontraditional assignments)

For specific ways of using these natural resources for executive development, see Hall (1995) and Seibert et al. (1995).

Using the Model Diagnostically: Assessment of SystemsWork's Resources for Leadership Development

Here, we consider the natural opportunities for leadership development that SystemsWork's environment provides for development. An overall general assessment of the current organization and culture regarding the previously discussed levels of resources for leadership might appear as shown in the following sections.

Natural Work Environment Factors: Very Strong

In a firm such as SystemsWork, with a successful track record of creating its own markets, the opportunities for learning in the everyday work environment are outstanding. The work assignments are extremely challenging. Coworkers are the best in their fields, which provides superb opportunities to learn through relationships at work, be they mentoring relationships, working together on project teams, or informal interacting in the cafeteria. The changes in the work environment (e.g., from individual to team functioning) and in products and technology demand continuous learning and development. Coaching, although just starting in a formal way in many firms, undoubtedly occurs often in informal interactions.

Organizational Factors: Mixed
(Some Very Strong; Some Underdeveloped)

The organizational factors involved in SystemsWork's young, fast-growing culture can be extremely strong: a compelling corporate mission, strong corporate values, and respect for the individual. There may be a high level of identification with the company, its purpose and its values, that may be quite unusual in today's downsized, "new contract" environment. Thus, this strong identification represents a tremendous competitive advantage for the firm in attracting and retaining executive and management talent. The importance of this advantage cannot be overstated.

At the same time, there may be a belief that because the company has changed so much, some people may have lost this feeling of identification—or of its importance. Also, there was a concern that new employees may not be experiencing it as well. Thus, it appears that such a firm might risk losing its advantage in this area.

Individual-Level Activities: Weak

In many newer, fast-growing firms such as SystemsWork, there is a paradox: Although the natural work challenges are strong growth facilitators, there is not a strong culture or value (or time) for development. In a world in which self-initiated continuous learning is becoming essential for career survival, this is an area that needs immediate attention.

There is good technology available to help managers and executives (and all employees) engage in personal reflection to capture learnings from experience, self-assessment, and career and life planning. There are also excellent executive education seminars available in areas such as strategy (e.g., at Northwestern's Kellogg School or Columbia's Arden House), managing organization change (e.g., at Columbia), and leadership development (e.g., at the Center for Creative Leadership, Boston University). These external programs, if used selectively, could assist senior executives and high-potential managers in acquiring the executive skills necessary to take the firm to its next level of growth.

Priorities and Recommendations: Seven Steps to Growth for Career Practice and Research

Research on executive careers has shown that of the previously mentioned ingredients, the following had the greatest impact on career success (Hall & Associates, 1996; McCall, 1998; McCall, Lombardo, & Morrison, 1988):

- Challenging assignments
- Formal training, education, development, and succession planning programs
- Developmental relationships

Therefore, I recommend as a first step that in most organizations efforts could profitably be made to create career development activities that will cover these three areas. Furthermore, initial efforts should be those that represent "low-hanging fruit" (i.e., can be done relatively quickly and easily).

These three areas also represent promising areas for additional research on careers. In particular, in recent years, the impact of relational influences on career development has become more clear. We need to get beyond mentoring and examine the wide range of naturally occurring relationships that a person experiences at work to better understand the processes by which these relationships affect the person's career growth.

There are seven initial basic principles for understanding career and organizational growth in any organization (Figure 10.2). These represent seven steps that could be used both to promote the business success and growth of the corporation through the growth of talent and to guide a research program on critical career system factors that affect an individual's career development.

Principle 1. Strong leadership of the human resources and of employee development function is necessary. (An organization that does not have strong leaders in these two key roles should get them now!)

Creating a strong career development process requires extremely strong leadership. This requires major culture change. Therefore, not only is strong leadership required but also these roles will demand outstanding skills in managing change. Within the human resource function, a clearly identified "point person" should be named to coordinate and integrate the various career development activities that are taking place throughout the company. The term "organization development" was included in the career development role to make it legitimate for the person to work as an organizational change agent, participating in activities such as strategic planning (as it relates to human resource planning), organization redesign, and team development, in addition to individual education and development activities.

This step is listed first in priority because it would help enable the human resource function to integrate the components of development (work, formal programs, and developmental relationships) to link the business strategy to career development.

Principle 2. A career development steering committee, chaired by a senior line executive and composed of key leaders in both line and human resource roles, can guide the implementation of the strategy for career development.

Because the goal here is to create more companywide development of talent and more companywide identification, a cross-functional, cross-business group should be assigned responsibility for leading this career development change process.

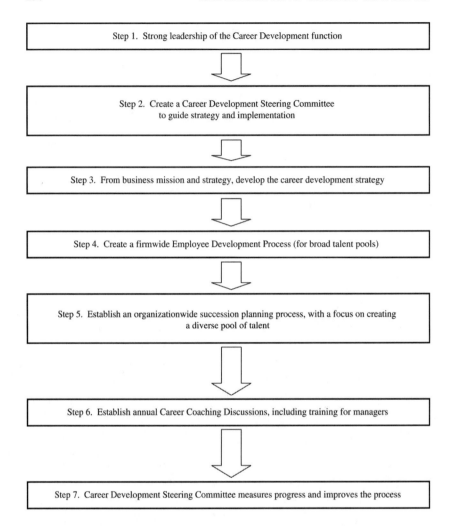

Figure 10.2. Steps in Career Development

For example, according to Ellen Johnston, Senior Manager of Executive Development, Sun Microsystems, has created what they call a leadership council, which is a group of 10 high-potential executives who meet quarterly to discuss the career development of leaders at Sun and to work on their own development. Each member serves a 2-year term, and the terms are staggered so that half of the council turns over each year: The "alumni" share what they have learned with their colleagues throughout the company. Thus, in addition to promoting the development of the council members, this structure provides a force for change at the top of the organization.

Ideally, as at Sun, the career steering committee should be a small group with a clear mandate and a specific timetable. Their charge would cover activities such as those discussed in the following principles.

Principle 3. Clarity on the mission and strategy of the business is critical, and the strategy for career development should be clearly linked to this business strategy.

A strategy for career development has no value or validity—indeed, it cannot properly be called a strategy—if it is not linked to the overall strategy and direction of the business. This is a critical stage at which the career development steering committee and the CEO need to work together to create a clear and compelling "theory of the case" for how the firm should approach the process of developing leaders. If this step is not taken, the firm will not have a strategic development process; it will be viewed as simply "the latest HR flavor of the month."

Principle 4. An employee development process (EDP), including career self-assessment workshops, can be a powerful method of implementing and giving visibility to career development. The process should focus on the development of metacompetencies rather than competencies. Attention should be given to career development for people at all levels, but it should start at the top to get strategic buy-in.

It is important to recognize that career development will cover all employees of the firm, although for tactical reasons you will probably want to start at one level and then extend the program to other levels later. Also, most firms start at the top to get senior executive buy-in and because other employees will take a process more seriously if top management starts and models the way.

Employee development can be a very simple process. It can be a conversation between employee and boss each year about the employee's work, aspirations, current and needed skills, current and needed experience, and mutual planning for the next steps in his or her development.

According to Charles Tharp (1999), Senior Vice President for Human Resources, such a process has recently been introduced at Bristol-Myers

Squibb, with a career dialogue serving as a replacement for a performance appraisal discussion. A 360-degree feedback process could be introduced as well, but at the beginning this element would not be as important as the manager-employee career development dialogue that the current EDP promotes. Developmental actions can include challenging assignments, formal education and development programs (e.g., "people skills," "change management skills," and "strategic skills"), and developmental relationships, depending on the individual's needs.

To support this EDP, career development seminars should be offered to assist employees and managers in self-assessment and career exploration and in building their skills in career self-management. The technology for these self-assessment and career management seminars has a long history and is well developed (Leibowitz, Farren, & Kaye, 1986) and can be provided on a large scale at a reasonable cost.

As this work continues, the employee would create and maintain a career portfolio, which would contain the record of these experiences along with the employee's reflections and lessons learned from them (a learning log). Research has shown that learning from experience is multiplied if the person is encouraged to reflect on it and to write his or her reflections in a journal (Daudelin, 1995; Seibert, 1999).

A central focus in capturing this developmental progress is on two metacompetencies: adaptability and identity growth. The actual experiences, especially if they contain variety and challenge, will promote adaptability, and the portfolio and the annual development conversations with the boss will promote identity learning (the person's self-awareness of new skills and development). Both these metacompetencies have to grow together. Adaptability without identity awareness can be blind reaction—the person may have adjusted to a new environment, but that reaction may take him or her away from the "path with the heart." Also, if the person becomes more aware of his or her skills and values but is unable to act on this self-knowledge, this can lead to psychological failure rather than success. Therefore, it is important to help the employee be mindful of these metacompetencies as the process unfolds because these two qualities are the ingredients in learning how to learn.

In fact, research at the Executive Development Roundtable (Briscoe & Hall, 1999) shows the incredible amount of effort that is currently being put into defining and measuring specific leadership competencies. Because companies often fail to adequately apply their competency models to a process of learning, however, I argue that much of this work on developing competency models is wasted. Also, the requisite competencies can change quickly as technology and business needs change. Thus, the process of how people learn is much more important than the elegance of the assessment models. The Bristol-Myers Squibb process of promoting a good boss-subordinate dialogue around development is an excellent example of working on the competencies of adaptability and identity learning. Through discussions such as these, the subordinate is encouraged to take a good look at himself or herself, and the boss acts as a coach in helping the person learn how to initiate successful change. (For more detail on developing metacompetencies, see Briscoe & Hall, 1999.)

Principle 5. Career development has greater legitimacy if it is done as part of an organizationwide human resources review and leadership succession planning process, with a focus on developing a diverse pool of talent.

An EDP will be implemented successfully to the extent that it meets a strong business need. A critical business need in most organizations is to build the bench strength of leadership talent to meet future business challenges. This means that the organization has a need to systematically assess the potential of its employees and make plans for developing them as future company leaders. A career planning process is a way to do this by marrying the development needs of both the individual and the organization. Succession planning integrates learning from challenging assignments, formal training and development, and developmental relationships.

A good career planning process has the following elements:

- It includes ownership by and involvement of senior line executives, with administration by the human resource organization.
- It includes a clear vision of the future business direction and strategy and the human capital requirements to take the company in that direction.
- It includes a process for organizational career review. This would cover the strengths and areas for improvement of managers and employees in a given unit in relation to the future strategic needs of the organization (with special attention given to the goal of increasing diversity in senior management so that the next generation of leaders will, in fact, be different from those now at the top).
- It includes the creation of a large, diverse talent pool. The old idea of a small number of "crown princes" and "crown princesses" no longer makes sense; no company

can predict its future skill needs so precisely that it can depend on a small range of talent. Companies need to cast their identification and development efforts widely to enable broad and deep bench strength, with all kinds of different people in the pool.

- It includes a process for sharing and discussing this talent review among senior management.

- It includes a process for planning and executing developmental action plans with senior management and key executives in other areas of the company (in which developmental job rotation moves might be needed).

- It includes a process for linking succession planning with the job assignment process. This can be a major "disconnect" in succession planning programs when, after much hard work goes into doing reviews and creating plans that are preserved in thick binders, key assignments are made without regard for these development plans. The person responsible for succession planning should be involved in the process of making key assignments.

- It includes linking of succession planning and executive/management performance appraisal (e.g., making the development of subordinates part of the executive's or manager's performance appraisal).

Although this process can be a series of one-on-one negotiations, it is done most effectively as a team process, with senior executives higher than the level of the managers being reviewed meeting as a group and conducting an organization review. Here, there is a process for sharing the information on the individual reviews and the developmental needs of the individuals. Then, as a group, the team discusses options for development and agrees on moves and "player swaps," with terms regarding pay, length of assignment, mentoring relationships, and the like.

It should be noted that this is a new kind of activity for a group of strong executives operating in a stovepipe culture, such as occurs in most corporations. It would take time and some training for such a group to learn to put on a "corporate hat," as opposed to their own functional or business hats.

It is also new for executives to actively work to identify and grow people who are different from them. The development of diversity in the management ranks calls for different kinds of challenge, support, and recognition (Morrison, 1992). An excellent guide to the development of minority managers can be found in Thomas and Gabarro (1999).

I recommend that companywide succession planning start at the level of the CEO and his or her staff, with the total group responsible for the organization and talent review. To keep it simple, the group could start with a small number of high-potential young managers, representing the most promising in each staff member's organization. The first step would consist of starting with the current organization and asking who are the possible successors to managers or executives at each level. Next, the group asks the following: What are these successors' development needs, and what action needs to be taken?

The following is a subsequent, more strategic question: What will our business look like in 5 or 10 years, and what are the gaps in our projected management talent? This would get the team to discuss how to blend internal development and external recruiting.

An attractive side benefit of having an executive team work together on succession planning and organizational reviews is that this activity provides a highly valued common strategic goal (developing the future leadership of the company) that can help create common purpose and team spirit. Thus, succession planning can be one effective way of doing team building.

Principle 6. Annual career coaching conversations between each employee and his or her boss represent a critical intervention point to provide relational development and to link the employee's career development needs with the company's business needs. The first step in these conversations should be self-reflection and self-assessment of career values and goals by the employee, which would be the starting point in the career conversation. A critical success factor is training for executives and managers in dialogue skills for implementing these career conversations.

In most firms, there is a developmental part to the regular annual performance appraisal process, which can be built on here. After discussing the employee's current performance, each manager should engage the employee in a discussion about his or her future goals and plans. Serious reflection by the employee should precede the conversation. This should be a dialogue process, not a feedback or persuasion attempt. The manager's role in this discussion should be that of coach, helping the employee problem solve about how best to achieve his or her future goals. In the discussion, the focus should be on steps the employee can take, not on what the manager can do to make things happen for the employee. (This is a key part of the employee empowerment process.)

Managers will need some training before they will feel comfortable with this kind of employee-centered coaching discussion. Without good training in how to conduct a career dialogue, this activity will not have its maximum value.

It is critical that part of the training include professional coaching for managers in how to conduct a career dialogue with employees, including how to ask exploratory, open-ended questions to draw out an employee's career aspirations, strengths, areas for development, and opportunities sought; how to put one's own perspective aside to enable one to truly hear the other's perspective; and how to actively "join" the other in supporting his or her growth. This development work should also include how to give realistic feedback on an employee's career aspirations.

Communications skills are especially critical here. In discussing an employee's development, it is important that a manager be able to establish open and trusting communication with the employee about his or her future aspirations and realism and the developmental steps necessary to work toward them.

Principle 7. Monitoring, assessment, and follow-up are critical to a career program's success. Program success will be positively related to the extent that the career development steering committee measures progress and revises career development activities as needed.

These activities represent only the "tip of the iceberg" of a full set of career development elements in a high-performing organization. There are many other components that might be deemed important to add as the work proceeds: addressing issues of diversity in career development, planning for the eventual departure of the current generation of top leadership, introducing career planning, formal mentoring programs, and expanded use of technology (e.g., the People Soft human resource information system already in use and decentralized human resources information and services).

Steps for Guiding the
Protean Careerist: Questions for
Career Self-Reflection or a Career Discussion

In commenting on the preceding section of this chapter, a good friend and colleague believed that it contained "no simple encouragement ... for the person to look after his or her own career agenda, or to stay in touch with industry trends or the market for one's talents" (Michael Arthur, personal communication, June 2001). Does the preceding material really "celebrate" the protean career? This is a good question to ponder. The previous steps, as summarized in Figure 10.2, do in fact focus on the organization. They are designed to help the organization capture what is known about career development to produce an organizationwide process for promoting organizational effectiveness through better development and use of people.

Is this consistent with the concept of the protean career? My view is that organizations still have a significant role to play in promoting protean careers. Also, the steps described here can potentially empower employees through the facilitation of informed search and exploration, support for mobility, provision of challenging experiences, developmental relationships, formal training and education, and the facilitation of identity growth and adaptability. If these organizational resources are provided with a view to building the capacities of the individual, as opposed to constraining and externally committing him or her, then the result can be win-win: career growth for the employee and business success for the organization. It is also important for the organization's management to realize that the successful development of employees will occasionally result in external offers and departures. Mobility in and out of the firm is to be expected. Enlightened organizations realize that by providing a strong developmental culture, this will make the organization more attractive to potential recruits while it grows people who will become targets for "raiding." If the developmental culture is vibrant and stresses freedom, individual identity growth, and personal adaptability, however, the net result over time will be a net inflow and retention—the talent will find the organization attractive and will want to be there.

Even if the organization provides all these good things for the development of its people, we still need to address the question of what do people need to do for themselves. We now turn to the individual to determine what actions the protean careerist might take. Consider that Rachel Thompson, mentioned at the beginning of the chapter, is now turning her attention to her own career as opposed to SystemsWork's career management process. What are some steps that Rachel could take to further her own learning and growth?

As noted in previous chapters, some of the most powerful influences on career development are new job challenges, relationships, and personal reflection to capture the lessons of experience. In the spirit of promoting dialogue and career conversations, either with another person or with oneself (through reflection), the following sections provide questions aimed at helping Rachel (and others—maybe even you) examine past, present, and future challenges and other sources of learning.

To Help You Decide if You Are Ready for a Change

Because career growth happens in short learning cycles, the following is an issue that Rachel will face often: Is it time to leave, or should I stay where I am? The following are questions for thinking about this issue:

- Are you still on a steep learning curve?
- Do you value what you are learning here?
- Do you like being here? Do you look forward to going to work each morning (or whenever you go to work)?
- What lies ahead for you where you are now? (If you do not know, ask a trusted person who might be in a position to know.)
- What are your four or five most important values in life?
- Write down each of those values. For each value ask, "Does this value support my staying here?" (Possible answers: yes, no, or not relevant). Examine the pattern of answers. If there are many no's, ask "Why haven't I taken action yet? What's stopping me?" If there are yes's and no's, ask "Can I redesign this job to convert some noes to yes's? Or am I willing to make some trade-offs in valued rewards to make a change?" If there are several not relevants, ask "How can it be that such an important decision is so unrelated to my most important values? Is my work that disconnected from my basic values?"
- What challenge(s) would you take on if you knew that you could not fail?

To Help You Decide Among Alternative Offers

If mulling over the previous questions suggests that it may be time to move on, here are questions to consider in choosing what to do next:

- How do those four or five most important values line up with each offer?
- In which alternative will you learn the most?
- Where will you find the most fun, stimulating colleagues?
- Why did the last person leave this job?
- Where might you get the most support for your professional development?
- Which option would contribute the most to your learning and development?

- Which option represents something that you have not done before? (Practice the "Mae West Rule": Mae West once said, "When I have to choose between two evils, I prefer to take the one I haven't tried yet.") The new and untried area produces more learning and excitement than the tried and mastered.

- What excites you the most— working with things, people, or ideas? How much challenge and support would each organization provide for the kind of work that excites you the most? Would there be pressures for you to focus in a different area? (For example, if you like ideas, would you have enough freedom and intellectual stimulation to stoke your creative juices, or would you be expected to spend your time managing people?)

- Look at your play (present and past). What do you do when you are not required to do anything? What does that tell you?

- Look at your life history. What were the high points? What were you doing then? What does that tell you about now?

- What do other people who know you well tell you about your interests and your strengths and weaknesses? What do they advise?

- If you have tried any career tests or inventories, what do they tell you? Try using a variety of sources and see what common themes occur.

To Help You Talk to Your Boss About a Possible Change

What about the delicate issue for Rachel of talking about leaving to Andrew Morton (chair of the board of directors and, thus, her boss)? When will you broach this subject, and how do you make this a developmental conversation for both parties rather than an angry parting of ways? Here are a few key questions to consider:

- Decide first if you can trust your boss. Have you taken a risk before in raising an issue with him or her, and did that discussion go well? If the answer is yes, you can trust your boss; if it did not go well, then do not discuss it, at least not until you have made a decision to leave.

- If you have a good relationship with your boss, ask if you can schedule a lunch or coffee out somewhere for a "career coaching" discussion. Say you would appreciate his or her help and advice on some career matters you have been thinking about. People appreciate being asked for advice, especially when they realize that you are not making any other demands on them.

- Let the boss know your dream or vision for your career future. You might talk about how much you have learned here and how much your boss has helped you with your development and how that has brought you to the point of thinking of next steps in your development. Also, if your dream for the future does not fit with staying in this organization, this should be pretty apparent to the boss.

- Have this discussion as early in your thought process as possible but after you know there is a good possibility that you might be leaving. This is a delicate balancing act. There is the risk that once the boss knows you might leave, you might get fewer of the choice assignments or other goodies; you do not want to be seen as a "lame duck" for too long. You do not want to leave the boss high and dry with a very short leave-taking process, either.

As we have discussed throughout this book, it is helpful to be engaging in dialogue with self and others on a regular basis, not just when major decisions must be made. These major decisions, however, such as whether or not to exit, do help focus the mind in a more compelling way than do everyday reflections or conversations.

11 Looking Back at Careers
In Organizations and
Looking Ahead:

TOWARD MORE SPIRITUAL CAREERS

Now, as we conclude this book, let us step back and reflect on where the whole field of careers is heading now, compared to where it was in 1976.

Looking Back at *Careers in Organizations*: Then and Now and Beyond

If the chapters in this book and the steps in career development shown in Figure 10.2 represent what we know about career dynamics at this point in time, how does this compare with what we knew in 1976 when *Careers in Organizations* was published? At that time, this was one of the first publications that linked the fields of careers and organizational behavior; there was no careers division in the Academy of Management, and there were no careers courses in schools of management and business (careers courses were found only in departments of education, psychology, and sociology). In Chapter 1, we discussed the changes in the context and the nature of careers during the past 25 years. Now, we step back, examine Figure 10.2, and reflect on some of the highlights of the change in the content of what we know about the process of career development.

The Protean Career Is No Longer Emergent: It Has Emerged. The last few pages of *Careers in Organizations* (Hall, 1976) referred to the protean career as "an emerging view of careers" (p. 200). At that time, this view was speculative but reasonable in light of the economic turbulence caused by oil embargoes and shortages, the economic downturn related to the end of the Vietnam War, and years of high inflation and high interest rates. Here, we review some of these speculations about the then future nature of careers:

> In the protean career ... attitudes, identity, and adaptability are simply more salient than they are in traditional careers. Almost by definition, since the protean person feels responsible for the long-run management of his life, he is more likely to be confronted by self-generated questions involving attitudes ("How do I feel about the work I am doing?"), identity ("Now that I'm 45, what do I want to be when I grow up?"), and adaptability ("How can I maintain my flexibility and freedom in the coming years?")
>
> In the traditional career, once the person commits himself to a career ladder in an organization, he can take a more passive role in managing his career; thus, as long as one concentrates on the performance dimension and is satisfied with one's rewards, there is little need to think about one's career attitude, identity, or adaptability until the career ladder begins to wobble, as it is in the many economy-minded organizations today. What this demonstrates is that along with the greater personal freedom found in the protean career also goes greater responsibility for one's choices and opportunities. This can entail greater feelings of insecurity and fear of failure than would be found in the traditional career, for the protean person knows that he cannot depend too heavily upon the employing organization for direction and security. (pp. 202-203)

These features of the protean versus the traditional career were summarized in a table, reproduced here as Table 11.1.

Reflecting on these predicted features of the protean career, I am not sure that I would change very much in describing the reality of the protean career today. The main change that I would make now is to

Table 11.1. The View From 1976: Differences Between the Traditional Career and the Protean Career

Issue	Protean Career	Traditional Career
Who's in charge?	Person	Organization
Core values	Freedom, growth	Advancement, power
Degree of mobility	High	Lower
Important performance dimensions	Psychological success	Position level, salary
Important attitude dimensions	Work satisfaction Professional commitment	Organizational commitment
Important identity dimensions	Do I respect myself? (self-esteem) What do I want to do? (self-awareness)	Am I respected by this organization? (esteem from others) What should I do? (organizational awareness)
Important adaptability dimensions	Work-related flexibility Current competence (measure: marketability)	Organization-related flexibility (measure: organizational survival)

SOURCE: Hall (1976, p. 202).

add more of the features of the protean career, now that we can see its details close up. In other words, we can now say more about the more differentiated features of this highly complex and adaptive view of Proteus in the career. Next, we discuss a few of these new features of the landscape.

Careers and Spirituality: We Now See Careers in the Service of Higher Purpose, Strategy, and Community. The organizational model used for Figures 10.1 and 10.2 suggests that careers are enacted by the individual to provide meaning and purpose, and they are managed by organizations to help carry out the mission and strategy of the institution. We now have a clearer sense of the relevance and importance of these micro and macro higher purposes as a way of integrating the goals and needs of the person and the organization. In 1976, only sociologists and "macro" organizational behavior scholars examined things such as organizational mission and strategy, and only humanistic psychologists in the tradition of Abraham Maslow examined the spirit and self-actualization of the individual. Now, there is more consensus from macro and micro scholars that we must consider both the person's path with a heart and the employer's path to profits.

We can state this even more strongly, however: One of the views that is currently emerging (as the protean view was just emerging in 1976) is the spiritual view of career as a calling (Weiss, Skelley, Hall, & Haughey, 2001). When I ask people today to imagine that their work and career represented a calling (putting aside the issue of whether they personally believe in the notion of a calling or not), I find that many people can identify quickly with this question. It is easy for people to slip into the language of "my vocation in life" and "my calling." This suggests that we all have a deep yearning to make meaning of the work we do. This is apparent in works such as Hillman's *The Soul's Code* (1997) and *The Force of Character* (1999), as well as in Ian Mitroff and Elizabeth Denton's *A Spiritual Audit of Corporate America* (1999) and Lee Bolman and Terry Deal's *Leading With Soul* (2001).

The calling notion, however, suggests a second new way of thinking about the career, beyond purpose. The calling also brings with it the idea that there is a community in which we do our work, and that our work should contribute to others in this community in some way. Thus, the path with a heart is not only about accomplishment and psychological success but also about service and contribution to others.

To give you a sense of how to help people think of their career as a calling, Box 10.1 shows a brief life/career planning exercise that I use. I usually precede this exercise with an approximately 30-minute discussion of the features of the protean career and encourage participants to think of their own careers and their own organizations.

BOX 11.1

**If Your Career Were a Calling:
A Self-Assessment Exercise**

Background

Many traditions and belief systems over the ages have included the idea that each of us has a reason or purpose for being in the world— that we were called here to do certain work in the world.

Now, you may or may not personally hold such a belief. Or maybe you haven't thought much about it.

Our Task

Well, regardless of what your personal beliefs are (we are not asking you about that), for our planning purposes today, we would like you to think about the following. For the sake of our discussion, assume that it were true that there is a calling behind the work you are doing and will do in the future. When you look back at the work you've done in the past, when you look at what your are doing now, and when you look ahead to what you might do next, if there is a calling behind that work, how would you describe that calling?

To help us think about our work in the world, let's do the following:

1. Take a few minutes and draw a *lifeline*, a graph that shows the ups and downs of our lives. You can label the vertical axis with any measure of life outcome (overall satisfaction? psychological success? connectedness? engagement? etc.) that you use to define a life worth living. The horizontal axis would be time (your age).

2. After you have drawn your lifeline, label the high points and the low points with a few words to describe what was happening in your life at that time. See if you can find any overall themes here that help explain the peaks and valleys for you.

3. Next, write 20 answers to the question, "Who am I?" (The first few will be easier. It gets harder later—and that's when you get into some good identity work!)

   Now, assume that you have had a good and long life. And like all good things, it will finally come to an end. Assume that you have accomplished all of the things that you are thinking about here today. Write your epitaph. (An epitaph is a few words that capture your essence, to be placed on a marker.)

4. Next, step back a bit and do some reflecting on our main question: If your work in the world reflects a calling, how would you describe that calling? Write it down in a sentence or two.

5. (20 minutes) Get together with a peer coach and share what you have just done. Each person will have 10 minutes to describe what she or he has written and discuss it with the partner. Then the other person will have 10 minutes to share and discuss his or her thoughts.

6. (30 minutes) Reconvene as a total group. (a) Go around the room and have everyone share how they described their calling. (b) Then discuss, as a group, any common themes we heard. Also ask the question, What does this all suggest for some shared activities that we might work on in the department?

We Are Now More Modest About the Organization's Role in Career Development, Using Career Resources in the Natural Work Environment. I admit that I had some misgivings about including in this book a chapter about an organizational process for career development. The reason is that career development can no longer be found as an explicit, managed activity in many contemporary organizations. In the 1980s, it was quite common to have a function, often in the human resources area, labeled "career development" or "employee development," and this was distinct from the training function, which was more specific and focused on skills acquisition. Now that corporate staffs, especially human resources staffs, have been downsized, organizational career development has virtually ceased to exist in many businesses.

The stated reason for this change is that we are now in the era of the self-managed or protean career, and it is all up to the individual. To that, I say, baloney! This is just a rationalization for removing organizational support for the kinds of development processes shown in Figure 10.2—processes that can build human capital and can make the difference between thriving and dying.

The fact is, however, that resources are tighter, and we must make the links between career development and corporate success correspondingly tighter. This is why the link to strategy and purpose is so critical. It is also why organizations need to use the steps shown in Figure 10.2 that use the everyday work of the business (strategy implementation, succession planning, selection of managers and leaders, and performance and career discussions) as the "engine" for career development. In the past, companywide career development seminars, generally 2 to 5 days long, were often held at corporate headquarters (with all the attendant travel and accommodation expenses) to get people to focus on career planning. Some of these (e.g., Travelers Insurance's 8-day career planning conferences) were described in *Careers in Organizations* (Hall, 1976). Now, organizations try to find ways to harness job assignments, existing work relationships, and individual reflection to promote career development.[1] Much of the work that had been done in corporate career planning seminars has been effectively "outsourced" to career consulting firms whose practice is largely driven by outplacement.

It Is Much Clearer That Challenging Job Assignments Drive Career Development, But We Still Do Not Know Exactly What to Do About It. Through research at AT&T (Berlew & Hall, 1966; Howard & Bray, 1988) and the

Center for Creative Leadership (McCall et al., 1988), it has become "ground truth" that the largest component in individual development comes from the stretching effects of challenging job assignments. *Careers in Organizations* used a lot of ink to discuss job challenge for career development, but this was a novel perspective at that time.

The bad news, however, is that we still do not have a clear sense of how to harness this knowledge. Although we do have some tools to help individuals recognize the developmental value from assignments that they have had, there is still no clear method for constructing sequences of jobs that would produce particular developmental effects. Currently, we know something about how to help individuals assess the developmental challenges that they have not yet experienced so that they can search for ways to obtain assignments that would provide those challenges. We know less, however, about how an organization can plan a series of appropriate developmental assignments for an individual.

A major reason for this state of affairs is that it is difficult to change the staffing processes in fast-moving businesses. Most managers and executives understandably want to select a person who will give the strongest performance in a key assignment. This often means picking a person who already has a track record of success in that kind of work, not a person who needs to develop those skills. Thus, it is difficult to gain acceptance for using the developmental needs of the candidate as an important criterion for selecting that person for an assignment. Only organizations with a strong culture for development will make that choice, and these tend to be the companies with strong human capital and histories of success (Pfeffer, 1998).

We Know More Now About Relational Development—That Everyday Work Relationships Can Be Harnessed for Development—But It Is Difficult to Do Something About This, Too. Perhaps the greatest career research progress during the past 25 years has been in the area of developmental relationships. Through the work of Kram (1988) and others, we know that mentoring has powerful effects on career growth. Also, the even better news is that it is not just the junior person who benefits: This is very much a mutual process, in which the senior person receives new skills and perspectives, fresh energy, recognition, generativity, and emotional support as well as other rewards.

We have also learned that career development can occur in a much wider set of work relationships, not just mentoring relationships. It can happen in peer relationships, with members of a task force or project team, with customers, with subordinates, in professional societies. In addition, it does not have to occur just in work settings. The learning can happen with family members (e.g., lessons from dealing with children or with aging parents can transfer over to learning how to deal with bosses, subordinates, and customers at work) and with friends (Hall & Kahn, 2001). Every person has a whole network of relationships that can be tapped for developmental purposes (Higgins & Kram, 2001). These developmental relationships can be especially powerful for the career progress of racial and ethnic minorities and other underrepresented groups in organizations (Thomas, 2001).

The problem is the same as that with assignments: It is difficult to know how best to intervene and use work relationships for development in a systematic way. The most promising aspect of relationships—their ubiquity—is precisely what makes them so difficult to "manage." When we try to formalize mentoring, the resulting relationships often feel forced for the participants. If we do not formalize them in some way, however, then some people are left out. The trick is to try to have "formal-informal" programs, in which perhaps the organization creates a process for participants to meet periodically (e.g., informal lunch gatherings) and provides support for their work together (e.g., training or readings in how to give and receive mentoring and reimbursement for monthly lunches or dinners together) and recognition for people who are known to be "great mentors." Even in organizations such as the military, in which extensive mentoring occurs informally, it has been difficult to find the appropriate organizationwide mentoring processes.

Work/Life Issues Are Now Clearly Part of the Career Landscape, Both in Research and in Practice. This area probably represents the starkest difference between *Careers in Organizations* (Hall, 1976) and this book. If you look at the table of contents of the 1976 book, you will see that the topic simply did not exist then (or at least not in my book). I had done research on women's life and work roles starting in 1971, and some of that work was presented in the 1976 book, but to the best of my recollection work/life (or work/family) did not exist as an area of research or practice.

As this book suggests, the relationships between work experiences and those in other parts of a person's life space are now the subject of a rich and extensive body of literature. This development is consistent with the current focus on the person-driven protean career: By putting the person at the center of the career dynamics process, by looking at things through the person's eyes, we see the person's whole life, not just the work career.

In this area, unlike assignments and relationships, we do have a clearer sense of what to do (but by no means do we have all the answers). There is legislation regarding leaves for parenting, organizations provide employees with information and resources for various kinds of family care, supervisors have learned to be more sensitive to personal and family needs, and employees have become more comfortable giving priority to these needs at times. Most organizations have a function, usually in human resources, for the coordination of work/life issues, albeit generally at the level of employee benefits rather than corporate strategy. At the societal level, it is now much more accepted and valued when a person makes a career sacrifice (e.g., turning down a promotion or a new job that would require relocation, more frequent travel, or more job stress) for the benefit of the family than it was in 1976.

In a similar vein, research on work/life issues is far more developed and differentiated, as Chapter 8 suggests. We have progressed from exploring types of conflict to examining the effects of stress on various types of employees and dual-career couples, the effects of flexible work schedules, the effects of formal work/life programs and practices, coping strategies, the effects of parents' working and child care arrangements on child development outcomes, and so on. There are still many work/life stressors, but the state of the research and the state of the practice has come a long way since 1976.

In Summary, Careers Are at Once "Tighter" and "Looser" Than They Were 25 Years Ago. What do I mean by this strange statement? By looser, I mean that individuals have more "slack" in enacting and managing their careers than they did in 1976. Under the protean career concept, which was introduced as a theoretical possibility at the end of *Careers in Organizations* and which is now much more common, the individual has much more self-control and is less tightly tied to a particular organization or occupation. Also, as discussed in the previous section, the person's family or personal life is less tightly controlled by work life. The person has more free choice to maximize personal and family outcomes.

At the same time, careers are tighter in several respects. Time frameworks for development and for accomplishing work objectives are much tighter. An example of this is the shorter career learning cycles that occur today as opposed to the longer career-spanning life cycles described in *Careers in Organizations*. Also, there is a much tighter connection between work, learning, and career development than existed 25 years ago. Now, it is clear that career development or growth is driven by learning, and learning is driven by new work challenges. Learning is not something that just happens (in school) before the career starts but, rather, a lifelong process. Also, development happens through doing one's work, all the time, not just in formal career development programs that may occur approximately every 10 years. There is also more tightness in the form of greater connection to other people, through teams and projects at work, through ongoing developmental relationships, and through professional networks outside of work.

Thus, ironically, just as the person is becoming more of a "free" agent in her work, she is simultaneously becoming more of a connected member of a larger career network. Any living system grows by becoming more differentiated or specialized and by becoming more integrated at the same time, thus moving up to a greater level of complexity. Therefore, human beings, in their careers, are becoming more highly developed by becoming more free, individualized, and self-directed and by becoming more integrated with their work and social environments.

Conclusion

One of the fortunate features of management systems is that they are all interdependent. This means that it is often not critical exactly where an organization starts on a new activity. If you start somewhere, you will see results. If you already have some of these elements in place, which most organizations do, you can leverage from them and add the others described here.

Providing support for the learning of employees and managers—both for helping their subordinates develop and for their own development—is a critical part of this whole process. The good news in using natural resources for development is that you do not need many large, special training facilities and programs; the bad news is that you have to invent relevant ways to build learning into everyday work. One of the most cost-efficient ways to do this is through self-assessment, reflection, and coaching, which can aid in the development of a wide range of individual skills and behaviors. (For a discussion of ways of using coaching, how it operates, and what works best, see Hall, Otazo, & Hollenbeck, 1999).

As you measure progress, you will see where changes, improvements, and additions have to be made. It is important (a) to have a clear goal and direction in which you want to move, and (b) to build on what you already have, and (c) to integrate and manage these development activities to serve companywide objectives. You can get there from here—and almost anywhere else.

The main difference between where we are now early in the 21st century and where we were in 1976, when *Careers in Organizations* was published, is that we have a solid understanding of the organizational intervention points (as shown in Figure 10.1) of the factors that enhance career development. We know that people grow as a result of challenging job assignments, from supportive and challenging relationships, from serious self-reflection, and from professional assessment of talent, with appropriate feedback and developmental planning. We also know that the boss-employee relationship, supplemented by good peer relationships, can be fertile ground for focusing the person's career development efforts. Finally, we know that the full weight of the organization's commitment will be brought to bear on the career development process when it is solidly grounded in a clear understanding of the overall strategy of the business so that it is clear to everyone that career development matters.

In 1976, we did not have a clear understanding of what had to be done to grow more successful careers. Now, we know what we need to do. Each individual step, as described in this chapter, is easy to do. Doing all of them is difficult. Doing them all together, in an integrated way and as a strategic way of managing people, requires caring, competent, and committed leadership—leadership that challenges, inspires, enables, models, and encourages members to celebrate and develop independent protean careers.

Note

1. Interestingly, *Careers in Organizations* (Hall, 1976) did describe some organizational practices, then in their early stages, that have become "mainstream" today. For example, it cites Joel Moses's work on pioneering assessment centers for development (vs. selection). In 2001, in his presentation for his Society for Industrial and Organizational Psychology Award for Contribu-

tions to Professional Practice, Dr. Moses summarized the lessons from this work, many of which involved the theme of using work experience in the development process (Moses, 2001). *Careers in Organizations* also described the early work of Alcan in framing layoffs as "outplacement" and using this traumatic event as a time when positive change in life and work can take place. This, too, has become established, and much career practice work is done in the context of downsizing and outplacement.

References

Abraham, J. D., & Hansson, R. O. (1995). Successful aging at work: An applied study of selection, optimization, and compensation through impression management. *Journal of Gerontology: Psychological Sciences, 50B,* 94-103.

Albert, S., & Whetten, D. (1985). Organizational identity. *Research in Organizational Behavior, 7,* 263-295.

Allen, N. J., & Meyer, J. P. (1990). Organization socialization tactics: A longitudinal analysis of links to newcomers' commitment and role orientation. *Academy of Management Journal, 33,* 847-858.

Allen, N. J., & Meyer, J. P. (1997). *Commitment in the workplace: Theory, research, and application.* Thousand Oaks, CA: Sage.

Anakwe, U. P., Hall, J. C., & Schor, J. (1999, August). *Career management in changing times: Role of self-knowledge, interpersonal knowledge, and environmental knowledge.* Paper presented at the annual meeting of the Academy of Management, Chicago.

Andrews, J. D.W. (1967). The achievement motive and advancement in two types of organizations. *Journal of Personality and Social Psychology, 6,* 163-169.

Argyris, C. (1954). Human relations in a bank. *Harvard Business Review, 32,* 63-72.

Argyris, C. (1957a). *Understanding organizational behavior.* Homewood, IL: Irwin-Dorsey.

Argyris, C. (1957b). *Personality and organization.* New York: Harper & Row.

Army Training and Leader Development Panel. (2001). *The Army Training and Leader Development Panel officer study report to the Army.* Washington, DC: Department of the Army.

Arthur, M. B., Inkson, K., & Pringle, J. K. (1999). *The new careers: Individual action and economic change.* Thousand Oaks, CA: Sage.

Arthur, M. B., & Rousseau, D. M. (Eds.). (1996). *The boundaryless career: A new employment principle for a new organizational era.* New York: Oxford University Press.

Ashford, S. J., & Taylor, M. S. (1990). Adaptation to work transitions: An integrative approach. *Research in Personnel and Human Resources Management, 8,* 1-39.

Ashforth, B. E. (2000). *Role transitions in organizational life: An identity-based perspective.* Hillsdale, NJ: Lawrence Erlbaum.

Ashforth, B. E., Kreiner, G. E., & Fugate, M. (2000). All in a day's work: Boundaries and micro role transitions. *Academy of Management Review, 25,* 472-491.

Ashforth, B. E., & Saks, A. M. (1996). Socialization tactics: Longitudinal effects on newcomer adjustment. *Academy of Management Journal, 39,* 149-178.

Ashforth, B. E., Saks, A. M., & Lee, R. T. (1997). On the dimensionality of Jones' (1986) measures of organizational socialization tactics. *International Journal of Selection and Assessment, 5*(4), 200-214.

Ashforth, B. E., Saks, A. M., & Lee, R. T. (1998). Socialization and newcomer adjustment: The role of organizational context. *Human Relations, 51*(7), 897-926.

Bailyn, L. (1993). *Breaking the mold: Women, men and time in the new corporate world.* New York: Free Press.

Baltes, P. B., & Baltes, M. M. (1990). Psychological perspectives on successful aging: The model of selective optimization with compensation. In P. B. Baltes & M. M. Baltes (Eds.), *Successful aging: Perspectives from the behavioral sciences* (pp. 1-34). Cambridge, UK: Cambridge University Press.

Baltes, P. B., & Schaie, K. W. (1975, March). The myth of the twilight years. *Psychology Today,* 35-40.

Bandura, A. (1986). *Social foundations of thought and action.* Englewood Cliffs, NJ: Prentice Hall.

Bandura, A. (1997). *Self-efficacy: The exercise of control.* New York: Freeman.

Barber, A. E. (1998). *Recruiting employees: Individual and organizational perspectives.* Thousand Oaks, CA: Sage.

Bardwick, J. (1980). The seasons of a woman's life. In D. G. McGuigan (Ed.), *Women's lives: New theory, research and policy* (pp. 35-55). Ann Arbor: University of Michigan, Center for Continuing Education of Women.

Barley, S. (1989). Careers, identities, and institutions: The legacy of the Chicago School of Sociology. In M. B. Arthur, D. T. Hall, & B. S. Lawrence (Eds.), *Handbook of career theory* (pp. 41-65). New York: Cambridge University Press.

Barnett, R., & Baruch, G. K. (1985). Women's involvement in multiple roles and psychological distress. *Journal of Personality and Social Psychology, 4*(91), 135-145.

Barnett, R., & Brennan, R. T. (1995). The relationship between job experiences and psychological distress: A structural equation approach. *Journal of Organizational Behavior, 16,* 259-276.

Barnett, R., & Brennan, R. T. (1997). Change in job conditions, change in psychological distress, and gender: A longitudinal study of dual earner couples. *Journal of Organizational Behavior, 18,* 253-274.

Barnett, R. C., & Gareis, K. C. (2000). Reduced-hours employment. *Work and Occupations, 27*(2), 168-187.

Barnett, R. C., & Gareis, K. C. (2001, April). *Career satisfaction among full-time and reduced hours professionals: A study of married women physicians with children.* Paper presented at the annual meeting of the Society for Industrial and Organizational Psychology, San Diego.

Barnett, R., Gareis, K. C., & Brennan, R. T. (1999). Fit as a mediator of the relationship between work hours and burnout. *Journal of Occupational Health Psychology, 4,* 307-317.

Barney, J. (1991). Firm resources and sustained competitive advantage. *Journal of Management, 17,* 99-120.

Bartlett, C. A., & Ghoshal, S. (1989). *Managing across borders: The transnational solution.* Boston: Harvard Business School Press.

Beck, K., & Wilson, C. (2000). Development of affective organizational commitment: A cross-sequential examination of change with tenure. *Journal of Vocational Behavior, 56,* 114-136.

Becker, H., Geer, B., Hughes, E., & Strauss, A. (1961). *Boys in white.* Chicago: University of Chicago Press.

Bell, E. L. (1986). *The power within: Bicultural life structures and stress among black women.* PhD dissertation, Case Western Reserve University, Cleveland, OH.

Bell, E. L. (1992). Myths, stereotypes, and realities of black women: A personal reflection. *Journal of Applied Behavioral Science, 28,* 363-376.

Bell, E. L., & Nkomo, S. M. (2001). *Our separate ways: Black and white women and the struggle for professional identity.* Boston: Harvard Business School Press.

Bellesi, B. E. (1999, March). The changing American workforce. *Management Review, 9.*

Berlew, D. E., & Hall, D. T. (1964, Fall). The management of tension in organization: Some preliminary findings. *Industrial Management Review,* 31-40.

Berlew, D. E., & Hall, D. T. (1966). The socialization of managers: Effects of expectations on performance. *Administrative Science Quarterly, 11,* 207-223.

Betz, N. E., Fitzgerald, L. F., & Hill, R. E. (1989). Trait-factor theories: Traditional cornerstone of career theory. In M. B. Arthur, D. T. Hall, & B. S. Lawrence (Eds.), *Handbook of career theory* (pp. 26-40). New York: Cambridge University Press.

Betz, N. E., & Schifano, R. S. (2000). Evaluation of an intervention to increase realistic self-efficacy and interests in college women. *Journal of Vocational Behavior, 56,* 35-52.

Black, J. S., & Gregersen, H. B. (1999). The right way to manage expats. *Harvard Business Review, 77*(2), 52-63.

Black, J. S., Gregersen, H. B., & Mendenhall, M. (1992). *Global assignments: Successfully expatriating and repatriating international managers.* San Francisco: Jossey-Bass.

Blanchard-Fields, F., Chen, Y., & Hebert, C. E. (1997). Interrole conflict as a function of life stage, gender, and gender-related personality attributes. *Sex Roles, 37,* 155-174.

Block, J., & Kremen, A. M. (1996). IQ and ego-resiliency: Conceptual and empirical connections and separateness. *Journal of Personality and Social Psychology, 70,* 349-361.

Blustein, D. L. (1997). A context-rich perspective on career exploration across life roles. *Career Development Quarterly, 45*(3), 260-274.

Bolman, L., & Deal, T. (2001). *Leading with soul: An uncommon journey* (Rev. ed.). New York: John Wiley.

Bond, J. T., Galinsky, E., & Swanberg, J. E. (1998). *The 1997 National Study of the Changing Workforce.* New York: Families and Work Institute.

Boyatzis, R. E. (1982). *The competent manager: A model for effective performance.* New York: John Wiley.

Boyd, E. M., & Fales, A. W. (1983). Reflective learning: The key to learning from experience. *Journal of Humanistic Psychology, 23*(2), 99-117.

Bray, D. W. (1972). *The management recruit: Early career and development.* Paper presented at the annual meeting of the American Psychological Association, Honolulu.

Bray, D. W., Campbell, R. J., & Grant, D. L. (1974). *Formative years in business.* New York: John Wiley.

Bray, D. W., & Grant, D. L. (1966). The assessment center in the measurement of potential for business management. *Psychological Monographs, 80*(17), 2.

Bridges, W. (1994). *Jobshift: How to prosper in a workplace without jobs.* Reading, MA: Addison-Wesley.

Brim, O. (1966). Socialization through the life cycle. In O. G. Brim & S. G. Wheeler (Eds.), *Socialization after childhood.* New York: John Wiley.

Brim, O. G., Jr., & Wheeler, S. (1966). *Socialization after childhood: Two essays.* New York: John Wiley.

Briscoe, J. P., & Hall, D. T. (1999, Autumn). Grooming and picking leaders using competency frameworks: Do they work? An alternative approach and new guidelines for practice. *Organizational Dynamics,* 37-52.

Brockner, J. (1988). *Self-esteem at work: Research, theory and practice.* Lexington, MA: Lexington Books.

Brown, D., & Brooks, L. (1996). *Career choice and development* (3rd ed.). San Francisco: Jossey-Bass.

Brush, C. (1992). Research on women business owners: Past trends, future directions, and a new perspective. *Entrepreneurship Theory and Practice, 16*(4), 5-30.

Brush, C. (1999). *Women's entrepreneurship. The second ILO enterprise forum, International Small Enterprise Programme.* Zurich, Switzerland: International Labour Organization.

Buchanan, B., II. (1974). Building organizational commitment: The socialization of managers in work organizations. *Administrative Science Quarterly, 19,* 533-546.

Buffington, P. W. (1992). Creating healthy change. In S. S. Gryskiewicz & D. A. Hill (Eds.), *Readings in innovation* (pp. 93-97). Greensboro, NC: Center for Creative Leadership.

Burnstein, E. (1963). Fear of failure, achievement motivation, and aspiring to prestigeful occupations. *Journal of Abnormal and Social Psychology, 67,* 189-193.

Cable, D. M., & Judge, T. A. (1994). Pay preferences and job search decisions: A person-organization fit perspective. *Personnel Psychology, 47,* 393-398.

Cable, D. M., & Judge, T. A. (1996). Person-organization fit, job choice decisions, and organizational entry. *Organizational Behavior and Human Decision Processes, 67,* 294-311.

Cable, D. M., & Judge, T. A. (1997). Interviewers' perceptions of persons: Organization fit and organizational selection decisions. *Journal of Applied Psychology, 82,* 546-561.

Cain, L. D., Jr. (1964). Life course and social structure. In R. Faris (Ed.), *Handbook of modern sociology.* Chicago: Rand McNally.

Cairo, P. C., Kritis, K. J., & Myers, R. M. (1996). Career assessment and the Adult Career Concerns Inventory. *Journal of Career Assessment, 4*(2), 189-204.

Campbell, D. P., Hyne, S. A., & Nilsen, D. L. (1992). *Campbell Interest and Skills Survey.* Minneapolis, MN: National Computer Systems.

Campbell, J. P., Dunnette, M. D., Lawler, E. E., III, & Weick, K. E., Jr. (1970). *Managerial behavior, performance, and effectiveness.* New York: McGraw-Hill.

Campbell, R. J. (1968). Career development: The young business manager. In J. R. Hackman (Chairman), *Longitudinal approaches to career development.* Symposium presented at the American Psychological Association annual convention, San Francisco.

Campbell, R. J., & Bray, D. W. (1967, March/April). Assessment centers: An aid in management selection. *Personnel Administration, 30,* 6-13.

Carr, P. L., Ash, A. S., Friedman, R. H., Scaramucci, B. T., Barnett, R. C., Szalacha, L., Palepu, A., & Moskowitz, M. A. (1998). The relationship of family responsibilities and gender to the productivity and career satisfaction of medical faculty. *Annals of Internal Medicine, 129,* 532-538.

Champy, J., & Hammer, M. (1995, January 17). Re-engineering the corporation. *Wall Street Journal,* p. B1.

Chartrand, J. M., & Camp, C. C. (1991). Advances in the measurement of career development constructs: A 20-year review. *Journal of Vocational Behavior, 39,* 1-39.

Clark, S. C. (2001). Work cultures and work/family balance. *Journal of Vocational Behavior, 58,* 348-365.

Cohen, A. (1993). Organizational commitment and turnover: A meta-analysis. *Academy of Management Journal, 36,* 1140-1157.

Cohen, M. S. (1993). The naturalistic basis of decision biases. In G. A. Klein, J. Oransanu, R. Calderwood, & C. E. Zsambok (Eds.), *Decision making in action: Models and methods* (pp. 51-99). Norwood, NJ: Ablex.

Cox, T., & Driver, M. J. (1994). Workforce personality and the new information age workplace. In J. A. Auerbach & J. C. Welsh (Eds.), *Aging and competition: Rebuilding the U.S. workforce* (pp. 185-204). Washington, DC: National Council on the Aging and the National Planning Association.

Crane, D. (1966). Scientists at major and minor universities: A study of productivity and recognition. *American Sociological Review, 30,* 699-714.

Crites, J. O. (1973). *Career Maturity Inventory.* Monterey, CA: McGraw-Hill.

Cuddihy, B. R. (1974). How to give phased-out managers a new start. *Harvard Business Review,* 61-69.

Dainty, A. R. J., Neale, R. H., & Bagilhole, B. M. (1999). Women's careers in large construction companies: Expectations unfulfilled? *Career Development International, 4*(7), 353-357.

Dalton, G. W. (1989). Developmental views of careers in organizations. In M. B. Arthur, D. T. Hall, & B. S. Lawrence (Eds.), *Handbook of career theory* (pp. 89-109). New York: Cambridge University Press.

Dalton, G. W., & Thompson, P. (1986). *Novations: Strategies for career development.* Glenview, IL: Scott, Foresman.

Dalton, G. W., Thompson, P., & Price, R. (1977, Summer). The four stages of professional careers. *Organizational Dynamics,* 19-42.

Dalton, M. (1959). *Men who manage.* New York: John Wiley.

Daudelin, M. (1995). Learning from experience through reflection. *Organizational Dynamics, 23,* 36-48.

DeFillippi, R. J., & Arthur, M. B. (1993). The boundaryless career: An inter-firm perspective on careers, entrepreneurship and cooperation. In *Proceedings of the 1993 Meeting of the Academy of Management.* White Plains, NY: Academy of Management.

Delbecq, A. L., & McGee, J. J. (2001, March 9-10). *Bridging the gap: Spirituality and business.* Conference sponsored by the Institute for Spirituality and Organizational Leadership, Santa Clara University, Santa Clara, CA.

Dix, J. E., & Savickas, M. L. (1995). Establishing a career: Developmental tasks and coping responses. *Journal of Vocational Behavior, 47,* 93-107.

Douvan, E., & Adelson, J. (1966). *The adolescent experience.* New York: John Wiley.

Downey, H. K., Hellriegel, D., & Slocum, J. W., Jr. (1975). Congruence between individual needs, organizational climate, job satisfaction, and performance. *Academy of Management Journal, 18,* 149-154.

DuBois, W. E. B. (1903). *The souls of black folks.* Chicago: Chicago University Press.

Duncan, R. B. (1971). Characteristics of organizational environments and perceived environmental uncertainty. *Administrative Science Quarterly, 17,* 313-327.

Eccles, R., Nohria, N., & Berkley, J. (1992). *Beyond the hype: Rediscovering the essence of management.* Boston: Harvard Business School Press.

Edwards, J. E., & Morrison, R. F. (1994). Selecting and classifying future naval officers: The paradox of greater specialization in broader areas. In M. G. Rumsey, C. B. Walker, & J. H. Harris (Eds.), *Personnel selection and classification* (pp. 69-84). Hillsdale, NJ: Lawrence Erlbaum.

Eisenhardt, K. M. (1989). Building theories from case study research. *Academy of Management Review, 14,* 532-550.

Ellington, J. E., Gruys, M. L., & Sackett, P. R. (1999). Factors related to the satisfaction and performance of temporary employees. *Journal of Applied Psychology, 83,* 913-921.

Erikson, E. H. (1963). *Childhood and society.* New York: Norton.

Erikson, E. H. (1966). The concept of identity in race relations: Notes and queries. *Daedalus, 95,* 145-171.

Evans, P. A. L., & Bartolome, F. (1981). *Must success cost so much?* New York: Basic Books.

Evans, P. A. L., & Bartolome, F. (1984). The changing pictures of the relationship between career and family. *Journal of Occupational Behavior, 5,* 9-21.

Evers, F. T., Rush, J. C., & Berdrow, I. (1998). *The bases of competence: Skills for lifelong learning and employability.* San Francisco: Jossey-Bass.

Featherman, D. L., Smith, J., & Peterson, J. G. (1990). Successful aging in a post-retired society. In P. B. Baltes & M. M. Baltes (Eds.), *Successful aging: Perspectives from the behavioral sciences* (pp. 50-93). Cambridge, UK: Cambridge University Press.

Fiol, C. (1991). Managing culture as a competitive resource: An identity-based view of sustainable competitive advantage. *Journal of Management, 17,* 191-211.

Fiol, C. (1994). Consensus, diversity, and learning in organizations. *Organization Science, 5,* 21-50.

Fisher, C. D. (1986). Organizational socialization: An integrative review. *Research in Personnel and Human Resources Management, 4,* 101-145.

Fletcher, J. (1994a). *Toward a theory of relational practice in organizations: A feminist reconstruction of "real" work*. Unpublished doctoral dissertation, Boston University, Boston.

Fletcher, J. (1994b). Castrating the female advantage: Feminist standpoint research and management science. *Journal of Management Inquiry, 3,* 74-82.

Fletcher, J. (1996). A relational approach to the protean worker. In D. T. Hall & Associates (Eds.), *The career is dead—Long live the career: A relational approach to careers* (pp. 105-131). San Francisco: Jossey-Bass.

Fletcher, J. (1998). *Disappearing acts*. Cambridge: MIT Press.

Fletcher, J. (1999). *Disappearing acts: Gender, power, and relational practice at work*. Cambridge: MIT Press.

Friedman, T. (2000). *The Lexus and the olive tree: Understanding globalization*. New York: Bantam Doubleday Dell.

Fuqua, D. R., & Hartman, B. W. (1983). Differential diagnosis and treatment of career indecision. *Personnel and Guidance Journal, 62,* 27-29.

Ginzberg, E., Ginsburg, J. W., Axelrad, S., & Herma, J. L. (1951). *Occupational choice*. New York: Columbia University Press.

Gist, M. E., & Mitchell, T. R. (1992). Self-efficacy: A theoretical analysis of its determinants and malleability. *Academy of Management Review, 17,* 183-211.

Glaser, B., & Strauss, A. (1971). *Status passage*. Chicago: Aldine/Atherton.

Glaser, B. G. (1964). *Organizational scientists: Their professional careers*. New York: Bobbs-Merrill.

Goffman, E. (1961). The moral career of the mental patient. In E. Goffman (Ed.), *Asylums*. New York: Anchor.

Goleman, D. (1995). *Emotional intelligence: Why it can matter more than IQ*. New York: Bantam.

Goleman, D. (1998). *Working with emotional intelligence*. New York: Bantam.

Goodman, J. (1994). Career adaptability in adults: A construct whose time has come. *Career Development Quarterly, 43*(1), 74-84.

Googins, B. K. (1991). *Work-family conflicts*. New York: Auburn House.

Gore, S., & Mangione, T. W. (1983). Social roles, sex roles, and psychological distress: Additive and interactive models of sex differences. *Journal of Health and Social Behavior, 34,* 300-312.

Gottfredson, L. S. (1978). An analytic description of employment according to race, sex, prestige, and Holland type of work. *Journal of Vocational Behavior, 13,* 210-221.

Gottfredson, L. S. (1996). Gottfredson's theory of circumspection and compromise. In D. Brown, L. Brooks, & Associates (Eds.), *Career choice and development* (3rd ed., pp. 179-232). San Francisco: Jossey-Bass.

Gould, S. B. (1975). *Organizational identification and commitment in two environments*. Unpublished PhD dissertation, Michigan State University, Lansing.

Gould, S. B., & Hawkins, B. L. (1978). Organizational career stage as a moderator of the satisfaction-performance relationship. *Academy of Management Journal, 21,* 434-450.

Gouldner, A. W. (1958/1959). Cosmopolitans and socials: Towards an analysis of latent social roles. *Administrative Science Quarterly, 2,* 446-450, 465-467.

Greenhaus, J. H., & Beutell, N. J. (1985). Sources of conflict between work and family roles. *Academy of Management Review, 10,* 76-88.

Greenhaus, J. H., & Callanan, G. A. (1994). *Career management* (2nd ed.). Orlando, FL: Dryden.

Greenhaus, J. H., & Parasuraman, S. (1999). Research on work, family, and gender: Current status and future directions. In G. N. Powell (Ed.), *Handbook of gender in organizations*. Thousand Oaks, CA: Sage.

Grezda, M. M. (1999). Re-conceptualizing career change: A career development perspective. *Career Development International, 4*(6), 305-311.

Gunz, H. P., Evans, M. G., & Jalland, R. M. (2000). Career boundaries in a "boundaryless" world. In M. A. Peiperl, R. Goffee, M. B. Arthur, & T. Morris (Eds.), *Career frontiers: New conceptions of working lives*. New York: Oxford University Press.

Hackett, G. (1995). Self-efficacy and career choice and development. In A. Bandura (Ed.), *Self-efficacy in changing societies*. New York: Cambridge University Press.

Haddad, T., & Lam, L. (1988). Canadian families—Men's involvement in family work: A case study of immigrant men in Toronto. *International Journal of Comparative Sociology, 29*(3-4), 269-281.

Hakim, C. (1994). *We are all self-employed: The new social contract for working in a changed world*. San Francisco: Berrett-Koehler.

Hall, D. T. (1968). Identity changes during the transition from student to professor. *School Review, 76,* 445-469.

Hall, D. T. (1971). A theoretical model of career subidentity development in organizational settings. *Organizational Behavior and Human Performance, 6,* 50-76.

Hall, D. T. (1972). A model of coping with role conflict: The role behavior of college educated women. *Administrative Science Quarterly, 17,* 471-486.

Hall, D. T. (1976). *Careers in organizations*. Glenview, IL: Scott, Foresman.

Hall, D. T. (1985). Project work as an antidote to career plateauing in a declining engineering organization. *Human Resource Management, 24,* 271-292.

Hall, D. T. (1986). Breaking career routines: Midcareer choice and identity development. In D. T. Hall & Associates (Eds.), *Career development in organizations* (pp. 120-159). San Francisco: Jossey-Bass.

Hall, D. T. (1993, November). *The new "career contract": Wrong on both counts*. Boston: Boston University Executive Development Roundtable.

Hall, D. T. (1994). *The new "career contract": Wrong on both counts?* (Tech. Rep.). Boston: Boston University School of Management, Executive Development Roundtable.

Hall, D. T. (1995). Executive careers and learning: Aligning selection, strategy, and development. *Human Resource Planning, 18,* 14-23.

Hall, D. T. (Ed.). (1996, February/1997, February). Careers in the 21st century [Special issue]. *Academy of Management Executive*.

Hall, D. T. (1996b). Protean careers of the 21st century. *Academy of Management Executive, 10*(4), 8-16.

Hall, D. T. (1999). Accelerate career development—At your peril! *Career Development International, 4,* 237-239.

Hall, D. T., & Associates. (Eds.). (1986). *Career development in organizations*. San Francisco: Jossey-Bass.

Hall, D. T., & Associates. (Eds.). (1996). *The career is dead—Long live the career: A relational approach to careers*. San Francisco: Jossey-Bass.

Hall, D. T., Briscoe, J. P., & Kram, K. E. (1997). Identity, values and learning in the protean career. In C. L. Cooper & S. E. Jackson (Eds.), *Creating tomorrow's organizations: A handbook for future research in organizational behavior* (pp. 321-337). London: John Wiley.

Hall, D. T., & Foster, L. W. (1977). A psychological success cycle and goal setting: Goals, performance, and attitudes. *Academy of Management Journal, 20,* 282-290.

Hall, D. T., & Gordon, F. (1973). Career choices of married women: Effects on conflict, role behavior, and satisfaction. *Journal of Applied Psychology, 58,* 42-48.

Hall, D. T., & Hall, F. S. (1976). The relationship between goals, performance, success, self-image, and involvement under different organization climates. *Journal of Vocational Behavior, 9,* 267-278.

Hall, D. T., & Hall, F. S. (1979). *The two career couple.* Reading, MA: Addison-Wesley.

Hall, D. T., & Hall, F. S. (1980). Stress and the two-career couple. In C. L. Cooper & R. Payne (Eds.), *Current concerns in occupational stress* (pp. 243-266). London: Wiley.

Hall, D. T., & Kahn, W. A. (2001). Developmental relationships at work: A learning perspective. In C. Cooper & R. J. Burke (Eds.), *The new world of work.* London: Blackwell.

Hall, D. T., & Louis, M. R. (1988). When careers plateau. *Research Management,* 41-45.

Hall, D. T., & Mansfield, R. (1971). Organizations and individual response to external stress. *Administrative Science Quarterly, 16,* 533-547.

Hall, D. T., & Mansfield, R. (1975). Relationships of age and seniority with career variables of engineers and scientists. *Journal of Applied Psychology, 60,* 201-350.

Hall, D. T., & Mirvis, P. H. (1993, October-December). The new workplace: A place for older workers? *Perspectives on Aging,* 15-17.

Hall, D. T., & Mirvis, P. H. (1994a). Careers as lifelong learning. In A. Howard (Ed.), *The changing nature of work.* San Francisco: Jossey-Bass.

Hall, D. T., & Mirvis, P. H. (1994b). The new workplace and older workers. In J. A. Auerbach & J. C. Welsh (Eds.), *Aging and competition: Rebuilding the U. S. workforce* (pp. 58-93). Washington, DC: The National Council on the Aging and the National Planning Association.

Hall, D. T., & Mirvis, P. H. (1995). The new career contract: Developing the whole person at midlife and beyond. *Journal of Vocational Behavior, 47,* 269-289.

Hall, D. T., & Mirvis, P. H. (1996). The new protean career: Psychological success and the path with a heart. In D. T. Hall & Associates (Eds.), *The career is dead—Long live the career: A relational approach to careers* (pp. 15-45). San Francisco: Jossey-Bass.

Hall, D. T., & Mirvis, P. H. (1998). Increasing the value of older workers: Flexible employment and lifelong learning. In J. A. Auerbach (Ed.), *Through a glass darkly: Building the new workplace for the 21st century.* Washington, DC: National Planning Association.

Hall, D. T., & Moss, J. E. (1998, Winter). The new protean career contract: Helping organizations and employees adapt. *Organizational Dynamics, 26*(3), 22-37.

Hall, D. T., & Nougaim, K. (1968). An examination of Maslow's need hierarchy in an organizational setting. *Organizational Behavior and Human Performance, 3,* 12-35.

Hall, D. T., Otazo, K., & Hollenbeck, G. P. (1999, Winter). Behind closed doors: What really happens in executive coaching. *Organizational Dynamics, 27*(3), 39-53.

Hall, D. T., & Richter, J. (1988). Balancing work life and home life: What can organizations do to help? *Academy of Management Executive, 2*(3), 213-223.

Hall, D. T., & Richter, J. (1990). Career gridlock: Baby boomers hit the wall. *Academy of Management Executive, 4,* 7-22.

Hall, D. T., & Schneider, B. (1972). Correlates of organizational identification as a function of career pattern and organizational type. *Administrative Science Quarterly, 17,* 340-350.

Hall, D. T., & Schneider, B. (1973). *Organizational climates and careers: The work lives of priests.* New York: Academic Press.

Hall, D. T., Schneider, B., & Nygren, H. T. (1970). Personal factors in organizational identification. *Administrative Science Quarterly, 15,* 176-190.

Hammer, L. B., Allen, E., & Grigsby, T. D. (1997). Work-family conflict in dual-earner couples: Within-individual and crossover effects of work and family. *Journal of Vocational Behavior, 50,* 185-203.

Handy, C. (1989). *The age of unreason.* Boston: Harvard Business School Press.

Handy, C. (1994). *The age of paradox.* Boston: Harvard Business School Press.

Hansen, L. S. (1997). *Integrative life planning: Critical tasks for career development and changing life patterns.* San Francisco: Jossey-Bass.

Harquail, C. V. (1991). Career paths and career success in the early career stages of male and female MBAs. *Journal of Vocational Behavior, 39,* 54-75.

Heifetz, R. A. (1994). *Leadership without easy answers.* Cambridge, MA: Harvard University Press.

Hesketh, B., & Neal, A. (1999). Technology and performance. In D. R. Ilgen & E. D. Pulakos (Eds.), *The changing nature of performance: Implications for staffing, motivation, and development* (pp. 21-55). San Francisco: Jossey-Bass.

Higgins, M. C. (1998). *Early career change: Toward a portfolio theory of relations* (Working Paper No. 98-016). Boston: Harvard Business School, Division of Research.

Higgins, M. C. (1999). *Changing careers: The effects of social context.* Unpublished manuscript, Harvard Business School, Boston.

Higgins, M. C., & Kram, K. E. (2001, April). Reconceptualizing mentoring at work: A developmental network perspective. *Academy of Management Review, 26*(2), 264-288.

Hill, L. A. (1992). *Becoming a manager: Mastery of a new identity.* Boston: Harvard Business School Press.

Hillman, J. (1997). *The soul's code: In search of character and calling.* New York: Warner.

Hillman, J. (1999). *The force of character and the lasting life.* New York: Random House.

Hipple, S. (1998). Contingent work: Results from the second survey. *Monthly Labor Review, 11,* 22-32.

Hoehn, M. (2000). *The role of agility in executive learning.* Boston: Boston University Executive Development Roundtable.

Holland, J. L. (1985). *The self-directed search.* Odessa, FL: Psychological Assessment Resources.

Holland, J. L. (1997). *Making vocational choices: A theory of vocational personalities and work environments* (3rd ed.). Englewood Cliffs, NJ: Prentice Hall.

Hollenbeck, G., & Hall, D. T. (2001). *Self confidence and leadership development* (Technical report). Boston: Boston University Executive Development Roundtable.

Hollenbeck, J. R., LePine, J. A., & Ilgen, D. R. (1996). Adapting to roles in decision-making teams. In K. R. Murphy (Ed.), *Individual differences and behavior in organizations* (pp. 300-333). San Francisco: Jossey-Bass.

Howard, A. (1992). Work and family crossroads spanning the career. In S. Zedeck (Ed.), *Work, families, and organizations* (pp. 70-137). San Francisco: Jossey-Bass.

Howard, A. (Ed.). (1995). *The changing nature of work.* San Francisco: Jossey-Bass.

Howard, A., & Bray, D. W. (1988). *Managerial lives in transition: Advancing age and changing times.* New York: Guilford.

Hrebiniak, L. C., & Alutto, J. A. (1973). Personal and role-related factors in the development of organizational commitment. *Administrative Science Quarterly, 18,* 555-572.

Hughes, E. C., & Coser, L. A. (Eds.). *On work, race, and the sociological imagination.* Chicago: University of Chicago Press.

Hullfish, H. G., & Smith, P. G. (1961). *Reflective thinking: The method of education.* New York: Dodd, Mead.

Jacobs, J. A., & Gerson, K. (1997). *The endless day or flexible office? Working hours, work-family conflict, and gender equity in the modern workplace.* New York: Alfred P. Sloan Foundation.

Jacques, E. (1965). Death and the mid-life crises. *International Journal of Psychoanalysis, 46,* 502-514.

Jacques, E. (1973). Equitable payment, 1961. In Task Force for the Secretary of HEW, *Work in America* (pp. 1-12). Cambridge: MIT Press.

Jennings, E. E. (1971). *Routes to the executive suite.* New York: McGraw-Hill.

Jones, C., Hesterly, W. S., & Borgatti, S. P. (1997). A general theory of network governance: Exchange conditions and social mechanisms. *Academy of Management Review, 22,* 911-945.

Jones, G. R. (1986). Socialization tactics, self-efficacy and newcomers' adjustments to organizations. *Academy of Management Journal, 29,* 262-279.

Judge, T. A., & Cable, D. M. (1997). Applicant personality, organizational culture, and organization attraction. *Personnel Psychology, 50,* 359-394.

Kahn, W. A. (1996). Secure base relationships at work. In D. T. Hall & Associates (Eds.), *The career is dead—Long live the career: A relational approach to careers* (pp. 158-179). San Francisco: Jossey-Bass.

Kaufman, H. G. (1974). *Obsolescence and professional career development.* New York: AMACOM.

Kegan, R. (1982). *The evolving self: Problems and process in human development.* Cambridge, MA: Harvard University Press.

Kegan, R. (1994). *In over our heads: The mental demands of modern life.* Cambridge, MA: Harvard University Press.

Kegan, R., & Lahey, L. L. (2000). *How the way we talk can change the way we work: Seven languages for transformation.* San Francisco: Jossey-Bass.

Knasel, E. G. (1980). A model, specifications and sample items for a measure of career adaptability in young blue-collar workers. *Canadian Counselor, 15*(1), 31-37.

Knasel, E. G. (1982, July 29). *Career maturity in adulthood.* Paper presented at the 20th International Congress of Applied Psychology, Edinburgh, United Kingdom.

Kobasa, S. (1982). The hardy personality: Toward a social psychology of stress and health. In G. S. Sanders & J. Suls (Eds.), *Social psychology of health and illness.* Hillsdale, NJ: Lawrence Erlbaum.

Koretz, G. (1997, January 27). Job mobility, American style. *Business Week,* 20.

Korman, A. (1967). Self-esteem as a moderator of the relationship between self-perceived abilities and vocational choice. *Journal of Applied Psychology, 51,* 65-67.

Korman, A. (1994). *Human dilemmas in work organizations.* New York: Guilford.

Korman, A., & Korman, R. (1980). *Career success/personal failure.* Englewood Cliffs, NJ: Prentice Hall.

Kouzes, J. M., & Posner, B. Z. (1995). *The leadership challenge: How to keep getting extraordinary things done in organizations* (2nd ed.). San Francisco: Jossey-Bass.

Kram, K. E. (1985). *Mentoring at work.* Glenview, IL: Scott, Foresman.

Kram, K. E. (1988). *Mentoring at work: Developmental relationships in organizational life.* Lanham, MD: University Press of America.

Kram, K. E. (1996). A relational approach to career development. In D. T. Hall & Associates (Eds.), *The career is dead—Long live the career: A relational approach to careers* (pp. 132-157). San Francisco: Jossey-Bass.

Kram, K. E., & Hall, D. T. (1991). Mentoring as an antidote to stress during corporate trauma. *Human Resource Management, 28*(4), 493-510.

Kram, K. E., & Hall, D. T. (1996). Mentoring in a context of diversity and turbulence. In E. E. Kossek & S. A. Lobel (Eds.), *Managing diversity: Human resource strategies for transforming the workplace* (pp. 108-136). Cambridge, MA: Blackwell.

Kram, K. E., & Isabella, L. A. (1985). Mentoring alternatives: The role of peer relationships in career development. *Academy of Management Journal, 28*(1), 110-132.

Kramer, D. A. (1986). A life-span view of social cognitions. *Education Gerontology, 12,* 277-289.

Krantz, D. (1977). The Santa Fe experience. In S. Sarason (Ed.), *Work, aging, and social change* (pp. 165-189). New York: Free Press.

Kuder, F. (1977). *Activity interests and occupational choice.* Chicago: Science Research Associates.

Kutner, D. H. (1971). *Crisis and decision at mid-life.* Unpublished manuscript, Yale University, New Haven, CT.

Labich, K. (1995, February 20). Kissing off corporate America: Why big companies can't hire the best and the brightest. *Fortune,* 44-52.

Lambert, C. (2001, March/April). The talent for aging well. *Harvard Magazine, 103*(4), 45-99.

Latack, J. C. (1984). Career transitions within organizations: An exploratory study of work, nonwork, and coping strategies. *Organizational Behavior and Human Performance, 34,* 296-322.

Latack, J. C. (1990). Organizational restructuring and career management: From outplacement and survival to inplacement. In G. R. Ferris & K. M. Rowland (Eds.), *Research in personnel and human resource management* (pp. 109-139). Greenwich, CT: JAI.

Lawler, E. E., III. (1997). *From the ground up: Six principles for building the new logic corporation.* San Francisco: Jossey-Bass.

Lawrence, P. R., & Lorsch, J. W. (1967). *Organization and environment: Managing differentiation and integration.* Boston: Harvard University, Graduate School of Business Administration.

Lee, S. M. (1971). An empirical analysis of organizational identification. *Academy of Management Journal, 14,* 213-226.

Lehman, H. C. (1953). *Age and achievement.* Princeton, NJ: Princeton University Press.

Leibowitz, Z. B., Farren, C., & Kaye, B. L. (1986). *Designing career development systems.* San Francisco: Jossey-Bass.

Levinson, D. J. (1959). Role, personality, and social structure in the organizational setting. *Journal of Abnormal and Social Psychology, 58,* 170-180.

Levinson, D. J. (1986). A conception of adult development. *American Psychologist, 41,* 3-13.

Levinson, D. J. (with Levinson, J.). (1996). *The seasons of a woman's life.* New York: Knopf.

Levinson, D. J., Darrow, C. N., Klein, E. B., Levinson, M. H., & McKee, B. (1978). *The seasons of a man's life.* New York: Knopf.

Levinson, H. (1962). *Men, management, and mental health.* Cambridge, MA: Harvard University Press.

Levinson, H. (1969). On being a middle-aged manager. *Harvard Business Review, 47,* 51-60.

Lewin, K. (1936). The psychology of success and failure. *Occupations, 14,* 926-930.

Lewin, K., Dembo, T., Festinger, L., & Sears, P. (1944). Level of aspiration. In J. McV. Hunt (Ed.), *Personality and behavior disorders.* New York: Ronald Press.

Linehan, M., & Walsh, J. S. (2001). Mentoring relationships and the female managerial career. *Career Development International, 4,* 348-352.

Lipsett, S. M., & Malm, F. T. (1955). First jobs and career patterns. *American Journal of Economics and Sociology, 14,* 247-261.

Livingston, J. S. (1976, July/August). Pygmalion in management. *Harvard Business Review, 47,* 81-89.

Lodahi, T., & Kejner, M. (1965). The definition and measurement of job involvement. *Journal of Applied Psychology, 49,* 24-33.

London, M. (1983). Toward a theory of work motivation. *Academy of Management Review, 8*(4), 620-630.

London, M. (1998). *Career barriers: How people experience, overcome, and avoid failure.* Hillsdale, NJ: Lawrence Erlbaum.

London, M., & Mone, E. M. (1987). *Career management and survival in the workplace.* San Francisco: Jossey-Bass.

London, M., & Mone, E. M. (1999). Continuous learning. In D. R. Ilgen & E. D. Pulakos (Eds.), *The changing nature of performance: Implications for staffing, motivation, and development* (pp. 119-153). San Francisco: Jossey-Bass.

Lynn, S. A., Cao, L. T., & Horn, B. C. (1996). The influences of career stage on the work attitudes of male and female accounting professionals. *Journal of Organizational Behavior, 17,* 135-149.

MacNeil, I. R. (1980). *The new social contract.* New Haven, CT: Yale University Press.

MacNeil, I. R. (1985). Relational contracts: What we do and do not know. *Wisconsin Law Review,* 483-525.

Major, D. A. (1999). Effective newcomer socialization into high performance organizational cultures. In N. M. Ashkanasy, C. Wilderom, & M. F. Peterson (Eds.), *The handbook of organizational climate and culture.* Thousand Oaks, CA: Sage.

March, J., & Simon, H. (1958). *Organizations.* New York: John Wiley.

Marx, M. H. (1963). The general nature of theory construction. In M. H. Marx (Ed.), *Theories in contemporary psychology* (pp. 4-46). New York: Macmillan.

Marx, M. H., & Hillix, W. A. (1963). *Systems and theories in psychology.* New York: McGraw-Hill.

Maslach, C. (1982). *Burnout: The cost of caring.* Englewood Cliffs, NJ: Prentice Hall.

Maslach, C., & Leiter, M. P. (1997). *The truth about burnout: How organizations cause personal stress and what to do about it.* San Francisco: Jossey-Bass.

Maslow, A. H. (1968, July). A theory of metamotivation. *Psychology Today, 2,* 38, 39, 58-61.

McCall, M. W., Jr. (1998). *High flyers: Developing the next generation of leaders.* Boston: Harvard Business School Press.

McCall, M. W., Lombardo, M., & Morrison, A. M. (1988). *Lessons of experience: How successful executives develop on the job.* New York: Free Press.

McCarthy, J. F. (2000). *Short stories and tall tales at work: Organizational storytelling as a leadership conduit during turbulent times.* Dissertation proposal, Boston University Graduate School of Management, Boston.

McClurg, L. N. (1999). Organisational commitment in the temporary-help service industry. *Journal of Applied Management Studies, 8,* 5-26.

McKinsey & Company. (1999). *The war for talent.* New York: Author.

Meyer, J. P., & Allen, N. J. (1984). Testing the "side-bet theory" of organizational commitment: Some methodological considerations. *Journal of Applied Psychology, 69,* 372-378.

Meyer, J. P., & Allen, N. J. (1997). *Commitment in the workplace: Theory, research, and application.* Thousand Oaks, CA: Sage.

Meyerson, D. E., & Fletcher, J. K. (2000, January/February). A modest manifest for shattering the glass ceiling. *Harvard Business Review, 78*(1), 126-136.

Mezirow, J. (1991). *Transformative dimensions in adult learning.* San Francisco: Jossey-Bass.

Miles, M. B., & Huberman, M. (1994). *Qualitative data analysis: An expanded sourcebook.* Thousand Oaks, CA: Sage.

Miller, J. B. (1986). *Toward a new psychology of women.* Boston: Beacon.

Miller, J. B. (1991). The development of women's sense of self. In J. V. Jordan, A. G. Kaplan, J. B. Miller, I. P. Stiver, & J. L. Surrey (Eds.), *Women's growth in connection.* New York: Guilford.

Mintzberg, H. (1990, March/April). The manager's job: Folklore and fact. *Harvard Business Review,* 163-176.

Mirvis, P. H., & Hall, D. T. (1994). Psychological success and the boundaryless career. *Journal of Organizational Behavior, 15,* 365-380.

Mitroff, I. I., & Denton, E. A. (1999). *A spiritual audit of corporate America.* San Francisco: Jossey-Bass.

Morrison, A. M. (1992). *The new leaders: Guidelines for leadership diversity in America.* San Francisco: Jossey-Bass.

Morrison, A. M. (1996). *The new leaders: Leadership diversity in America* (Reprint). San Francisco: Jossey-Bass.

Morrison, R. F. (1974, June). *A career development model: Implications for practicing physicians.* Invited address to the Colloquium on the Career Development of Physicians, Association of American Medical Colleges, Washington, DC.

Morrison, R. F. (1977). Career adaptivity: The effective adaptation of mangers to changing role demands. *Journal of Applied Psychology, 62,* 549-558.

Morrison, R. H., & Hall, D. T. (2001). *Adaptability: Toward a conceptual model* (Tech. Rep.). Boston: Boston University School of Management, Executive Development Roundtable.

Morrow, P. C., & McElroy, J. C. (1987). Work commitment and job satisfaction over three career stages. *Journal of Vocational Behavior, 30,* 330-346.

Moses, Joel (2001). "Distinguished professional contribution award: How to assess (and develop) leaders better."Paper presented at the 16th Annual Meeting of the Society for Industrial and Organizational Psychology, San Diego, CA, April 27.

Mowday, R., Porter, L., & Steers, R. (1982). *Employee-organization linkages: The psychology of commitment, absenteeism, and turnover.* New York: Academic Press.

Mumford, M. (1991). *Attributes conditioning the capacity for effective development: Background data measures of predicting performance in variable situations* (Contract No. N00014-91-5-1435). Arlington, VA: Office of Naval Research.

Mumford, M., Baughman, W. A., Threfall, K. V., Uhlman, C. E., & Costanza, D. P. (1993). Personality, adaptability, and performance: Performance on well-defined and ill-defined problem-solving tasks. *Human Performance, 6,* 241-285.

Munley, P. H. (1975). Erik Erikson's theory of psychosocial development and vocational development. *Journal of Counseling Psychology, 22,* 314-319.

Murphy, P. R., & Jackson, S. E. (1999). Managing work role performance: Challenges for twenty-first century organizations and their employees. In D. R. Ilgen & E. D. Pulakos (Eds.), *The changing nature of performance: Implications for staffing, motivation, and development* (pp. 325-365). San Francisco: Jossey-Bass.

Near, J. (1989). Organizational commitment among Japanese and U.S. workers. *Organizational Studies, 10,* 281-300.

Nelson, P. D. (1975, April). *Biographical constructs as predictors of adjustment to organizational environments.* Paper presented at the Research Seminar on Social Psychology of Military Service, University of Chicago, Chicago.

Nevill, D. D., & Super, D. E. (1986). *The salience inventory manual: Theory, application, and research.* Palo Alto, CA: Consulting Psychologists Press.

Nicholson, N., & West, M. A. (1988). *Managerial job change.* London: Cambridge University Press.

Nicholson, N., & West, M. (1989). Transitions, work histories, and careers. In M. B. Arthur, D. T. Hall, & B. S. Lawrence (Eds.), *Handbook of career theory* (pp. 133-201). New York: Cambridge University Press.

Nkomo, S., & Cox, T. (1996). Diverse identities in organizations. In S. Clegg, W. Hardy, & W. Nord (Eds.), *Handbook of organization studies.* Thousand Oaks, CA: Sage.

Noer, D. (1993). *Healing the wounds: Overcoming the trauma of layoffs and revitalizing downsized organizations.* San Francisco: Jossey-Bass.

O'Connell, D. J. (2001). *FAST stages in contingent employment: Finding, adapting, staying, and transforming.* Davenport, IA: St. Ambrose University, College of Business.

O'Reilly, C. A., & Chatman, J. A. (1996). Culture as social control: Corporations, cults, and commitment. *Research in Organizational Behavior, 18,* 157-200.

O'Reilly, C. A., Chatman, J., & Caldwell, D. F. (1991). People and organizational culture: A profile comparison approach to assessing person-organization fit. *Academy of Management Journal, 34,* 487-516.

Organ, D. W. (1988). *Organizational citizenship behavior: The good soldier syndrome.* Lexington, MA: Lexington Books.

Organ, D. W., & Konovsky, M. (1989). Cognitive versus affective determinants of organizational citizenship behavior. *Journal of Applied Psychology, 74,* 157-164.

Orlofsky, J. L., & Windle, M. T. (1978). Sex-role orientation, behavioral adaptability and personal adjustment. *Sex Roles, 4,* 801-811.

Ornstein, S., Cron, W. L., & Slocum, J. (1989). Life stages versus career stage: A comparative test of Levinson and Super. *Journal of Organizational Behavior, 10,* 117-133.

Ornstein, S., & Isabella, L. (1990). Age v. stage models of career attitudes of women: A partial replication and extension. *Journal of Vocational Behavior, 36,* 1-19.

Osherson, S. (1980). *Holding on or letting go: Men and career change in midlife.* New York: Free Press.

Ozer, E. M., Barnett, R. C., Brennan, R. T., & Sperling, J. (1998). Does childcare involvement increase or decrease distress among dual-earner couples? *Women's Health: Research on Gender, Behavior, and Policy, 4,* 285-311.

Patchen, M. (1970). *Participation, achievement and involvement on the job.* Englewood Cliffs, NJ: Prentice Hall.

Peiperl, M., & Baruch, Y. (1997, Spring). Back to square zero: The post-corporate career. *Organizational Dynamics,* 23-34.

Peiperl, M., & Lidewey, V. S. (1999, August). *The navigation of boundarylessness: Job change, extrinsic and intrinsic career success among early-career MBAs.* Paper presented at the annual meeting of the Academy of Management, Chicago.

Peiperl, M. A., Arthur, M. B., Goffee, R., & Morris, T. (Eds.). (2000). *Career frontiers: New conceptions of working lives.* New York: Oxford University Press.

Pelz, D. C., & Andrews, F. M. (1966). *Scientists in organizations.* New York: John Wiley.

Peres, S. H., (1966). *Factors which influence careers in General Electric.* Crotonville, NY: General Electric Company, Management Development and Employee Relations Service.

Pervin, L. A. (1968). Performance and satisfaction as a function of individual-environment fit. *Psychological Bulletin, 69,* 56-68.

Pfeffer, J. (1998). *The human equation: Building profits by putting people first.* Boston: Harvard Business School Press.

Phillips, S. D. (1997). Toward an expanded definition of adaptive decision making. *Career Development Quarterly, 45*(3), 275-287.

Porter, L. W., & Lawler, E. E., III. (1968). *Managerial attitudes and performance.* New York: John Wiley.

Pratt, M., & Foreman, P. (2000). Classifying managerial responses to multiple identities. *Academy of Management Review, 25,* 18-42.

Pulakos, E. D., Arad, S., Donovan, M. A., & Plamondon, K. E. (2000). Adaptability in the workplace: Development of a taxonomy of adaptive performance. *Journal of Applied Psychology, 85*(4), 612-624..

Quinn, J. B. (1992). *Intelligent enterprise: A knowledge and service based paradigm for industry.* New York: Free Press.

Rabinowitz, S., & Hall, D. T. (1977). Organizational research on job involvement. *Psychological Bulletin, 84*(2), 265-288.

Raelin, J. (1984). *The salaried professional.* New York: Praeger.

Raelin, J. (1985). Work patterns in the professional life cycle. *Journal of Occupational Psychology, 58,* 177-187.

Raelin, J. (1991). *The class of cultures: Managers managing professionals.* Boston: Harvard Business School Press.

Rapoport, R., & Rapoport, R. N. (1969). The dual-career family: A variant pattern and social change. *Human Relations, 22,* 3-29.

Rapoport, R., & Rapoport, R. N. (1975). Men, women, and equity. *The Family Coordinator, 24,* 421-432.

Reichheld, F. F. (1996). *The loyalty effect.* Boston: Harvard Business School Press.

Reidy, M. T. V., & White, L. C. (1977). The measurement of traditionalism among Roman Catholic priests: An exploratory study. *British Journal of Sociology, 28*(2), 226-241.

Roberts, P., & Newton, P. (1987). Levinsonian studies of women's adult development. *Psychology and Aging, 2*(2), 154-163.

Roe, A. (1957). Early determinants of vocational choice. *Journal of Counseling Psychology, 4,* 212-217.

Roethlisberger, F. J., & Dickson, W. J. (1939). *Management and the worker.* Cambridge, MA: Harvard University Press.

Rothstein, H. R. (1999). Recruitment and selection: Benchmarking at the millennium. In A. I. Kraut & A. K. Korman (Eds.), *Evolving practices in human resource management: Responses to a changing world of work* (pp. 69-89). San Francisco: Jossey-Bass.

Rousseau, D. M. (1990). New hire perceptions of their own and their employer's obligations: A study of psychological contracts. *Journal of Organizational Behavior, 11,* 389-400.

Rousseau, D. M. (1995). *Psychological contracts in organizations: understanding written and unwritten agreements.* Thousand Oaks, CA: Sage.

Rousseau, D. M., Schalk, R., & Schalk, R. (Eds.). (2000). *Psychological contracts in employment: Cross cultural perspectives.* Lanham, MD: University Press of America.

Saks, A. M., & Ashforth, B. E. (1997). Socialization tactics and newcomer information acquisition. *International Journal of Selection and Assessment, 51,* 48-61.

Sarason, S. (Ed.). (1977). *Work, aging, and social change.* New York: Free Press.

Savickas, M. L. (1990). The use of career choice measures in counseling practice. In E. Watkins & V. Campbell (Eds.), *Testing in counseling practice* (pp. 373-417). Hillsdale, NJ: Lawrence Erlbaum.

Savickas, M. L. (1997). Career adaptability: An integrative construct for life-span, life-space theory. *Career Development Quarterly, 45*(3), 247-259.

Savickas, M. L., & Super, D. E. (1993). Can life stages be identified in students? *Man and Work: Journal of Labor Studies, 4,* 71-78.

Schein, E. H. (1964). How to break the college graduate. *Harvard Business Review, 42,* 68-76.

Schein, E. H. (1965). *Organizational psychology.* Englewood Cliffs, NJ: Prentice Hall.

Schein, E. H. (1967). Attitude change during management education: A study of organizational influences on student attitudes. *Administrative Science Quarterly, 11,* 601-628.

Schein, E. H. (1970). *Organizational psychology* (2nd ed.). Englewood Cliffs, NJ: Prentice Hall.

Schein, E. H. (1971). The individual, the organization, and the career: A conceptual scheme. *Journal of Applied Psychology, 7,* 401-426.

Schein, E. H. (1978). *Career dynamics: Matching individual and organizational needs.* Reading, MA: Addison-Wesley.

Schein, E. H. (1996). Career anchors revisited: Implications for career development in the 21st century. *Academy of Management Executive, 10*(4), 80-88.

Schneider, B. (1972). Organization climate: Individual preferences and organizational realities. *Journal of Applied Psychology, 56,* 211-217.

Schneider, B. (1987). The people make the place. *Personnel Psychology, 40,* 437-453.

Schneider, B. (1999). Is the sky really falling? A view of the future. In A. I. Kraut & A. K. Korman (Eds.), *Evolving practices in human resource management: Responses to a changing world of work* (pp. 328-357). San Francisco: Jossey-Bass.

Schneider, B., & Bowen, D. E. (1995). *Winning the service game.* Boston: Harvard Business School Press.

Schneider, B., & Konz, A. M. (1989). Strategic job analysis. *Human Resource Management, 28,* 51-63.

Schneider, B., Kristof-Brown, A., Goldstein, H. W., & Smith, D. B. (1997). What is this thing called fit? In N. Anderson & P. Herriott (Eds.), *International handbook of selection and assessment* (pp. 393-412). London: Wiley.

Schneider, B., & Rentsch, J. (1988). Managing climates and cultures: A futures perspective. In J. Hage (Ed.), *Futures of organizations* (pp. 181-200). Lexington, MA: Lexington Books.

Schneider, B., Smith, D. B., Taylor, S., & Fleenor, J. (1998). Personality and organizations: A test of the homogeneity of personality hypothesis. *Journal of Applied Psychology, 83*(3), 462-470.

Scott, W. R. (1992). *Organizations: Rational, natural, and open systems* (3rd ed.). Englewood Cliffs, NJ: Prentice Hall.

Seibert, K. W. (1996a). *The nature of managerial reflection in learning from developmental job experiences in organizations.* Unpublished doctoral dissertation, Boston University School of Management, Boston.

Seibert, K. W. (1996b). Experience is the best teacher, if you can learn from it: Real-time reflection and development. In D. T. Hall & Associates (Eds.), *The career is dead— Long live the career: A relational approach to careers* (pp. 246-264). San Francisco: Jossey-Bass.

Seibert, K. W. (1999). Reflection-in-action: Tools for cultivating on-the-job learning conditions. *Organizational Dynamics, 27*(3), 54-65.

Seibert, K. W., & Daudelin, M. W. (1999). *The role of reflection in managerial learning: Theory, research, and practice.* Westport, CT: Quorum.

Seibert, K. W., Hall, D. T., & Kram, K. E. (1995). Strengthening the weak link in strategic executive development: Integrating individual development and global business strategy. *Human Resource Management, 34*(4), 549-567.

Sekaran, U. (1986). *Dual-career families.* San Francisco: Jossey-Bass.

Sekaran, U., & Hall, D. T. (1989). Asynchronism in dual-career and family linkages. In M. B. Arthur, D. T. Hall, & B. S. Lawrence (Eds.), *Handbook of career theory* (pp. 159-180). Cambridge, UK: Cambridge University Press.

Sheehy, G. (1995). *New passages.* New York: Random House.

Sheldon, M. E. (1971). Investments and involvements as mechanisms producing commitment to the organization. *Administrative Science Quarterly, 16,* 143-150.

Shepard, H. A. (1984). On the realization of human potential: A path with a heart. In M. B. Arthur, L. Bailyn, D. J. Levinson, & H. A. Shepard (Eds.), *Working with careers.* New York: Columbia University, Graduate School of Business.

Slocum, J., & Cron, W. L. (1985). Job attitudes and performance during three career stages. *Journal of Vocational Behavior, 26,* 126-145.

Slocum, J., Cron, W. L., Hansen, R. W., & Rawlings, S. (1985). Business strategy and the management of the plateaued performer. *Academy of Management Journal, 28,* 133-154.

Smith, E. M., Ford, J. K., & Kozlowski, S. W. J. (1997). Building adaptive expertise: Implications for training design. In M. A. Quinones, A. Ehrenstein, et al. (Eds.), *Training for a rapidly changing workplace* (pp. 89-118). Washington, DC: American Psychological Association.

Soelberg, P. O. (1966). *Unprogrammed decision making.* Paper presented at the 26th annual meeting of the Academy of Management, San Francisco.

Sofer, C. (1970). *Men in mid-career.* London: Cambridge University Press.

Spencer, L. M., McClelland, D. C., & Spencer, S. M. (1996). *Competency assessment methods: History and state of the art.* Boston: Hay/McBer Research.

Staw, B. M., & Barsade, S. G. (1993). Affect and managerial performance: A test of the sadder-but-wiser vs. happier-and-smarter hypotheses. *Administrative Science Quarterly, 38,* 304-331.

Steiner, G. A. (Ed.). (1965). *The creative organization.* Chicago: University of Chicago Press.

Stevens, M. (1981). *The big eight.* New York: Macmillan.

Strauss, A. (1970). *Mirrors and masks: The search for identity.* San Francisco: Sociology Press.

Stroh, L. K., Brett, J. M., & Reilly, A. H. (1994). A decade of change: Managers' attachment to their organizations and their jobs. *Human Resource Management, 33,* 531-548.

Stroh, L. K., Gregersen, H. B., & Black, J. S. (1998). Closing the gap: Expectations versus reality among expatriates. *Journal of World Business, 33*(2), 11-24.

Stumpf, S. A., & Rabinowitz, S. (1981). Career stage as a moderator of performance relationships with facets of job satisfaction and role perceptions. *Journal of Vocational Behavior, 18,* 202-218.

Sullivan, G. R., & Harper, M. V. (1997). *Hope is not a method: What business leaders can learn from America's army.* New York: Broadway Books.

Super, D. E. (1955). The dimensions and measurement of vocational maturity. *Teachers College Record, 57,* 151-163.

Super, D. E. (1957). *The psychology of careers*. New York: Harper & Row.

Super, D. E. (1990). A life-span, life-space approach to career development. In D. Brown & L. Brooks (Eds.), *Career choice and development* (pp. 197-261). San Francisco: Jossey-Bass.

Super, D. E. (1992). Toward a comprehensive theory of career development. In D. H. Montross & C. J. Shinkman (Eds.), *Career development: Theory and Practice* (pp. 35-64). Springfield, IL: Charles C Thomas.

Super, D. E., & Bohn, M. J., Jr. (1970). *Occupational psychology*. Belmont, CA: Wadsworth.

Super, D. E., Crites, J., Hummel, R., Moser, H., Overstreet, P., & Warnath, C. (1967). *Vocational development: A framework for research* (pp. 40-41). New York: Teachers College Press.

Super, D. E., & Knasel, E. G. (1979). *Specifications for a measure of career adaptability in young adults*. Cambridge, UK: National Institute for Careers Education and Counseling.

Super, D. E., & Knasel, E. G. (1981). Career development in adulthood: Some theoretical problems and a possible solution. *British Journal of Guidance and Counseling, 9*, 194-201.

Super, D. E., Savickas, M. L., & Super, C. M. (1996). The life-span, life-space approach to careers. In D. Brown, L. Brooks, & Associates (Eds.), *Career choice and development* (3rd ed., pp. 121-178). San Francisco: Jossey-Bass.

Super, D. E., Thompson, A. S., & Lindeman, R. H. (1988). *Adult Career Concerns Inventory: Manual for research and exploratory use in counseling*. Palo Alto, CA: Consulting Psychologists Press.

Tenbrunsel, A. E., Galvin, T. L., Neale, M. A., & Bazerman, M. H. (1999). Cognitions in organizations. In S. R. Clegg, C. Hardy, & W. R. Nord (Eds.), *Managing organizations* (pp. 63-87). Thousand Oaks, CA: Sage.

Tharp, C. (1999, May 7). *The role of performance management in organizational change at Bristol-Myers Squibb*. Paper presented to the Boston University Human Resources Policy Institute, Boston.

Thelen, E. (1992). Development as a dynamic system. *Current Directions in Psychological Science, 1*, 189-193.

Thoits, P. A. (1992). Identity structures and psychological well being: Gender and marital status comparisons. *Social Psychology Quarterly, 55*(3), 236-256.

Thompson, A. S., Lindeman, R. H., Super, D. E., Jordaan, J. P., & Myers, R. A. (1984). *Career Development Inventory: Technical manual*. Palo Alto, CA: Consulting Psychologists Press.

Thomas, D. A. (2001, April). The truth about mentoring minorities: Race matters. *Harvard Business Review, 79*(4), 98-107.

Thomas, D. A., & Alderfer, C. P. (1989). The influence of race on career dynamics: Theory and research on minority career experiences. In M. B. Arthur, D. T. Hall, & B. S. Lawrence (Eds.), *Handbook of career theory* (pp. 133-158). New York: Cambridge University Press.

Thomas, D. A., & Gabarro, J. J. (1999). *Breaking glass: The making of minority executives in corporate America*. Boston: Harvard Business School Press.

Tiedeman, D. V., & O'Hara, R. P. (1963). *Career development: Choice and adjustment*. New York: College Entrance Examination Board.

Topel, R. H., & Ward, M. P. (1992). Job mobility and the careers of young men. *Quarterly Journal of Economics, 197*(2), 439-479.

Turban, D. R. (2001). Organizational attractiveness as an employer on college campuses: An examination of the applicant population. *Journal of Vocational Behavior, 58,* 293-312.

Turban, D. R., & Keon, T. L. (1993). Organizational attractiveness: An interactionist perspective. *Journal of Applied Psychology, 78,* 184-193.

Vaillant, G. E. (1977). *Adaptation to life.* Boston: Little, Brown.

Vaillant, G. E. (1993). *The wisdom of the ego.* Cambridge, MA: Harvard University Press.

Vaillant, G. E. (2002). *Aging well: Surprising guideposts to a happier life from the landmark Harvard study of adult development.* Boston: Little, Brown.

Van Gennep, A. (1960). *The rites of passage.* Chicago: University of Chicago Press.

Van Maanen, J. (1976). Breaking in: Socialization to work. In R. Dubin (Ed.), *Handbook of work, organization, and society* (pp. 67-130). Chicago: Rand McNally.

Van Maanen, J., & Schein, E. H. (1979). Toward a theory of organizational socialization. *Research in Organizational Behavior, 6,* 287-365.

Von Hipple, C., Mangum, S. L., Greenberger, D. B., Heneman, R. L., & Skoglind, J. D. (1997). Temporary employment: Can organizations and employees both win? *Academy of Management Executive, 11*(1), 93-104.

Voyandoff, P. (1988). Work role characteristics, family structure demands, and work/family conflict. *Journal of Marriage and the Family, 50,* 749-761.

Vroom, V. (1966). Organizational choice: A study of pre- and post-decision processes. *Organizational Behavior and Human Performance, 1,* 212-225.

Vroom, V., & Deci, E. (1971). The stability of post-decision dissonance: A follow-up study of job attitudes of business school graduates. *Organizational Behavior and Human Performance, 6,* 36-49.

Walker, B. A., & Hanson, W. C. (1992). Valuing differences at Digital Equipment Corporation. In S. Jackson & Associates (Eds.), *Diversity in the workplace: Human resource initiatives* (pp. 50-65). New York: Guilford.

Wanous, J. P. (1992). *Organizational entry: Recruitment, selection, and socialization of newcomers* (2nd ed.). Reading, MA: Addison-Wesley.

Ward, S. P., Wilson, T. E., Jr., & Ward, D. R. (1994). Perceptions of retirement satisfaction: Data from retired certified public accountants. *Perceptual and Motor Skills, 78,* 525-526.

Weick, K. E. (1984). Small wins: Redefining the scale of social problems. *American Psychologist, 39*(1), 40-49.

Weick, K. E., & Berlinger, L. R. (1989). Career improvisation in self-designing organizations. In M. B. Arthur, D. T. Hall, & B. S. Lawrence (Eds.), *Handbook of career theory* (pp. 313-328). New York: Cambridge University Press.

Weiss, J. W., Skelley, M. F., Hall, D. T., & Haughey, J. C. (2001, March 9). *Vocational calling, new careers, and spirituality: An integrated perspective for organizational leaders and professionals.* Paper presented at the conference, "Bridging the gap: Spirituality and business," Institute for Spirituality and Organizational Leadership, Santa Clara University, Santa Clara, CA.

Wellbank, H. L., Hall, D. T., Morgan, M. A., & Hamner, W. C. (1978, March/April). Planning job progression for effective career development and human resources management. *Personnel*, 54-64.

Whetten, D. A., & Godfrey, P. A. (Eds.). (1998). *Identity in organizations: Building theory through conversations.* Thousand Oaks, CA: Sage.

White, R. W. (1952). *Lives in progress.* New York: Dryden.

White, R. W. (1959). Motivation reconsidered: The concept of competence. *Psychological Review, 66,* 297-323.

Williams, C. P., & Savickas, M. L. (1990). Developmental tasks of career maintenance. *Journal of Vocational Behavior, 36,* 166-175.

Williams, M., & Etzion, D. (1995). Crossover of stress, strain and resources from one spouse to another. *Journal of Organizational Behavior, 16,* 169-181.

Wilson, G. (1991). Old age and change in home and neighbourhood: Personal adaptability by frail older people in response to the legacies of social and economic policies. *Housing Studies, 6*(4), 263-272.

Witchel, A. (1994). By way of Canarsie, one large hot cup of business strategy. *New York Times,* pp. C1, C8.

Wright, T. A., & Cropanzano, R. (1997). Well-being, satisfaction and job performance: Another look at the happy/productive worker thesis. In *Academy of Management best paper proceedings* (pp. 364-368). Boston: Academy of Management.

Yan, A., Hall, D. T., & Zhu, G. (2000). *International assignments for career building: Agency relationships and psychological contracts* (Working paper). Boston: Boston University School of Management.

Yin, R. K. (1994). *Case study research: Design and methods.* Thousand Oaks, CA: Sage.

Index

About the Author

Douglas T. (Tim) Hall is Professor of Organizational Behavior and Director of the Executive Development Roundtable in the School of Management at Boston University. He is a recipient of the American Psychological Association's James McKeen Cattell Award (now called the Ghiselli Award) for research design. His research and consulting activities have dealt with career development, the new employer-employee contract, executive succession, management of diversity, and work/life issues. He is a fellow of the Academy of Management and the American Psychological Association and is currently serving on the board of governors of the Center for Creative Leadership. He is author of *Careers in Organizations* (1976) and *Career Development* (1994); coauthor of *Organizational Climates and Careers* (1973), *The Two Career Couple* (1979), *Experiences in Management and Organizational Behavior* (4th ed., 1997), *Human Resource Management* (1986), *Career Development in Organizations* (1986), *Turbulence in the American Workplace* (1991), and *The Career is Dead—Long Live the Career* (1996); and coeditor of *Handbook of Career Theory* (1989). His research interests include work/life balance, career planning and development, leadership development and executive succession, and managing diversity. In 2001, he won the Everett Cherrington Hughes Award from the Academy of Management for his research on careers. He will hold an Erskine Visiting Fellowship at the University of Canterbury in Christchurch, New Zealand, in 2002.